DRESSAGE THE COWBOY WAY

The Complete Guide to Training and Riding with Soft Feel and Kindness

EITAN BETH-HALACHMY &
JENNI L. GRIMMETT, DVM

FOREWORD BY JACK BRAINARD

TRAFALGAR SQUARE
North Pomfret, Vermont

First published in 2018 by
Trafalgar Square Books
North Pomfret, Vermont 05053

Copyright © 2018 Eitan Beth-Halachmy and Jenni L. Grimmett

All rights reserved. No part of this book may be reproduced, by any means, without written permission of the publisher, except by a reviewer quoting brief excerpts for a review in a magazine, newspaper, or website.

Disclaimer of Liability
The authors and publisher shall have neither liability nor responsibility to any person or entity with respect to any loss or damage caused or alleged to be caused directly or indirectly by the information contained in this book. While the book is as accurate as the authors can make it, there may be errors, omissions, and inaccuracies.

Trafalgar Square Books encourages the use of approved safety helmets in all equestrian sports and activities.

Library of Congress Cataloging-in-Publication Data
Names: Beth-Halachmy, Eitan, author.
Title: Dressage the cowboy way : the complete guide to training and riding with soft feel and kindness / by Eitan Beth-Halachmy and Jenni L Grimmett, DVM ; foreword by Jack Brainard.
Description: North Pomfret, Vermont : Trafalgar Square Books, 2018. | Includes index.
Identifiers: LCCN 2017059440| ISBN 9781570768576 (paperback) | ISBN 9781570769061 (ebook)
Subjects: LCSH: Dressage. | Western riding. | Horses--Training.
Classification: LCC SF309.5 .B48 2018 | DDC 798.2/3--dc23
LC record available at https://lccn.loc.gov/2017059440

All photographs by Lesley Deutsch, except p. xiv (Debby Zarate); pp. vi, 24, 122, 143, 145 (Lee Folino); p. 86 (Ralf Schaefer); p.119 (Margaret Fabion); pp. 176, 182, 185, 192, 193 (Chris Holloway)
All illustrations by Eitan Beth-Halachmy
Book design by DOQ | Layout by Lauryl Eddlemon
Cover design by RM Didier
Index by Andrea M. Jones (www.jonesliteraryservices.com)
Typeface: Chaparral Pro

Printed in China

10 9 8 7 6 5 4 3 2 1

*This book is lovingly dedicated
to the horses.*

For the lessons they've taught us,

for the memories we've made,

for the trails we've journeyed,

and the forgiveness they gave.

—JENNI LYN GRIMMETT, DVM

CONTENTS

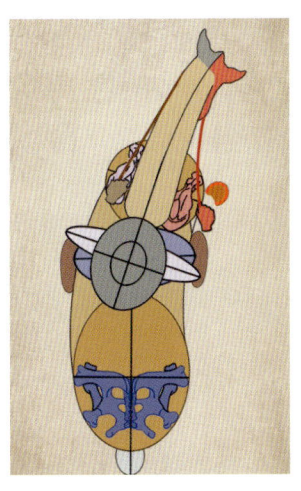

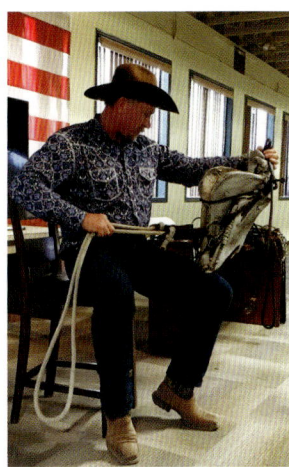

Foreword xi
Introduction: My Journey to Cowboy Dressage 1
   Special Section: Soft Feel 4

1: TACK. 7
   Halter and Lead. 8
   Saddle 9
   Special Section: Saddle Fit 10
   Bridle. 13
   Apparel 22

2: WISDOM TREE. 25
   Special Section: Skeletal Maturation 27
   Level 1: Partnership and Groundwork. 33
   Level 2: Communication and Moving the Feet 33
   Level 3: Lightness and Acceptance of the Aids 34
   Level 4: Ride Them Forward. 34
   Level 5: Balance and Straightness 35
   Level 6: Soft Feel and Self-Carriage 35

3: GROUNDWORK AND PARTNERSHIP ON THE GROUND . . . 37
    Leading the Horse 37
    Maneuvering the Horse's Body on the Ground 42
    Groundwork Exercises 45

4: AIDS 49
    Special Section: Behavior Modification Terms *51*
    The Hands 57
    The Legs 63
    Seat and Weight and Energy 65
    The Voice 70
    How the Horse Communicates with Us 70

5: THE COWBOY DRESSAGE COURTS 75
    Setting Up Your Court 76
    Challenge Court 81
    Half-Court 85

6: CADENCE AND GAITS OF THE COWBOY DRESSAGE HORSE 87
    Cadence 88
    Forward and Frames 89
    The Queen of Gaits: The Walk 90
    Special Section: Muscles of Balance *97*
    The Jog 109
    The Lope 113
    Final Thoughts on the Free Frame 117

7: STRAIGHTNESS AND BEND 121
    Straightness 121
    Bend 123
    Counter-Bend 135

8: LATERAL MANEUVERS 139
- Turn-on-the-Haunches 140
- Turn-on-the-Forehand 145
- Shoulder-In 147
- Shoulder-Out 149
- Shoulder-Fore 150
- Leg-Yield 151
- Haunches-In 151
- Haunches-Out 152
- Half-Pass 152

9: SHORTENING THE FRAME 155
- Teaching the Short Frame 157

10: THE GATHERINGS 165
- Family 165
- Education 166
- Celebration 167
- Divisions 168
- *Special Section: Picking Your Tests* **169**
- Judging 174
- *Special Section: The Cowboy Dressage Horse* **176**

11: BEYOND THE COURT 181
- Trail Riding 182
- Mountain Trail 183
- Cattle Work 184
- *Special Section: More About Musical Freestyles* **186**
- Retreats and Getaways 191

12: THE FUTURE OF COWBOY DRESSAGE 195

Appendix I: Glossary 200

Appendix II: Cowboy Dressage Exercises and Maneuvers. 206
    10-Meter Figure Eight 206
    Quarterline Loop 208
    20-Meter Circles 209
    Square with 5-Meter Bend 210
    20-Meter Diamond. 211
    10-Meter Serpentine. 212
    Broken Arrows 213
    Circle Inside the Box 214
    Bow-Tie 215
    Circles 216
    Turkey Tail 217

Acknowledgments 218
Personal Note by Dan Grimmett. 219
Index 221

NOTE TO READERS

Eitan and I would like to thank every one of you who are about to embark on this journey with us. This book has been a labor of love and we hope that it helps you to advance your partnership, horsemanship, and enjoyment of your equine partner. I have done my absolute best to put into words the artistry that Eitan has in the saddle. At times, it has been akin to transcribing the notes of Mozart or the colors of Monet. Eitan—known by many as just "8"—is a true artist in his horsemanship, and it is his wish that we all aspire to such art within ourselves. The tools, advice, and exercises that are included in this book are but a scratch on the surface of a lifetime of knowledge built out of trial and error and an elevated sense of feel and timing. When a personal point of view is included in the book, it is my own, but all the educational tools provided for the rider are straight from Eitan. All of the illustrations are of Eitan's own design, and they provide a glimpse into how his mind works when he is riding his horses.

May the trail rise up to meet you and the wind be at your back.

— Jenni L. Grimmett, DVM

"Eitan Beth-Halachmy, who grew up riding mules out of the fields in a far-off land, spent his lifetime as a horseman. His expertise is now recognized internationally. As a veterinarian who has seen countless horses crippled due to excessive stress in the competitive world of horse shows, racing, and other equestrian sports, I have become a great supporter of Eitan's creation: Cowboy Dressage. Why? Because, unlike many disciplines, if performed correctly as Eitan conceived of it, it can only benefit the horse, mentally and physically."

— Dr. Robert M. Miller, DVM,
Father of Imprint Training

Dr. Bob Miller, DVM, and wife Debby at a Cowboy Dressage Gathering at Rancho Murieta Equestrian Center. Debby competes at many of the Gatherings each year.

FOREWORD

These were my thoughts when I first learned of Eitan's decision to write a new book. It will surely be a good one. Who else has better qualifications? What will be the format? How will he slant it? It surely shouldn't be for a beginner, amateur, novice, or about basic horsemanship. The horse world is full of this kind of book. I wonder if he will get down to the how and why, which he knows so well? Will he go from green to finished? What about horse psychology, which he is a master of? These along with a dozen more thoughts occupied my mind.

Now here comes a phone call, "Jack, will you write a little something for my new book?" Hell yes, but I'd like to see the new book. Here comes the copy and I was awestruck. It is the "how-to" dictionary of proper horse training. Since a horse learns through training exercises, here they are—A to Z!

Probably the most important facts of the book are the illustrations. Eitan's phenomenal camera knowledge gives proof of the authenticity of what he is teaching. These photos and diagrams are second to none. No other book equals this in its illustrations.

It's about equipment, Soft Feel, cadence, footfall, conformation, anatomy, kindness, training exercises, plus hundreds more vitals that are so important to the schooling of the horse, and written by a man who has made a lifelong determined search for the ultimate in the art of true horsemanship.

In giving any kind of instruction on training the horse, whether it be oral, written, or through demonstration, the "why" is always as important as the "how." The collaboration between Eitan and Jenni Grimmett, DVM delves deeply into the "why" and then the "how."

I am so happy to have 8 for one of my closest friends. We have much in common. We both like to have fun, we have a sense of humor, we like good food, we agree on how the horse should be trained, we love horses and nothing gives us a greater sense of satisfaction than seeing someone ride a better horse because of our efforts.

The only downside is that we are about "used up." Time has taken its toll, but we are determined to "hang in." So, here it is: the best book of its kind and written by a man who could hardly speak English 30 years ago.

My hat is off to you, 8.

— Jack Brainard
*Legendary Trainer
and Clinician*

INTRODUCTION

MY JOURNEY TO COWBOY DRESSAGE

By Jenni L. Grimmett, DVM

Cowboy Dressage is the dream and life work of Debbie and Eitan Beth-Halachmy. It was gloriously inspired by Eitan's unique riding style and his flamboyant and entertaining performances with his lovely Morgan horses. Eitan and Debbie dreamed of bringing this style of horsemanship to the public, creating a place for riders that would like to embrace lightness, kindness, and Eitan's love of the cowboy tradition. Through their hard work, dedication, and the support of fellow enthusiasts, Cowboy Dressage has blossomed into what is now a thriving worldwide phenomenon.

    I came to Cowboy Dressage, like so many others, by meeting and riding with Eitan. I was searching for a better way of being with my horses and had bounced from one natural horsemanship trainer to another looking for just the right blend for my Morgans and me. Being a fan of the Morgan horse, I was familiar with Eitan and his gorgeous Morgans, Holiday Compadre and the stately Santa Fe Renegade.

I didn't know what to expect when I rode with Eitan for the first time. I was hoping for help with some of the spots I was having trouble with. Like so many other students that go to learn from one of the best, I wanted to be doing flying lead changes by the time I was done with the clinic! I had so very much to learn. Eitan spent that weekend teaching me how to feel for softness and reward for it when it is finally there. He asked me to feel where each of the horse's feet were and cue in time with the footfalls of the horse, which at the time was a completely foreign concept to me.

I probably missed most of what 8 was trying to teach me that day. The subtleties are often lost in the quagmire as you are feeling your way along with new concepts. My "aha" moment came when I watched 8 get on a particularly bothered little mare that belonged to another clinic participant. I was worried at first because 8 hadn't been out of the hospital for very long and this little mare was HOT and distracted and worried. 8 got on this mare and sat there with her. Not talking, not walking, not moving. He just sat there with her for a moment before he quietly asked her to walk off. The change in the mare was so drastic it looked like magic. Here was a mare that, moments before, had been unable to do anything but prance stiff-legged around the round pen. Ten minutes with 8, and she was walking on a loose rein.

I've seen 8 do some amazing and fancy things with his horses: gorgeous extended trots, canter pirouettes, and sliding stops, but it was his ability to talk to that troubled mare and have her go with him in softness that struck me the most that day. That was the day I realized that being a great horseman has as much to do with who you are as what you can do. If you can find the softness, kindness, and calmness within yourself to communicate with these spirited, talented animals, the sky is truly the limit.

We are so blessed to have as our leader in Cowboy Dressage a horseman of Eitan's caliber. There are many talented and great horsemen out there but I believe there are few that have what 8 has in his ability to relate to the horse on the horse's level. Eitan is a unique blend of European riding instruction and cowboy lore. He is a lifelong student always happy to learn something new, and constantly changing, adapting, and searching for that one thing to help his horse understand and learn what he is trying to teach him to do. He is patient and understanding with his horses, allowing them to be who they are while they develop their talents in their own time.

Cowboy Dressage is as unique as its founding father. Eitan and Debbie have assembled around them a perfect core group of horsemen coming from different corners of the equestrian world to create the Cowboy Dressage World partners. Like reading each horse to take the very best he has to offer, Eitan and Debbie excel at finding the very best in the people who are working so hard to bring Cowboy Dressage to the world. It takes a village to keep this train rolling and the Cowboy Dressage World train is rolling ahead on full steam and picking up new passengers at every stop.

The Cowboy Dressage Handshake is our Code of the West. By agreeing to the Handshake principles of try, kindness, trust, and being the very best you can be, each member becomes a part of the Cowboy Dressage family. The Cowboy Dressage Handshake can be found on the Cowboy Dressage World website (www.cowboydressageworld.com). In this day and age, we use an "electronic handshake."

The history and development of Cowboy Dressage have been discussed in previous publications. In this book, we would like to help those who may have already given their Handshake and started their Cowboy Dressage journey to reach their goals of "Soft Feel." But there is also value for the rider brand new to Cowboy Dressage and the rider looking to improve test scores: This book will serve as a companion to your arena time helping you to better understand how to ride with partnership, harmony, and balance. From the very basics like making decisions on which bridle to grab from the tack room to how to correctly ride some of the more advanced maneuvers, this book will have something for every rider, whether you compete at Cowboy Dressage Gatherings or not.

Before we head to the tack room, it is important to have a discussion on the driving principle of Cowboy Dressage, which is kindness. Kindness needs to be at the forefront of every interaction you have with your horse from the minute you lift the latch on the stall door. Always keeping kindness in your heart and mind will change the interactions you have with people, horses, and most importantly the private conversations you are always having with yourself. When you embrace kindness in all your dealings, you open your heart and mind to the journey that is Soft Feel. The goal for every Cowboy Dressage rider

Soft Feel

The mission of Cowboy Dressage is written at the top of every Cowboy Dressage test score sheet. It reads: "Soft Feel (or Fresh Rein) is the guiding principle of Cowboy Dressage. It is a wordless, intimate communication within the partnership between horse and rider. Soft Feel is not only sending messages but also having the sensitivity and awareness to feel the message the horse sends back.

"The timing and use of the Release, Relaxation, Preparation, and Execution are the basic fundamentals of Soft Feel.

"Since Soft Feel is the mission of Cowboy Dressage, it will be scored with emphases on lightness, harmony, finesse, and partnership as a priority. Balance, cadence, carriage, control, and performance are additional areas where the horse and rider will be judged and scored."

While the definition of Soft Feel is officially provided, you will find that it means something a little different to every one of our Cowboy Dressage riders, professionals, and judges. Here is some insight from a few of our Cowboy Dressage professionals and judges who define Soft Feel in their own words:

"The feeling of you and the horse working together as one!" Martina Bone, Cowboy Dressage Clinician and Recommended Judge, Somerset, California.

"Physical, mental, emotional, spiritual connection. Those moments of Soft Feel, where it seems effortless for horse and rider to become something we then compare every other moment to. It begins to be a lifelong journey to continually recreate." Marcia Moore Harrison, Cowboy Dressage Clinician and Recommended Judge, Potlatch, Idaho.

"When I reach for my horse he reaches for me, when I think about my vision he is there and our minds meld as one. It's all about the dance, the lightness, and the connection." Dale Rumens-Partee, Cowboy Dressage Clinician, Redmond, Washington.

"Soft Feel is the relationship between horse and rider where the connection they share is one of a kind, based on trust and communication." Megan Gallagher, 2015 Top Hand Winner, Grass Valley, California.

"Soft Feel to me is the journey toward perfection." Phil Monaghan, Cowboy Dressage Clinician, Coffs Harbor, New South Wales.

"Soft Feel happens in those moments when I can listen to what my horse is saying and then respond with communication that results in him understanding what I want. It took longer to write that than for it to happen!" Dee Meyers, Cowboy Dressage Clinician and Recommended Judge, Baker City, Oregon.

"For me, Soft Feel is an unseen communication between horse and rider. I can think of a maneuver and my horse will transition to it. Almost a spiritual connection as one being." Wyatt Paxton, Cowboy Dressage World Partner, Redding, California.

"Soft Feel is that 'aha' moment in riding that we are always trying to capture. It is a lifetime journey." Nonny Largent, Cowboy Dressage Clinician and Recommended Judge, Cottonwood, California.

is to cultivate Soft Feel in their partnership with their horse to maximize communication and achieve effective riding. This is why a book on Cowboy Dressage cannot begin without a discussion of this important principle.

The definition of Soft Feel is elusive and is something that every student of horsemanship must find within themselves. It is the dance. It is the wordless bond between horse and rider. It is the sound of two souls touching. It is love. It is respect. It is partnership. Seek Soft Feel with your horse and you will find it helps you to seek Soft Feel in all your dealings—both equine and human. Make kindness your byword, and the world becomes a kinder place. So, pick up a Soft Feel and let's move into the barn. Soft Feel isn't a look, head set, draped rein, or style. It's a promise and a commitment from the rider to the horse—and ultimately from the horse to the rider—that they will go together as one through all things (see sidebar to discover what Soft Feel means to some of our Handshake members and Cowboy Dressage professionals).

Jenni L. Grimmett, DVM

1

TACK

*"It isn't the bit
that creates the softness,
it is the hands."*

EITAN BETH-HALACHMY

As any artist or skilled craftsman will tell you, the tools of your trade are of great importance in the creation of the art. For the serious horseman, the selection of tack is no mere passing fancy at the mercy of whims or trends except where the communication with the horse is directly affected. While all horsemen, just like artists, have their own preferences for their gear selections, the resounding lesson is quality and ease of use to facilitate communication and Soft Feel. Each of our choices in tack should focus on clear communication and clarity of signal to the horse.

All the tack requirements for Cowboy Dressage exist either to ensure ease of communication in the pursuit of Soft Feel or to honor the traditions of the American Cowboy. There is plenty of room for personal choice and selection of tack and appointments in Cowboy Dressage and we encourage you to make the choices that best suit you, your horse, and your place in your personal journey. What follows is a discussion of the tack pieces most commonly selected by folks who are Handshake members of the Cowboy Dressage World, and some of the rules that will apply to a rider in a competition setting at a Cowboy Dressage Gathering.

Halter and Lead

This most basic piece of equipment is important in Cowboy Dressage because Soft Feel starts from the ground when you first take your horse from the stall or pasture. While ultimately the halter choice is up to the rider with the only requirement in Cowboy Dressage being that there is no chain on your lead shank, the type of halter you use can help you to cultivate Soft Feel and communication in your ground work. By and large the most common halter choice is the rope halter. This isn't due to just fad or trend. There are some very good reasons why we choose to use a rope halter: It can be fitted better to the horse's head for groundwork and lungeing, and it provides a clear, consistent signal and release, unlike a traditional leather or web halter. For the groundwork exercises that help the horse to develop bend, softness, and partnership, a soft rope halter provides the very best communication.

Not all rope is created equally. Students of natural horsemanship quickly find that the dexterity in some types of lead ropes is different than others. Soft, lovely cotton leads that feel so good on the hand turn to mushy handfuls when used to direct a horse around in a circle with bend. Stiff halters with a fancy large bedazzled noseband speak to the horse only when given a resounding tug. None of those things are helpful when helping to create Soft Feel in the horse. We want our signals through the halter to be subtle yet easily understood. A good rope halter with a nice, lively, long yachting rope lead will send better feel to the horse and result in better timing of the release.

While traditional lungeing on a long rope lead has its place in helping horses develop consistency and cadence in gaits in the early stages of their education, groundwork performed on a shorter 12-foot lead provides an opportunity to help the horse begin to read the handler's body language and energy as well as creating bend, softness, and correct footfall in maneuvers such as turn-on-the-forehand and turn-on-the-haunches. The soft construction of the rope halter and the subtle communication of the rope lead allow for development of Soft Feel in the execution of these exercises. But, these are suggestions and not requirements in Cowboy Dressage. You are welcome to do your groundwork with whatever tack you find promotes Soft Feel and partnership between you and your horse.

Learning how to properly fit and tie a rope halter will help to increase your success and comfort with this tool. The rope halter is designed so that should the horse pull excessively against the overhand knot on the crown piece, it will always be easily freed when it is tied properly. A proper tie will also prevent the halter from slipping under pressure. The pictures on the next page walk you through proper fitting of a traditional rope halter:

Step 1: Run the crown piece down through the loop tied in the halter. Hold the tail in your right hand (fig. 1.1).

Step 2: Run the tail back behind the loop, creating a new loop that you hold open with your right hand. Hold upward tension on the crown piece to keep the halter snug behind the angle of the jaw as you tie the knot (fig. 1.2).

Step 3: Run the tail end through the loop you are holding open with your right hand so that the tail now points toward the horse's tail (fig. 1.3).

Step 4: When pulled tight the tail should point away from the horse's face toward the tail and the overhand knot should be tied around the halter loop. When tied in this manner, the knot will not slide or give under pressure but can always be untied, even after extreme pressure is applied (fig. 1.4).

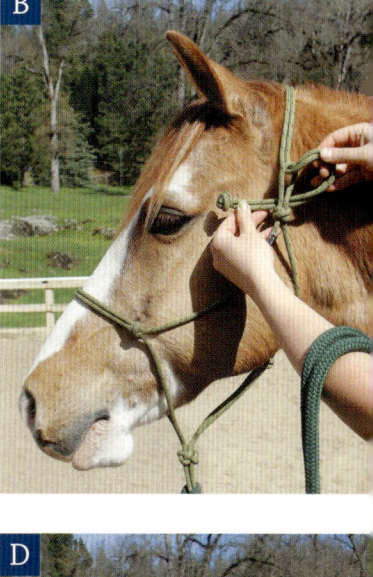
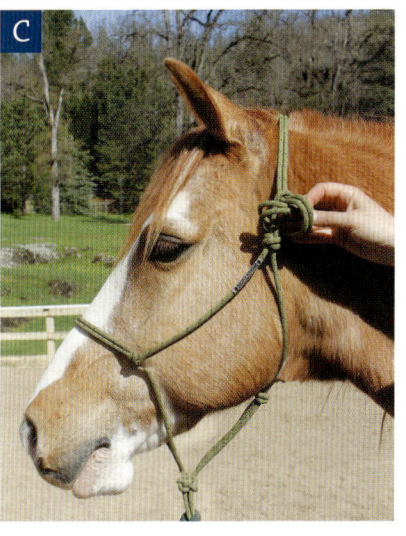
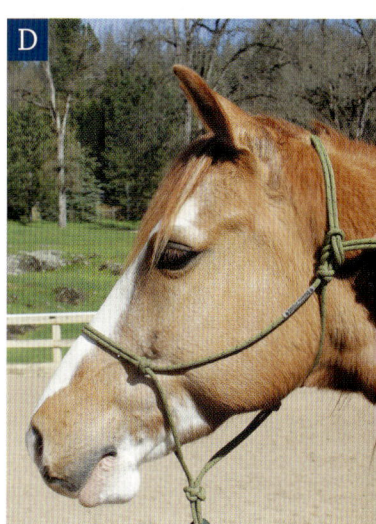

1.1–1.4 – *Proper fitting of a traditional rope halter: Step 1 (A); Step 2 (B); Step 3 (C); Step 4 (D).*

Saddle

All saddles should be Western in style, meaning they include a horn. Both single rigged and double rigged Western saddles are found on the Cowboy Dressage Court. There is no need for fancy silver or expensive saddles. Good, working, serviceable tack that fits horse and rider well is of primary importance. The most important aspect of the saddle you choose should be *fit*. Having a saddle that comfortably fits both the horse and rider makes the conversation that involves the seat, leg, and weight aids that much clearer for the horse. Western saddles, by design, are meant to spread the weight of the rider over a larger area of the back than English all-purpose or dressage saddles, or even the Australian stock saddle. The Western saddle grew out of a need for very long days in the saddle and carrying fairly heavy loads, as well as dallying off and restraining animals as needed.

Saddle Fit

First in saddle fit, it is important to consider the anatomy of your horse's back. Back length, withers height, and shoulder angle are all very important in saddle fit. The bars of the saddle should ride along the top of the rib heads supported by the long muscles of the back. The front of the bars sits in the pocket just behind the shoulder and below the withers. The bars should not extend beyond the flank nor should they create pressure on the loin. The paddle-like portion of the scapula moves in an arch over the front of the rib cage with the horse's stride. The flatter (more laid back) the shoulder is, the longer the stride length and the more movement of that shoulder. Pressure in this area will affect stride length.

There is a wide variation in body types and styles within our equine population. Some horses are high-withered and narrow-shouldered; some are mutton-withered with huge bulldog shoulders. It may be hard to believe but horses used to be selected for breeding based on their backs. A horse was said to have a good back for riding with moderate withers and a good pocket behind the shoulder for the saddle bars. Mutton-withered horses were considered cart horses because it was difficult to get saddles to stay in place on their backs.

Often, in the discussion of saddle fit, you will hear horsemen talk about how the horse's conformation today is much different than it used to be, presumably because people have quit selecting for back conformation in their horses. We don't believe this to be a universal problem across the breeds. Many families of the Quarter Horse have lost the nice withers that they were bequeathed from the Thoroughbred, and certainly, there has been increased selective pressure in that breed for that "bulldog" look. Today's Quarter Horse often doesn't resemble the foundation type in many ways, back conformation among them. They tend to be lower-withered with wider, flatter backs than their ancestors, so using an old saddle or one of the old type will have a bar angle that is too steep for a flatter-backed horse.

The majority of horses are left-handed. Usually, you can tell the horse's handedness by the direction that the mane falls naturally. When the mane falls to the right, the horse is left-handed. If you stand on a stool at the rump and sight down his back toward the shoulders, you can see any difference that might exist in the two shoulders. A horse that is dominant to one side or the other may have a shoulder that is larger to the dominant side. Lameness or conformation defects may also contribute to lack of symmetry in the horse. This asymmetry can cause a saddle to slip to one side or the other, and when the rider's weight is carried with that saddle slip, the problem is compounded. Being aware of how the saddle is riding on the horse while he is being worked can help to identify saddle-fit issues as well, and help riders compensate for slippage by adjusting their weight and helping the horse to develop balance and symmetry through proper body use.

White hairs (saddle spots) are caused by pressure points from the saddle and indicate chronic pressure damage, or damage that was inflicted months ago. It takes some time for those white hairs to show up. A common spot for white hairs to develop is at the hollow behind the shoulders where poorly fitting saddles have been interfering with shoulder movement. Behavioral or gait changes are often the reason a vet must be called out to evaluate a horse for back pain and saddle fit. Hollowing of the back during saddling, dancing around, pulling away, or puffing up at the cinch during tightening can all be indications that your saddle is causing your horse physical discomfort. While there are many other reasons for back pain or referred back pain, you should always rule out saddle fit as a cause first.

Under saddle, a sudden reluctance to lope, extend gait, or pick up a certain lead may indicate pain due to saddle fit. Sometimes the horse has spent so much time in pain from a bad saddle that he becomes a chronic bucker. If your horse is kicking out or bucking suddenly, ruling out physical pain should be your first thought before trying to "train" the buck out of him. Other signs of back pain can include head-tossing, teeth-grinding, agitation as the ride progresses, or carrying the head too low trying to stretch out those back muscles.

After riding and removing your saddle, you should always examine your horse's back. Is his sweat pattern even? In a horse with a healthy back with no previous damage, there should be even sweat patterns on both his sides, especially where the bars are located. If it's been a long ride, the entire area under the pad will probably be sweated up, but it's the bar areas that you are most concerned with. Unfortunately, if a horse has experienced previous saddle damage, these areas will not sweat—and they don't recover through correcting the saddle-fit issue. Check all along your horse's back for areas of raised lumps, excessive heat, rubbed hair, or tenderness to the touch.

In Cowboy Dressage, we are doing everything we can to promote healthy muscle structure and balance. Making sure the horse is comfortable enough to do the things we are asking is so important. A horse that isn't comfortable will be resistant and bracing, and your partnership and harmony will suffer.

The wood and rawhide tree (in traditional Western saddles) that helps the saddle withstand those forces is the skeleton that first acts to establish the fit of the saddle on the horse's back. Obviously, not all horses are created equal, and there is quite a bit of difference in the back of a little Arabian and a stocky Quarter Horse! It is, therefore, of the utmost importance that informed Cowboy Dressage riders choose their saddle with good fit in mind (see sidebar for more tips on saddle fit).

As well as having a saddle that fits, having one that allows you to be in the proper position with good balance is also very important. Effective riders develop a balanced seat in their saddles, neither bracing on the stirrups, nor leaning on the cantle. A too-small saddle can inhibit the development of a balanced seat because it holds you in place without the aid of your balance. A saddle that is too large can also inhibit a balanced seat as you will brace yourself to maintain a seat in the middle of the saddle.

Often, in a Western saddle, this pushes you back into a "recliner" position where your legs are too far in front of your body. When we begin discussing bend and proper rider position, the importance of this will become quite clear. If you are struggling to stay balanced and in position in the saddle, you become less effective.

The Cowboy Dressage rider is encouraged to find a saddle that places the rider's legs directly below the rider's hips with stirrups that swing freely, thus allowing the rider to properly communicate with all parts of the horse's body, especially during training for the lateral maneuvers. While there are no rules about double rigged saddles and many riders find success in a double rigged saddle, the back cinch can sometimes interfere with leg aids when speaking to the horse's hindquarters. If you find you are having trouble with these maneuvers with your horse, consider removing the hind cinch for a time until the horse better understands. Most double rigged saddles function just as well with the back cinch removed. Just remember to put the cinch back on before you dally off to anything.

Bridle

Snaffle

The most common bit choice in Cowboy Dressage for all ages and stages of horses is the snaffle bit. The Western snaffle bit consists of two rings and a jointed mouthpiece. The comfort snaffle (fig. 1.5) is also a common choice among Cowboy Dressage riders. Whatever style of snaffle bit you

1.5 – *A comfort snaffle and alpaca fiber mecate with slobber straps.*

choose, it is important to understand how to properly communicate to the horse through the rein to the snaffle bit.

When used alone, the snaffle is the simplest of bits that applies just as much pressure to the mouth as the rider applies by hand, meaning there is no leverage effect that increases the pressure on the horse's mouth or poll. It is the most common choice for young horses because it simplifies directions by causing direct guiding pressure to the side of the horse you would like to communicate with. When affixed with reins that can slide up and down the ring of the snaffle, you can use three levels of communication to the horse.

You can talk to the bottom, middle, and upper portion of the bit, effectively separating messages to different parts of the horse's head, neck, and shoulders and, eventually, speaking directly to the front legs of the horse. At the bottom of the bit, you encourage the horse to both soften and lower his head. By lowering your hands and allowing the rein to slide to the bottom of the bit, you change the weight of the bit in the horse's mouth, as well as weight on the poll. Even rein weight on the bottom of the bit will eventually signal to the horse to relax and drop the head and neck to stretch out the topline in the free frame.

The middle of the bit is used for lateral flexion, creating bend, and guiding the horse's head, neck, and shoulders in the direction of travel. When connecting to the middle of the bit, the horse learns to seek the rider's hand, looking into the bend. Pressure created on the middle of the bit transmits a signal to the tongue and bars on the inside of the direction of the horse's bend and to the contralateral cheek. The inside rein tells the horse to look to the hand and to the inside of the bend, while the outside rein connects to the outside shoulder completing the turn. When riding in the snaffle, it is wise to use one hand at a time on the reins. If you hold the horse, pull with both hands without first preparing the horse, or if you fail to use release and reward, you can create bracing in the horse. With the traditional two-piece snaffle, pressure on both reins simultaneously will also cause a nutcracker effect, pulling the two pieces of the bit close together and causing the joint to poke into the upper palate of the horse's mouth. "Over-bridling," during which the horse's head is behind the vertical, is a form of evasion and can be the result of methods that have inflicted pain in the horse. The Cowboy Dressage horse should travel with his head in front of the vertical line.

It is also important to remember not to create pain or discomfort as you teach the horse to soften and bend in the snaffle. Instead, be gentle and consider the horse is learning to trust the rider's hands and the bit. Fear and pain are the enemies of long-term learning.

Snaffle Bit Action

There are three rein positions on the snaffle: The *top* of the bit is for raising the horse's head and shifting the horse's weight back to the hindquarters. The *middle* of the bit is for lateral flexion and direction. The *bottom* of the bit is for lowering the head and softening at the poll (fig. 1.6).

The *top* of the bit has less to do with direction and more to do with helping the horse elevate his head, neck, and shoulders, and shift his weight back onto the hindquarters. You can communicate with the top of the bit by raising your hands and applying upward pressure with the reins. When used with good timing and feel, you can help a horse that naturally tends to carry his head too low raise his head and move to a better balance. Making contact with the top of the bit creates a signal on the horse's lips rather than on

1.6 – *There are three distinct rein positions on the snaffle bit: top (gray), middle (green), and bottom (brown).*

the bars of the mandible and tongue. A quick soft lift that contacts the lips can encourage the horse to follow that pressure upward into your hands rather than over-bridle and shift his weight toward the forehand.

This is a good time to talk about placement of the bit in the horse's mouth. Traditionally, the school of thought with the snaffle bit was the "two wrinkle" rule. The idea was to place the bit in the horse's mouth so that it raised the corners of the mouth, creating two wrinkles. Instead, we like to place the bit comfortably within the horse's mouth so that he can pick the bit up and carry and support it himself with the tongue. This increases the horse's feel of the bit so that the slightest change in rein weight will be conveyed to him with lightness. With this bit placement, you can raise your hands slightly and make connection to the top of the bit and the corners of the mouth. If the bit was already raised to that position and held there, the raising of the hands and change in rein weight would be less significant to the horse.

Two-Handed Western Bit

The two-handed Western bit has been around a long time (fig. 1.7). It has been touted as a way to transition between the snaffle and the more widely common curb bits used on the Western horse. In Cowboy Dressage, the two-handed Western bit has found a more permanent home than just as a transition bit. With a horse that has a good understanding of bend and the basic maneuvers and is ready for a little more refinement, the two-handed bit is a very good choice. There are as many different options for mouthpieces and shank styles as there are colors of wild rags, and the final choice will depend on each individual horse-and-rider combination.

Unlike a traditional solid mouthpiece Western bit, the two-handed Western bit allows you to continue to facilitate communication to one side of the horse's mouth at a time as you refine your other aids in building a horse with Soft Feel and self-carriage. The movement in the bit allows you to lightly lift and apply pressure to one commissure at a time. Used properly, the horse can carry and perform quite comfortably in this bit when ridden with light contact. Many Cowboy Dressage riders will transition between this bit and the snaffle and back again, as needed, depending on the horse and the goals of the rider. It is important to note that the choice to transition up to a two-handed shanked bit from a snaffle bit is not because the horse "needs a bigger bit" but rather that the horse is ready for a little more refinement in his communication. When a horse doesn't understand softness and bend in a snaffle bit, you aren't likely to find success in a two-handed bit either (see sidebar on leverage bits for more on this concept).

1.7 – *This is an example of the two-handed Western bit. It is broken in the middle so each side moves independently. The shanks are also loose, as opposed to fixed, allowing for more variations in communication. There are multiple variations of this bit type available.*

Leverage Bits

While bit choice is often just a matter of personal preference between horse and rider, the differences between the bits are much more significant. Before choosing your bit, it is important to consider your goals, your horse's level of training, and reason for changing bit type. Typically, the horse learns in the simplest training tool, either a snaffle or a bosal, and transitions to a leverage-type bit as his training is refined, but more importantly, as his understanding of pressure and release and rider expectation grows. It is essential that you understand the mechanism of action of the tools being used to get the most effectiveness out of the exchange between horse and rider.

No matter what kind of bit you are using, you are effecting a change on the horse's poll. If you look at the horse's head as a long rod connecting the muzzle to the poll, you can imagine that moving the poll would be easier and require less energy the farther away you are from the poll. This is the principle of leverage (fig. 1.8). The bosal sits closest to the poll and requires the most direct pressure to affect the poll. A shanked bit's action is farthest from the poll and can, therefore, exert the most action on the poll with the least amount of pressure from the rider. The longer the shank, the more leverage it applies.

The misconception that many riders fall victim to is that because the rider is exerting less pressure manually, the horse is "lighter." This is not the case because of the leverage effect. If this were true we would not hear the complaint when transitioning a horse from the shanked bit back to the snaffle that the rider has no control or that the horse is so much heavier in the snaffle. When the horse is heavy in the snaffle, transitioning to a leverage bit is only going to make the rider feel better about that heaviness because she must pull less to get the same effect. But from the horse's perspective, he isn't learning to

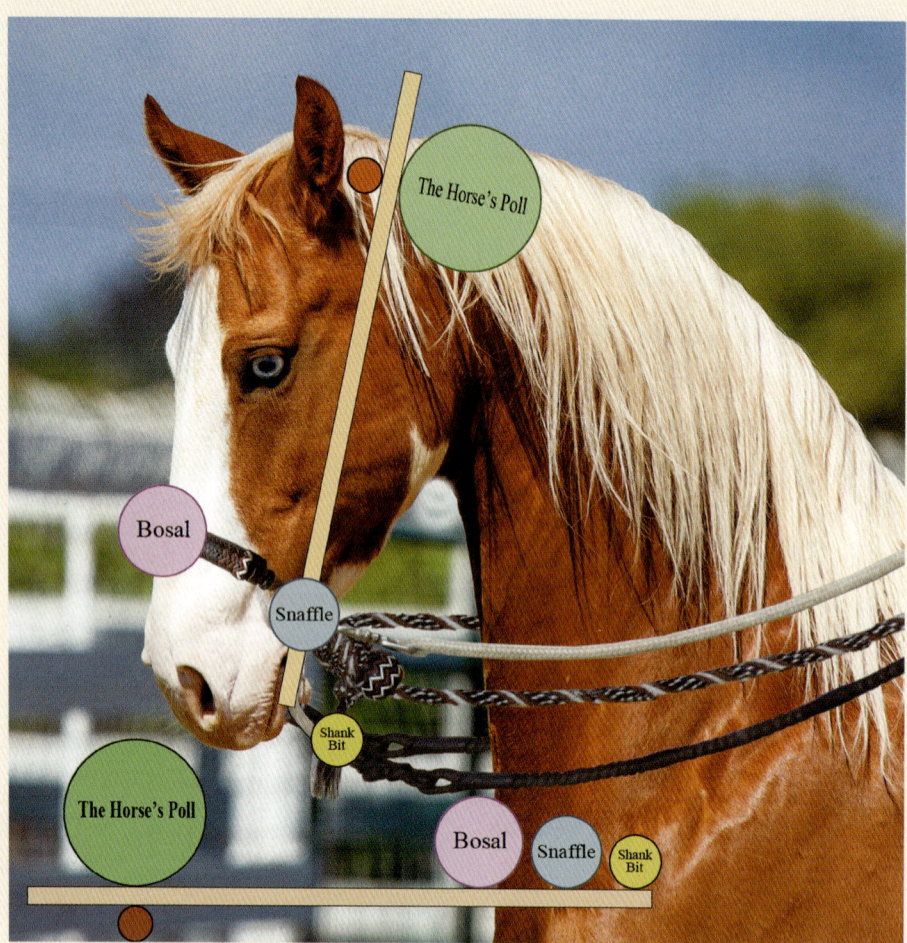

1.8 – *The fulcrum point is at the horse's poll and the bar of leverage is the horse's head. Each of the different pieces of tack is represented by a circle, the size of which represents the amount of force applied by the rider to exert force on the horse's poll. The bosal requires the most force to exert action on the poll and the leverage bit requires the least amount. It is important to remember that just because you are pulling less does not mean the horse is experiencing less pressure.*

be lighter and more responsive, he is learning how to deal with ever increasing amounts of pressure.

Once the horse understands pressure and how to relax his poll and give to the pressure, he is ready for the refinement of the leverage bit. The lighter signal allows for more subtlety of cues and more infinite variation in the conversation between horse and rider.

1.9 – *The closer to the poll, the more effort is required to exert the same effect on the horse's poll. Farther away from the poll, and less effort is required by the rider to exert the same effect on the horse's poll. This is the principle of leverage.*

The poll is directly affected by the pressure on the long rod that is the plane of the horse's face from poll to muzzle (fig. 1.9). The bosal requires the most relative force to apply a given amount of pressure to the poll. The snaffle requires slightly less pressure for the same effect, but both are direct pressure devices. As you move into a shanked bit, you really emphasize the effect of leverage action on the poll, and this effect is amplified most by the length of the shank.

Bosal and Loping Hackamores

Currently the only bitless options available to the Cowboy Dressage rider in the show ring are the *traditional bosal* and the *loping hackamore* (figs. 1.10 and 1.11). The bosal is a traditional piece of cowboy gear that is most commonly made of a rope or rawhide core overbraided with rawhide. The bosal is an important step in the California and Vaquero bridle horse traditions that aims to transition the horse into the spade bit. Many horses perform very well in the bosal. It can be ridden either one- or two-handed. Traditionally the mecate is made of twisted mane hair but other natural fibers such as mohair or alpaca fiber have also been used. Some of the working cowboys prefer a paracord mecate due to its all-weather durability. If you choose to ride in a bosal, you may find you enjoy the Vaquero division that exists to showcase the tack and traditions of the early Vaqueros, but

1.10 – *The traditional rawhide bosal with a mane hair mecate.*

1.11 – *The loping hackamore.*

bosals are welcome in all divisions and classes.

A properly fitted bosal is important to ensure proper communication with the horse. The well-fitted bosal will fit the horse's face like a hat does a head with good contact points all along the bridge of the nose with good balance and movement of the heel knot.

The loping hackamore is typically more of an exercise piece of equipment that originated as a tool for riders who were "loping down" performance horses before their run, either in the cutting pen or reining pen. It loosely resembles the bosal without the weight and signal of the heel knot.

Spade Bits and Other One-Handed Western Bits

The epitome of the Western performance horse has always been the bridle horse, from the tradition of the California bridle horse to the reining and cutting performance horses featured in the World's Greatest Horseman competitions. We believe that to show a horse straight up in the bridle takes an enormous amount of training and time. For this reason, horses younger than five cannot be shown in a bridle bit in Cowboy Dressage. If the rider chooses to enter a class straight up in the bridle, riding one-handed, he is required to finish the test the same way. Some examples of one-handed bridle bits are the spade, Mona Lisa, and the half-breed.

It takes a very accomplished horseman and a well-trained and prepared horse to successfully ride with bend and balance in the spade bit (fig. 1.12). While we honor those horsemen that are

1.12 – *The traditional spade bit—only to be used on a properly prepared bridle horse.*

able to achieve that success, we caution others that these tools can be misused if the horse is not well prepared, or if the rider doesn't have a thorough understanding of the way the spade is designed to work in the horse's mouth.

Reins

Reins can be a very personal decision for the horseman and in Cowboy Dressage they are the rider's choice. Whether you ride with traditional harness leather split reins or the popular natural fiber mecate is irrelevant as long as the bit and rein combination are appropriate. For the snaffle bit, split reins, braided loop reins, and mecate style reins are all suitable. When riding in a single-braided loop rein, be sure that the rein length is long enough to allow for enough release of rein for the free frame without causing the rider to be too far out of position.

Many Cowboy Dressage riders prefer a rein with some weight in it, either in the form of slobber straps or tassels to aid in asking the horse to follow the bottom of the bit down and out in the free frame. A rein style with a little weight in it will also provide clearer and quicker release. The romal reins in the tradition of the bridle horse are appropriate only on a one-handed bridle bit such as the spade or equivalent bit, and are not appropriate on a snaffle or a two-handed bit.

There are no requirements for how you hold your reins other than in the Vaquero division as it applies to both the two-rein and the bridle bit with romal reins. The Cowboy Dressage rider is encouraged to use whatever rein is easiest for communication and rein management. When riding a test in front of a judge, you are required to stay either one-handed or two-handed throughout the test. The way you enter the Court is the way you ride the entire test.

Apparel

Here is one of the places Cowboy Dressage riders express their own unique background and journey to Cowboy Dressage. There is no uniform or standard look, and we see everything from riding skirts to equitation chaps at a Cowboy Dressage Gathering. The only requirements are Western apparel, long sleeve shirt, a tie of some sort, Western boots, and hat or helmet. The rest is up to the riders (figs. 1.13–1.18).

Many riders embrace the vintage Cowboy culture and outfit themselves as Dale Evans might have done. Others, with a more modern show ring background, will bring their "blingiest" slinky and shiny saddle. While fancy show clothes or tack are not required at a Cowboy Dressage show, they are not discouraged either. They do not give you any extra credit with the judges whose eyes are for Soft Feel, the partnership, and the good ride, but if you like to dress up in shiny stuff, why not?

Chaps, chinks, and armitas are common at a Cowboy Dressage show but not required. Boots with a heel are required for safety except for ground classes requiring jogging, during which we allow riders to wear a riding shoe for ease moving over the arena floor. You are also required at the Gatherings to have a cowboy hat or helmet and some form of tie, be it bolo, necktie, or wild rag. If your clothes are neat and tidy and your tack clean and serviceable, you have everything you need to head to a Cowboy Dressage Gathering.

We strive to keep the rules to a minimum where Cowboy Dressage tack and apparel are concerned, but in the interest of fairness to horse and rider and fellow competitor, we find our rules are evolving all the time. Current recommendations and rules for tack and apparel are always available at www.cowboydressageworld.com.

1.13–1.18 – *Cowboy Dressage members showing off their personal style at Cowboy Dressage Gatherings.*

2

WISDOM TREE

"The most beautiful thing you can do with your horse is nothing. We are always in such a hurry. Take your time. Stop and do nothing sometimes."

EITAN BETH-HALACHMY

When teaching the horse, we often talk about the "foundation" of that education. The analogy is perfect because like a house with a poor foundation, the horse with a poor foundation is a shaky entity ready to collapse (or explode!) when you least expect it. While we all long to have a finely tuned and perfectly trained horse, this level of perfection is not something that can be attained in a short period. Time is the enemy of teaching horses because they are animals that live in the moment. We as humans try to force horses to fit into our schedule, and learn at what we deem a reasonable pace, only to be confounded again and again by their "stubbornness." In truth, each horse learns at his own unique pace. It is up to us to feel our way along and make the horse's education as individualized as the horse.

This principle of taking your time is one of the traditions of the California Vaquero horsemen of old. They called it *mañana*, which means "tomorrow" in Spanish. The idea is that tomorrow is always another day. When working with a horse, it is important to remember that it doesn't have to happen today. The horse often learns best slowly, one step at a time. By taking it slowly and rewarding the slightest try, you can keep the horse happy and willing in his work. In today's world of competitive futurities, it can be hard to see the progress that is happening slowly. By keeping the foundation and the goals of progression firmly in your mind you can avoid the pitfalls that come with quickly slapping down a poor foundation. "Slow and steady wins the race," and this principle holds true in working with your horse, as well.

In Cowboy Dressage we are interested in building our equine partners slowly, and we expect them to be with us for a very long time. Longevity, strength, and soundness take the place of fast-paced learning. By considering the rate of growth of the equine skeleton and the time it takes to properly prepare a horse for the ultimate in Soft Feel and self-carriage, we feel it is important that we do not start horses too young. All horses, regardless of breed, develop at the same skeletal rate. While a thick-bodied young Quarter Horse may appear stout and mature at three, his skeleton doesn't stop growing until he is five-and-a-half or six years of age (see sidebar on rate of skeletal maturation).

Futurities do not exist in Cowboy Dressage and there is no reward given for a young horse that excels at a Gathering. In fact the overwhelming attitude is to not push young horses too far or too fast. We bring our horses along slowly, allowing them to grow and mature to their full potential before asking them to perform more than just the basic tests.

Part of our education with our horses is teaching them to learn. The old adage, "You can't teach an old dog new tricks," is founded in the belief that all species need to learn to learn. This is part of the reason that horses tend to get started before their bodies are ready for heavy work. Their minds, like young children's, are like sponges and behavior modification can become more challenging as they age. But, we can teach our horses to learn and use their body without the added stress of carrying a rider. Groundwork allows us to begin to build that partnership and establish the basics of communication and response to our aids without adding undue stress to the horse's body. While we carefully lay the foundation for our horses through groundwork exercises, we help them learn to learn. Groundwork, then, is the very bottom of the foundation that we lay in our teaching programs.

We have borrowed the concept of the "training scale" from classical dressage but have adapted it to fit the Cowboy Dressage horse and rider (fig. 2.2). The "scale" or "tree" (as we call it) illustration is so apt because it not only illustrates the lineal progression of training but the relative time that is spent in training at each step. Only the horse can tell you if that relative time translates to months or years, but you can bet a successful "tree" starts with much more time spent on the ground than in the saddle.

Skeletal Maturation

By Jenni L. Grimmett, DVM

It's interesting to me that now that horses are used primarily for pleasure, sport, or entertainment instead of as a work partner or means of transportation, we are less patient when training them. Perhaps this reflects our throwaway society. Or, maybe, it is the fault of the veterinary community that has perfected the band-aids necessary to keep a horse working when he shouldn't be. Or maybe it's the fault of the high-end competitive venues that have turned toward making money off equine "children" (young horses) rather than encouraging owner, riders, and trainers to compete their horses once they've reached adulthood. Or maybe it is the fault of the rest of us… who just follow suit.

I'm talking about the very controversial issue of skeletal maturation and the optimum age for starting a young horse. There are many widely spread misunderstandings in this area—the modern horse world seems to be more and more impressed with the advanced abilities of a young horse as showcased in a futurity. We prize the young horse that achieves enormous amounts of money earnings early in his career and then retires to the breeding shed before reaching maturity.

You can see this change in almost every aspect of the horse industry, but maybe nowhere so dramatically as in the American racing industry. Where racehorses used to have to be at least four before they began competing in long heats of 4-mile feats of endurance, the concept of the quick sprint futurities was introduced to allow bettors a "glimpse" of the talent coming up. Racing of two- and three-year-olds in shorter, more "humane" races became the norm, and were immensely popular for their ability to stage a shorter race on a track that could seat more people, allow for more prospective bettors, and overall increase the excitement of the race. Soon, the only horses racing at maturity were cheap claimers or geldings that didn't have a career in the breeding shed to look forward to. What has occurred in the racing industry is a significant drop in the number of starts a horse will have in his life paired with an increase in the number of breakdowns.

The same has occurred in the Western Reined Cow Horse industry. What used to be a competition for a mature bridle horse (generally six or older) was then turned into a futurity for hackamore horses. As the snaffle bit increased in popularity for its ability to accomplish more advanced training more quickly, the snaffle bit futurity was born. This is a high-dollar competition for young stock horses that are three years of age. In order to compete in this highly demanding and physical sport these horses are often started under saddle at 18 months. One of the sad parts about this is that right there on the first page of the NRCHA (National Reined Cow Horse Association) rule book is the purpose of the association: "The purpose of the NRCHA is to improve the quality of the Western reined stock horse: to perpetuate the early Spanish traditions of highly trained and well reined working cow horses." It has traveled quite a way from the goals at its inception.

The tradition of the early Spanish horsemen was to not put any metal in their horses' mouths until age five or six, and to bring them along slowly to protect not only their physical well-being but mental well-being, too. Spanish tradition would start a horse at three or four with very light riding with a hackamore until he was ready to move into the two-rein at five or six, and only after he was carefully prepared would he be straight up in the bridle and riding one-handed. For many horses, this wasn't until they were seven or older. Today, a seven-year-old reined cow horse is likely ready to retire from the show ring. Not always, but often.

But it's not just high-dollar performance horses that are being started as two-year-olds. Conventional wisdom seems to push folks to start their backyard pleasure horses sometime during their two-year-old year. The conscientious owner knows to wait until "the knees are closed." This piece of equine wisdom is referring to the growth plates at the distal radius. While you can't actually tell by palpating the horse if that growth plate has fused or not, many folks feel that you can, and they use this colloquial rule of thumb for starting youngsters under saddle.

What we know about the rate of skeletal maturity is that the growth plates in the equine body slowly fuse between one-and-a-half and six years—across the board. There is no truth to the myth that some breeds of horses mature faster than others. All horses reach skeletal maturity at about five-and-a-half to six years of age. This really shouldn't surprise us as we know that horses continue to erupt molars until they are five. Why shouldn't the timing for completion of growth be about the same?

What may not be common knowledge is that it's not the legs that are the slowest maturing part of the body. The growth plates of the knees mature (or close) at about two years for the small bones and three years for the distal radius and ulna. The very last growth plates to fuse are in the equine vertebrae. All 32 of them! The last of those are the ones in the base of the neck.

The reason this is relevant to our young horses that we plan to ride well into their advanced years is that the process of riding our young horses can contribute to not only excessive wear and tear on their young joints (the hocks also don't fuse until three-and-a-half years) but strain to their backs and necks as well (fig. 2.1).

The process of teaching a horse to be ridden at a very young age teaches the horse to protect himself from back pain. To do this, the horse braces his back and drops his shoulders and hollows out so that he can help take the weight off his vertebral column. It's a minor thing at first and one that every young horse being started under saddle goes through to a certain degree until his back muscles get better at carrying weight. But if you persist in riding a young horse whose vertebral column is not able to bear that weight—even with muscular conditioning—you create a habit caused by pain that becomes deeply ingrained and prevents the horse from properly learning to round up and use his body.

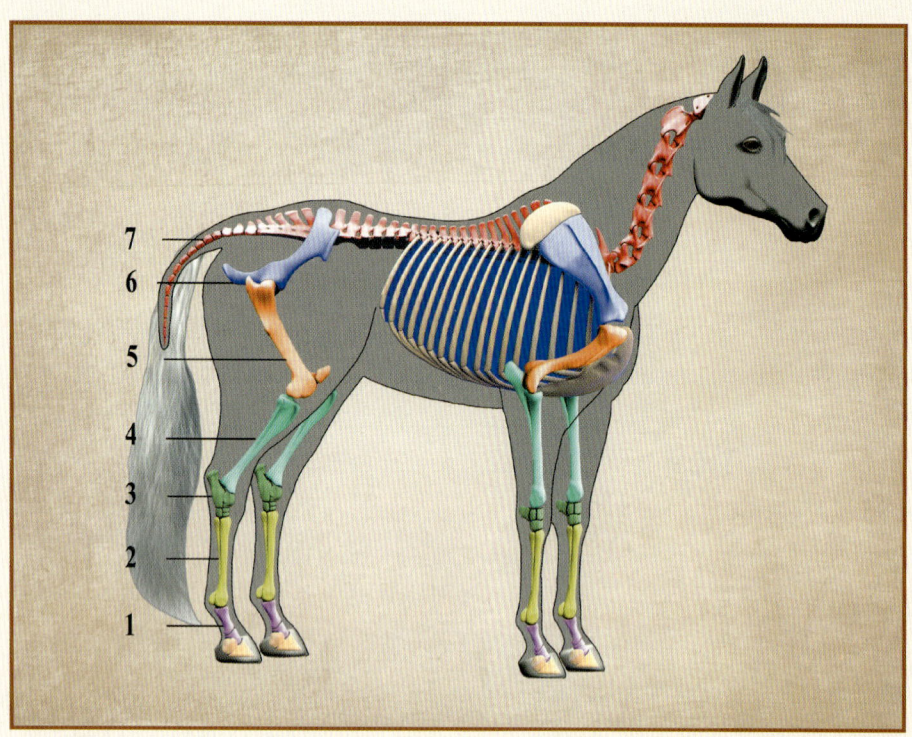

2.1 – *Rate of Equine Skeletal Maturation: 1) Pasterns fuse at about six months old. 2) Metacarpus/metatarsus (commonly called the cannons) fuse at one-and-a-half years. 3) The carpus/tarsus, knees and hocks: one-and-a-half to two years. 4) Radius and tibia: two-and-a-half to three years. 5) Humerus and femur: three to three-and-a-half years. 6) Scapula and pelvis: three-and-a-half to four years. 7) Vertebrae fuse from back to front from three-and-a-half to six years.*

The next step in training a young horse after getting on his back (especially in many of today's "natural horsemanship" methods) is the one-rein stop. This is accomplished by repetitively pulling the horse's head over to your foot and limbering up the neck until it is quite soft and "rubbery." Isn't this putting added stresses on the last vertebrae to fuse in the horse's entire body? Pain here causes stiffness in the bridle that makes the horse flex by turning his head at the atlas rather than flexing his entire vertebral column. With vertical flexion, he then learns to brace his withers, and instead of flexing along his entire column, will flex at the third vertebra to protect the rest of the cer-

vical vertebrae. All of this might look like a broke young horse to the uninitiated, but in truth it is a horse with reflexes built on pain. These horses can never move in a true collected frame.

So while the now common and widespread practice of putting a two-year-old to work in a rigorous training program undoubtedly leads to increased incidences of breakdowns in racehorses, the widespread practice of injecting young horses' joints to try to stave off juvenile osteoarthritis—the other long-lasting effects of bracing and consequent pain through their back and neck—are less often addressed.

Does this mean that we shouldn't start our horses until they are fully skeletally mature? This, for me, is a hard question to answer.

Paired with the data of skeletal maturity is the data that exists on mental maturity. Horses can and do learn to learn. One of the great things that have been bred into the Quarter Horse performance horses is their ability to calmly and easily learn what is expected of them. They are almost "born broke." This is because they have been selected for trainability, which is really the capacity to learn. (Whether this makes them the smartest breed of horse or just the most trainable is a discussion for another time!) For most folks that work with young horses and start colts, the ones that have had an introduction to good handling and training as yearlings are much easier to start as two- or three-year-olds. This ability to retain a lesson and understand what is being taught is a learned behavior. The younger they learn this, the easier they seem to be to train and quicker they come to trust human handlers.

Therefore, I believe the answer lies in moderation, as with most things. I think you must take into consideration your youngster and your training program. I am 100 percent *not* in favor of futurities that demand a horse be put into rigorous training as a two-year-old. I am also *not* in favor of any practice that deems it common and prudent to inject a young horse's joints to maintain joint health or cover up lameness and keep him working. But, that's just me. I have many colleagues happily performing these procedures and building their retirement accounts much faster than I am.

I don't think you necessarily need to completely stay off your horse until he is four. I think you can teach a young horse some valuable lessons, expose him to important stimuli and situations, and in general, build his confidence and ability to learn as a young horse. I don't feel that lack of skeletal maturity means no work or riding at all, but I think it means *conscientious* riding and training to preserve not only your horse's mind but his physical ability to be able to be a good sound partner throughout his entire life. I want to be riding my horses well into their second decade and possibly longer. There is nothing sadder to me than a six-year-old that is too lame to be ridden in the show pen anymore because he was ridden too hard as a youngster. That's like seeing a teenage girl who trained too hard as a gymnast and now has collapsed bones in her wrists and a deformed radius. Too much work too soon. We need to be smarter than this for our horses. Increasing the usable upper-age limits of our horses through smart training will go miles to decreasing the numbers of unwanted or crippled horses out there.

From the groundwork we establish response to *pressure and release*. We establish *forward*. We build *partnership* and *try*. We also help our horses to begin to establish an attention span and a work ethic by commanding and directing their attention for a period of time during which they can be successful. This means, again, that we must pay attention to the horse and his body language. A young horse can only be expected to successfully pay attention for a short span of time. Requiring more out of him sets him up for failure. Give your lessons in small bite-sized pieces and it will be better digested and retained.

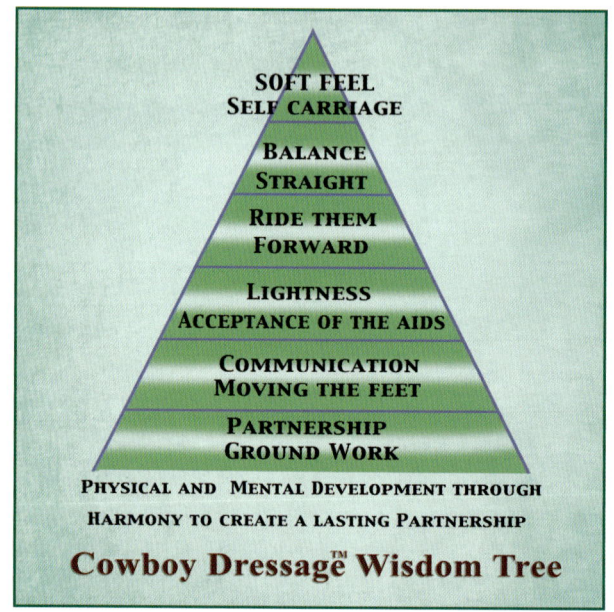

2.2 – *The Cowboy Dressage Wisdom Tree.*

Level 1: Partnership and Groundwork

Every interaction that you have with your horse, from haltering to grooming to leading, can be considered groundwork. From the moment you greet your horse at the gate, he is either learning good habits and being rewarded for good behavior, or learning bad habits that will crop up later when you least expect it. Groundwork isn't only when you are in the round pen or on the longe line. If you can remember to be a conscientious handler each time you interact with your horse, you will be a better horseman for it (fig. 2.3).

Good handling makes everything that you want to do with your horse later in his career that much easier. Groundwork serves not only to begin his training but throughout his life to introduce new things. Groundwork should also be a part of your daily ride warm up. It allows you to politely check out your horse before you get on and ask him, "How are you today?" (See chapter 3 for more on groundwork.)

Level 2: Communication and Moving the Feet

From the ground, and in the saddle, you progress to moving the horse's feet with purpose (fig. 2.4). Driving and directing the horse's movement, you can begin to connect aids to each of the feet and build responsiveness and lightness. You can help to develop and maintain *forward*. All of the lateral maneuvers can be started on the ground. Groundwork gives you the tools that you then take into the saddle to begin directing the horse through maneuvers or obstacles. The Cowboy

2.3 – Sending the horse around us in a circle is the basis of all our groundwork maneuvers. We ask the horse to walk, using driving pressure from the hindquarters to establish frame and gait, and guiding pressure on the lead rope to establish direction. The horse should move off with light contact on the lead, never taking the slack out of the lead rope, and maintaining a consistent distance from the handler. The horse should look to the inside of the circle and bend from head to tail.

2.4 – The handler increases the difficulty of the manuevers on the ground by asking for bend through the gaits. Here she is asking the horse to maintain bend and pick up the working jog. In this moment we can see there is too much bend through the horse's head and neck, and the handler will have to work to balance the bend and the drive to help the horse create the perfect balanced circle.

Dressage Challenge Court provides multiple obstacles and ground poles that can be used to help direct the horse's feet and build responsiveness. (See chapter 3 for a discussion on the introduction of lateral maneuvers on the ground, as well as groundwork exercises using the octagon.)

Level 3: Lightness and Acceptance of the Aids

Learning a new shared language takes time and patience. You must be consistent in your aids and timely in your release to guide the horse to understand how you guide him with the use of your body through your aids (fig. 2.5). When the horse learns to seek the quiet place within your aids, he is ready to move on to more advanced skills and maneuvers. (See chapter 4 for a discussion of the aids.)

Level 4: Ride Them Forward

As the horse's confidence grows, and his response and lightness improves, you begin to ride the horse forward into the other gaits. By keeping the horse moving forward in lightness and harmony, you can begin to ask the horse for more in each of the frames and in each of the gaits (see p. 89 for a discussion of frames). Transitions between frames and between gaits are the key to developing these within the horse. Developing cadence through the gaits, as well as frame, takes time and encouragement and confidence in the horse. You can't rush this stage of development and each horse will progress at his own pace (fig. 2.6). Take your time and let the horse be your guide in this stage. (See chapter 6 for a discussion on cadence and gaits.)

2.5 – *From the saddle, the rider begins to introduce each of the aids while using maneuvers already introduced on the ground. Here she is asking for slight lateral flexion through the horse's head and neck while driving the horse forward. This will eventually become a shoulder-in (see p. 139).*

2.6 – *As lightness and acceptance of aids develops, this rider asks the horse for more "forward" by transitioning to the faster gaits. Here she asks the horse to jog.*

Level 5: Balance and Straightness

Building balance, suppleness, and straightness happens through the use of bend (fig. 2.7). Horses are not born straight. You must help them to evenly strengthen and develop their bodies and their balance by teaching them bend and building the muscles of balance using the lateral maneuvers. (See chapter 7 for further discussion of straightness and the development of bend.)

Level 6: Soft Feel and Self-Carriage

Finally, the horse can carry himself in self-carriage and is the example of Soft Feel and partnership and all that is possible between horse and rider (fig. 2.8). There is no timeline for this development, and each horse and rider must progress at his or her own pace. Properly developing the horse through lightness can only happen when you pay close attention to the horse's body development and make sure that you are building the right muscles for self-carriage. You are sculpting an equine masterpiece through your work in Cowboy Dressage. (For a discussion on lateral maneuvers and developing the muscles and strength, see chapter 8. For information on the short frame and collection on the journey to Soft Feel, see chapter 9.)

2.7 – *Riding the horse in a perfectly straight line like Eitan is here cannot happen without preparation and suppling through bend.*

2.8 – *They say a picture is worth a thousand words, and this picture couldn't have happened without thousands of hours of dedicated work both on the ground and in the saddle. There are no shortcuts to a finished horse.*

3

GROUNDWORK AND PARTNERSHIP ON THE GROUND

"Everything you do on the ground you should do in the saddle, and vice versa."

EITAN BETH-HALACHMY

Cowboy Dressage believes in a solid foundation on the ground from the very beginning in educating the horse. To that end, the Partnership on the Ground division was developed. Partnership is more than just a halter class and another division at a Gathering. It is an opportunity for the handler and the horse to work on basic principles and elements of Soft Feel that will certainly translate to their time under saddle. Whether a rider ever has any dreams of competition, the Partnership on the Ground tests are excellent check lists and warm-up ground exercises for any rider in any discipline (fig. 3.1).

Leading the Horse

One of us is a veterinarian and one a horseman, and so between us we see horses of every discipline, from talented upper-level dressage horses to ponies that are passed from eight-year-old to eight-year-old. No matter the skills the horse possesses under saddle, the skills that

3.1 – *In Cowboy Dressage we strongly believe that groundwork is the foundation of all the work we will later do under saddle. Groundwork needs to establish a connection and a foundation that will later be carried over into the saddle. When you are working with your horse on the ground you always need to be considering how that will translate to ridden work. So even while our feet are on the ground, we keep our minds thinking toward them being in the stirrups.*

are sure to win our hearts every time are respectful ground manners. Handling a horse that is patient, light on the halter, and respectful to the handler on the ground is such a joy that we have trouble imagining why anyone would wish to forgo this very basic handling skill. *Any* horse and *any* handler can learn the basics of proper ground manners and safe handling, and carry that essential connection into their work in the saddle. Partnership begins on the ground with a solid connection to cues and aids that will eventually be used in the saddle.

Teaching a young horse to lead or re-teaching a horse that hasn't previously learned how to lead lightly can be a very rewarding experience. The tools needed are a lead rope and halter (preferably a rope halter and lead; see the discussion on tack on p. 8); and an extension of your arm: stick and string, flag, or dressage whip. It is also very helpful to have a fence or straight wall to work along when the horse is very new to proper leading.

When working with a horse on the ground, you can either *lead* or *drive* the horse. Leading occurs when you are at or near the horse's head. Driving occurs when you are back near or behind the shoulder in a closer position to where you would be in the saddle. Your goal in groundwork is to create a connection that feels like the connection you will eventually have under saddle. So, while you often will have to begin by leading the horse by walking up near the head, you want to always be thinking about driving and moving back to the shoulder as soon as possible. If you are thinking about driving rather than leading, you will avoid the common pitfall of dragging the horse along behind you. Instead the two of you move as a unit.

In a definite *leading* position, the handler is leading and the horse is following (fig. 3.2 A). In this position, you cannot see the horse without looking back at him nor can you make significant changes to the horse's body position. For many horses, this becomes a position from which they learn to drag behind the handler like they would in a pack string. Driving the horse forward is much more difficult in this position and the handler may compensate by pulling on the horse.

In a *driving* position, the horse is leading and the handler is following (fig. 3.2 B). The rider is in a similar position to where she would be in the saddle. In this position, you can more closely train using the same cues and energy that you would use to communicate from the horse's back. Obviously, this is also an easy position for the horse to choose to ignore your cues by rushing past you. This is a position that we work toward in our leading exercises, and it is a useful position for initiating driving exercises.

Going together is the position that you would like to be using most of the time (fig. 3.2 C). This is the position that is your goal in Cowboy Dressage Partnership on the Ground classes to show that you are establishing partnership, softness, and a willing forward-moving horse. You can drive from this position as well as influence the horse's front feet and rib cage. Using a dressage whip or stick, you can drive the horse's hindquarters forward.

Body Language Cues

Just as when you ride your horse, you want the horse to respond to more than just rein cues, and when you lead the horse, you want the horse to respond to more than just cues on the lead rope. Therefore, consistency in body language cues is important when handling and teaching the horse proper ground manners.

To ask the horse to go forward, you first cue the horse by leaning slightly forward with the

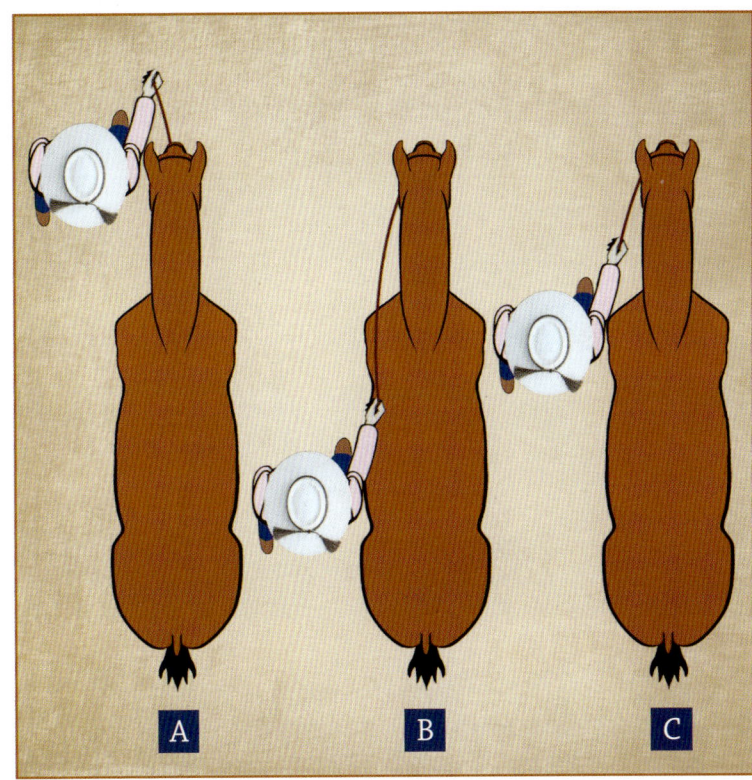

3.2 – *The three positions of leading the horse: leading (A), driving, (B), and going together (C).*

body. If the horse does not move forward from this signal with body language, ask the horse to step forward using the dressage whip with a very gentle tap at the hindquarters using the left hand when standing on the horse's left side. Once the horse is moving forward, relax the "go" body position and walk with your shoulder at the horse's neck, staying between the jaw and the shoulder.

If the horse moves off past you or doesn't move at the pace you've established, there are two options for correction. The first option is to stop and allow the horse to continue to travel past you, making a small circle until he is back into the original position. Once there and standing quietly, praise the horse and walk off again. If you are

3.3 – *Partnership on the ground and in the saddle is an excellent way to introduce children to the joys of the Cowboy Dressage Court. Lead-line classes are offered at Gatherings in the Partnership Division.*

using this technique, be sure that you are driving the horse away from you and not pulling him into you. If the horse is crowding your space and you continue to pull him in around you, this situation will get worse instead of better. For the horse that doesn't appreciate the extra energy expenditure of additional steps, this technique may work quite well. For the horse that enjoys, and even seeks those moments of extra energy expenditure, this technique may not work as well. For these horses, you may be better off stopping that forward movement and asking the horse to take a few steps backward using pressure on the lead rope, then asking the horse to step forward back into position next to you again by driving him forward from the hindquarters rather than pulling. Allow the horse to settle and then set off again at a walk. You may need to repeat either of these techniques and maybe a combination of them until the horse is comfortably walking beside you and moving forward off consistent body language.

Another tool at your disposal in correcting a horse that wants to rush past you is the dressage whip. If you have tried the other techniques, sometimes, using the dressage whip as an extension of your hand and creating a physical barrier is a good way to reinforce the lesson on a horse that is rushing. You can either hold the whip up in front of the horse in his line of sight or tap the horse on the chest. Do not hit the horse on the head or neck with the dressage whip.

"Old Man Walk"

A great exercise for helping the horse to learn to rate his speed to your speed is an exercise called "Old Man Walk." In this exercise, you vary the speed of your walk and the energy in your body, asking the horse to stay with you on a soft lead. You can go from slowly walking one step at a time to walking off quite rapidly and see if the horse can adjust to match your speed. Be sure you are playing fair by intentionally increasing and decreasing the energy in your body so your horse learns to rely on those cues. If you are having trouble figuring out how to tap into your inner body language and energy center, think of walking forward with a purpose to increase energy; not in a hurry, but with a true destination in mind. Breathing out your energy and walking slowly is usually less difficult to tap into!

Jogging in Hand

You teach the horse to jog beside you in exactly the same manner as you teach him to walk beside you. Pulling the horse into a jog does not encourage a light and willing partner. Driving the horse forward from the hindquarters improves the overall drive and movement of the horse on the ground in a manner that will carry forward once you are in the saddle. You accomplish this again by using the dressage whip with the left hand (when leading on the left), making contact with the hindquarters. This is best achieved along a fence because often the horse will move sideways away from the contact with the dressage whip instead of forward. Once the horse is moving forward, it is important to go with the horse and make sure you don't discourage that forward movement by pulling on the lead rope. You can often teach the horse to jog by using a partner to help drive the horse from the hindquarters until he understands the body language cue from you.

Remember when teaching your horse to lead at the walk and the jog, do it from both sides. In Cowboy Dressage everything you do on the left you must do again on the right. Smoothly transitioning lead rope and dressage whip from one hand to the other takes a bit of practice. You will want to spend some time getting smooth and fluid at this so as not to interfere with the horse.

Halt on the Ground

Teaching the horse to stop from the ground when you stop is also best accomplished by helping the horse to understand your body language rather than by pressure on the lead rope. Again, working along a fence line at the walk, prepare your horse to stop by first releasing your forward energy then slowing the feet to melt to a stop. If the horse fails to stop with this body language cue, then a gentle downward pressure on the lead rope should follow. If the horse continues to walk right on by, you can use the dressage whip as the extension of your hand in front of the horse. A young horse, or one long accustomed to leading the person—not vice versa—may continue forward through all of these commands until he walks a circle around you. As the handler, calmly keep your own feet still. You have stopped and it's up to the horse to stop with you. Keep your own feet still, and use the lead rope and dressage whip to guide the horse back into position next to you until he stops his feet and stands where you stopped initially. Once he has stopped there let him rest, and praise him before moving on.

These elemental principles are the skills practiced on the Court in Partnership on the Ground. Leading in a straight line from the correct position with Soft Feel without dragging the horse forward or yanking him to a stop are the basic

3.4 – *Partnership on the Ground serves as a starting point for the Cowboy Dressage journey for both horse and rider new to the discipline.*

purposes of the Partnership test (fig. 3.4). The same accuracy in transitions that you aim for under saddle begins through adequate preparation and soft execution from the ground. You also begin to teach bend from the ground in the Partnership tests.

Maneuvering the Horse's Body on the Ground

Once the horse has learned to lead with Soft Feel in the correct position, he is ready to start to learn to bend from the ground as well. You create bend in your mount from the ground by establishing bend in your body as you lead your horse. When entering into a 10-meter circle, your head and shoulders rotate on the bend just as they would if you were riding the 10-meter circle. The leading hand can make a small contact on the lead rope laterally to initiate bend in the head and neck. The dressage whip can function as your inside leg, making contact with the rib cage to ask the horse to bend. When creating bend on the ground it is common to see the horse bend primarily through the head and neck and to a lesser degree through the rib cage, while the hindquarters often drift slightly to the outside of the circle. This deviation in bend will be corrected as the horse's training progresses, but it is difficult to fix from the ground.

Turn-on-the-Haunches in Hand

The other basic exercise included in the Partnership tests that will eventually be very important under saddle is the turn-on-the-haunches. Horse and handler are required to execute this turn from both directions. Using a fence or the rail, ask the horse to stop and move to the other side of the horse. Standing at the horse's shoulder, you direct your body language and energy to the horse's forehand. You don't want to either push or drag the horse backward through the turn. Generally, using a dressage whip or even your hand, you can tap the horse at the junction of shoulder and neck right where the rein will eventually make contact when the horse is under saddle. Your other hand helps to direct the horse's head around in the turn.

For example, if you are teaching your horse to

do a turn-on-the-haunches to the left, you will stand on the horse's right side (fig. 3.5). Create energy through body language directed at the horse's head, neck, and shoulders by facing the horse's neck. Your left hand will direct the horse's shoulder over in the turn by tapping at the junction of neck and shoulder with feel and timing, releasing pressure as soon as the horse steps over with his outside front leg. The right hand can alternately lift to direct the horse's head away from you and into the turn, or with gentle pressure on the lead, keep the horse from walking forward in the turn.

As with teaching turn-on-the-haunches in the saddle, you want to take the turn-on-the-haunches on the ground one step at a time (figs. 3.5, 3.6, 3.7, and 3.8). We use the rail in Partnership on the Ground to assist us through the turn by supporting the horse's haunches. Once the turn is completed, the horse-and-handler pair should walk right off in the working walk, maintaining forward energy through the turn.

The Partnership on the Ground tests are practiced on the challenge Court to help provide visual direction to both horse and rider and to help give purpose to the test for the young horses. For the more advanced Partnership on the Ground

3.5 – *Turn-on-the-haunches to the left. The rider stands on the right side, directing the horse's forehand away using driving pressure on the shoulder at the junction to the neck right where the rein will eventually contact when the rider is in the saddle.*

3.6 – *The rider moves the horse one step at a time. Be careful not to rush the horse through the turn. The front legs should cross over in front of one another, maintaining forward through the turn, while the hind feet stay in place with the inside hind foot being either the pivot foot or stepping in place.*

test (Two), the horses are asked to walk over the ground poles. This is how we begin to introduce lengthening of stride and foot placement from the ground. The quarterline ground poles can be difficult for some of the younger, greener horses to navigate. Consistent ground-pole work helps the horse to become responsible for his own feet without the added distraction of a rider on his back.

Groundwork or in-hand work in both long lines and driving reins has been a tradition in equine training for centuries. There are so many different theories and exercises that can be used by the savvy horseman to help establish connection and partnership on the ground. We leave the selection of those exercises up to the handler. You will find a rainbow of different exercises being performed in the warm-up arena at a Cowboy Dressage Gathering, depending on the horsemanship background of the handler. It is important to be creative and not just drill the horse with ground exercises. Always change things up and find new ways to challenge the horse and yourself to continue to grow your partnership. The exercises that follow are a few that you can use. Keep Soft Feel and partnership as your primary goal and many different exercises will aid in helping the horse to learn some of the basic maneuvers that will serve you well in all you do.

3.7 – *Turn-on-the-haunches to the right. The handler moves to the horse's left side and asks the forehand to move to the right. Here you can see Indy's front right foot stepping out and back slightly to make room for the left front foot to step across. The handler's body position is driving the horse's forehand through the turn.*

3.8 – *Turn-on-the-haunches to the right. Indy's left front foot is reaching over and crossing in front of his right front foot.*

3.9 – *Using the octagon for groundwork. Here the handler stands inside the octagon and asks the horse to travel around the outside. The physical barrier of the poles helps to encourage the horse to bend.*

3.10 – *Here the handler is asking the horse to jog through the octagon while the handler is outside it. As the horse travels to the outside of the octagon, the handler could step back into the center and change the exercise again to the horse traveling around the outside.*

Groundwork Exercises

The Octagon

That eight-sided box in the middle of the Cowboy Dressage Challenge Court is the perfect tool for groundwork (fig. 3.9). We often use the octagon as a "pre-flight check" before getting into the saddle. With a 12-foot diameter, it is the perfect size for in-hand work with most of our 12-foot natural horsemanship rope halter and leads. The presence of the ground poles helps the horse in many ways during groundwork on the lead. The poles create a visual for the horse to bend around on the lead, just as he does under saddle. For the horse that tends to crowd the handler, it also establishes a physical barrier to help remind him to stay on the circle.

Circle around and change direction: After a few circles around the outside of the octagon, you can ask the horse to step through the center and change direction. You can also have the horse change direction by stopping and making a turn-on-the-haunches where the poles help the horse to remember not to step forward out of the turn.

Walk and jog through the octagon: Asking the horse to travel through the center of the octagon at both the walk and the jog helps the horse to be more aware of his foot placement and stride length (fig. 3.10). Smoothly transitioning from jogging around the octagon to stepping through the octagon is an excellent exercise for any horse.

3.11 –*Shoulder-in on the circle. You can see the horse is bent through the head and neck, and the inside hind leg is traveling on the same track as the outside front leg.*

Shoulder-in on the circle: The octagon is also useful for teaching and practicing the shoulder-in on the circle (fig. 3.11). By asking the horse to walk around the octagon you can drive the hindquarters deeper under the horse using a dressage whip as an extension of your hand. The horse ends up walking around the octagon, creating two circles. The forehand walks a circle close to the octagon while the hindquarters walk a circle farther from the octagon. This helps build strength in the hindquarters and balance in the horse and makes this exercise easier for the horse once under saddle (fig. 3.12).

3.12 – *Another view of the shoulder-in on the circle, demonstrating the three tracks.*

Quarterline Ground Poles

I also like to use quarterline ground poles in my ground work exercises by working my horse first at a walk and then a working jog in a 10-meter oval over the ground poles (fig. 3.13). This is an excellent exercise for perfecting drive, straight lines, and bend from the ground. The goals for this exercise are for the handler to remain on midline between I and G while the horse travels from C to 8 with 10-meter bend at the ends of the oval and a straight line down the quarterlines over the ground poles (see p. 77 for a map of the Court).

And as said before, the Partnership on the Ground tests are a great way to warm your horse up on the ground and test out your partnership for the day before climbing into the saddle. We will often run through one or both of the Partnership on the Ground tests at the beginning of our open arena nights.

3.13 – *The handler is driving the horse through the quarterline ground poles and doing a fine job of asking the horse to stay centered over them.*

4

AIDS

"Riding your horse should be a conversation that nobody else can see."

EITAN BETH-HALACHMY

Your aids are the collection of tools that you use to communicate with your horse. You use your body to speak directly to different parts of the horse's body. Your aids include hands, legs, seat, weight, energy, and voice. At its simplest, the *application of an aid* is termed a *cue*. For example, when you apply a leg *aid* directly to the side of the horse, you can create a *cue* the horse understands to mean "move forward." In this scenario, cues are very black-and-white and create a single reliable, specific response from the horse. But in truth, the application of aids is infinitely more subtle and complex than this. Here's why: Aids actually say more than a cue. A cue is a single action with a single response, but your aids are "sentences" with inflection and emotion. Initially, for both horse and rider, when the rider applies pressure with the leg (her aid) and the horse moves off the leg, the aid was a cue to move. But eventually the same aid is refined, and a simple flexing of the rider's leg speaks to the horse with many different meanings, depending on the position of the leg, the balance of the rider, and the intention in the rider's seat. Less pressure is applied, making the aid more subtle but also more complex, because there is an infinite number of things the rider can be saying with that same leg.

In this chapter, we will discuss aids as a bridge in the language barrier between horse and rider (fig. 4.1).

Building an effective relationship between horse and rider is much like two people with no common language learning how to communicate through a new, shared language. While people are primarily creatures of the spoken language, the horse is a creature almost entirely of the unspoken language of body signals. Both horse and rider must learn and adapt to a common means of communication for the conversation to be more than cues and conditioned responses.

For many people, the spoken language is a difficult thing to forego. We love to talk to our horses, and we believe the horses like to hear us speaking to them. Horses are not completely without an oral language. The deep-throated nicker between a mare and her newborn foal or the far-reaching scream of a stallion are oral communications that ring out universally in the evolutionary history of the horse. Horses will often greet their owners with nickers and whinnies like the calls they would use between herd mates. A horse can learn to recognize the voice of his owner and respond accordingly. But, the prevailing communication observed in a herd setting is through body language, and the inference of motive behind simple gestures that are shaded in meaning by the social standing within the herd.

The horse has a wide range of body-language vocabulary that is universal and easily understood by other members of his species. It is also known that horses, as a prey species, can read the body language of other animals quite easily. This is how a lion may walk among a herd of zebras (part of the *Equidae* family, along with

4.1 – *In a perfect world, your skeleton mirrors and guides the horse's skeleton. Your aids speak directly to the horse's body in a simple-to-understand, if not simple-to-achieve, universal language.*

Behavior Modification Terms

It is often said that as equestrians we are either training or untraining a horse while we are riding him. While most horse enthusiasts do not consider themselves trainers, we all must take on the mantle of a trainer to a certain degree every time we handle or ride our horse. Therefore, a basic understanding of behavior modification is helpful for any student of horsemanship. All trainers are amateur behaviorists, and all horsemen are at least amateur horse trainers—whether they want to be or not. Here are some basic terms and concepts used in any discussion of behavior modification and horsemanship:

Modification is the process of changing a given behavioral response through either positive or negative reinforcement. When training our horses, we modify their behavioral responses.

Positive reinforcement is the addition of something desirable in response to a desired behavior. The positive is almost always a food reward but can also be the promise of a food reward delivered at an unspecified time. This is the basis for clicker training and the way most performing marine mammals are trained. It is widely considered by behaviorists to be the most effective training modality, creating a long-lasting and fairly predictable response. It has an interesting history in horse training, with people firmly in the camps both for and against this form of training.

We see positive reinforcement more commonly (and incorrectly) used as a distraction technique. This is not how positive reinforcement is meant to be applied. Your acting as a human PEZ® dispenser to keep the horse standing quietly is not positive reinforcement—it is bribery. Giving a treat to reward a horse that has stood quietly through a procedure is positive reinforcement. There are a few big name natural horsemanship trainers that are adamantly opposed to positive reinforcement ("treating") in training because it "spoils" the horse. When used ineffectively (like the human PEZ dispenser) that can certainly be the case.

Negative reinforcement is the removal of something undesirable in response to a behavior. This is the classic training paradigm that is used in almost all of our work with our horses. Our aids are effectively the "undesirable" that is removed in response to the desired behavior. Many people balk a little at the "negative" in negative reinforcement. If it helps, think of it as "subtractive" reinforcement. When used with effective timing and feel, there is nothing abusive about negative reinforcement. This is not a pain or fear-based training paradigm. It is the addition of pain or fear that moves negative reinforcement closer to punishment. As with all behavior modification, a positive experience makes the behavior more likely to be accepted and repeated. When fear and pain are introduced into the equation, those become the stronger association making the behavior association unpredictable.

Within the natural horsemanship movement there is a teaching paradigm that really emphasizes the theory that any time a horse doesn't immediately respond to your request he is being disrespectful and dull, and that we need to follow it up in any way we can to get the results we desire from our horse. The phrase "do as little as possible and as much as necessary" can escalate quickly from application of negative reinforcement training to punishment.

Punishment can be in one of two forms. You can have *negative punishment*, which is the removal of something, generally a treat or food reward, in response to an undesirable behavior. A good example would be removing a treat from the horse's reach when he takes it too abruptly. *Positive punishment* is the addition of something due to an undesirable behavior and is much more common in training our horses. An example of positive punishment is jerking on the bit when the horse pushes on your hands, or spurring or kicking repetitively when the horse ignores your leg. Probably the most common punishment we see, especially in natural horsemanship circles, is aggressively backing the horse that crowds you out of your space.

The problem with punishment as a behavior modifier is that it is almost impossible to apply accurately to change or affect the undesirable behavior. In order for punishment, either positive or negative, to be effective both contingency and contiguity must be well paired with the behavior. *Contingency* means that every time the behavior is exhibited, the punishment is administered. *Contiguity* means that the punishment is delivered right away rather than delayed. For punishment to be effective, it must be delivered within one to two seconds of the behavior, and the horse must understand the relationship between the action and the handler's reaction. If the punishment is delayed, several other behaviors may occur before punishment, making it confusing to the horse as to which behavior is being discouraged by the punishment.

The horse, in almost all instances, simply does what he thinks he has to in order to get by. It is our anthropomorphism that projects motive onto horses. We want to believe our horses love us. We want to believe that we "know" what is going on in their heads. This is exactly what gets us into trouble when we are in a training situation. This is why great horsemen seem to have the patience of Job when dealing with a horse that the rest of us may look at and say, "Man, that horse is a jerk!" The horseman knows the horse is only doing what he thinks he has to, and is in "search mode," trying to find the right answer to this new herd dynamic he is faced with.

All horse training, from the very first haltering experience to developing a flying lead change, is the result of rewarding the horse for desired behavior. In most instances, we cannot force a horse into a behavior. The better the horse is at searching for behaviors (we call that "try") and the better the trainer is at rewarding those behaviors (timing and feel), the faster and further the training will go.

When we change our training paradigm from negative or positive reinforcement to negative or positive punishment, we change the rules on the horse. Punishment can actually produce unwanted behavior as the horse responds to the action of the punishment without understanding the behavior that induced the punishment in the first place.

A good example of punishment resulting in an undesirable behavior is the head-shy horse. Obviously, biting is a dangerous and undesirable trait that we see in young horses. It is a natural extension of their teething and a learning phase of development. It's as natural to the horse as it is to the toddler gnawing on whatever is within reach. It is very difficult to effectively punish the horse for biting without creating undesirable behavior. Hitting or flicking the young horse that is biting will either induce a fun game of "see who can bite the quickest," or if you hit hard enough or often enough, produce a horse that is difficult to handle around the head, eyes, ears, or mouth.

Most people will agree that the very best and effective horsemanship comes from a place devoid of human emotion. Anger, fear, or frustration has no place in horse training. Punishment comes from those places within us. In an attempt to sterilize these actions of emotion, we see some trainers who laugh as they punish the horse or make a joke of it. "Oh, I'm sorry, did you run into my stick?" Laughing or playfully saying, "Oops!" after punishment is for the owner, not the horse. It makes us feel better about inflicting punishment for an action that we couldn't prevent, redirect, or avoid.

We are not advocating that you hand over leadership to your horse. He still needs to understand that you are the leader and he is the follower in your little herd of two. He needs to understand this and accept it, not because he will be punished if he doesn't, but because you will keep him safe and secure if he does.

So, how do we use the theories of positive and negative reinforcement and avoid resorting to punishment to produce the most effective and long-lasting behavior modifications in our horses? In all cases of behavior modification, it is the motivation behind the behavior that the horse is most likely to remember, paired with the timing of the release or reward. The most common and effective method to date is negative reinforcement *without* punishment. In order to prevent negative reinforcement from becoming positive punishment, we have to learn to *wait*. This is how we build "try" and softness in our horses without developing fear or pain. We retain their trust and their desire to follow

our lead because we build a place where it feels good to be with us. We wait for the "try," and we reward it when it happens.

From the very beginning when working with our horses, some will have more "try" than others. We must hold on to whatever "try" they are born with and attempt to cultivate it by always rewarding the smallest amount of it. If we keep the horse searching with "try," he will be more likely to stumble upon and remember the right answers to our directives without the need to resort to pain-associated negative reinforcement or positive punishment. We are such an impatient species. We have agendas and goals and checklists. The horse does not. The horse desires the bare necessities and puts up with us for reasons that only God could expound on. We owe it to the horse to be the very best humans we can be. Sometimes that means letting go of all the things that make us human in the first place: emotion; impatience; agenda; drive; anger; frustration. Let go of it and just *wait* and be with the horse.

There will be times in any training program when things go south. That's the nature of attempting to align the mind and soul of two very different creatures. Punishment will happen out of necessity, frustration, or desperation. That's okay. Recognize it for what it is, and try to see how it perhaps could have been avoided. As luck would have it, we are dealing with one of the most forgiving of all beasts on the planet. Just don't excuse it as good training. Punishment is a last resort and is the least effective of all the training modalities.

horses) without spooking the herd. As Dr. Robert Miller is much quoted as saying, "Horses fear predatory behavior, not predators." Zebras can read the intention in the lion's body language and know there is no danger until the lion begins to display hunting and stalking characteristics.

The study of body language, and how our horses read and respond to it, is the basis of the natural horsemanship movement. The attempt to communicate with horses through their "natural" language explains the derivation of the term "natural horsemanship." By learning how to read and respond to our horses we have also learned how to work within their understanding of

4.2 – This illustration demonstrates the concept of the rider's hands directing the horse's front feet through the rein aids, while the rider's legs direct the horse's hind feet as the seat drives those hind legs forward. The visual representation of the rider's hands speaking directly to the horse's feet through the reins is important to understand because proper timing of these aids is paramount to creating lightness. Imagine this rider attempting to pull the horse's feet off the ground. It would be impossible. But we can influence the placement of those feet once they are in travel off the ground. The "gears" of the seat encouraging and riding the horse forward are instrumental in all other communication with the horse's feet through our aids. Only through "forward" can those aids be effective.

pressure and release, and positive and negative reinforcement, to improve our training and our relationship with them.

In a perfect world, when the horse is right where we want him to be, our aids are quiet. The horse learns to seek that quiet place of relaxation as the correct response to any direction given. It is our better understanding of body language and how to communicate with our horse that has changed how we think of our aids in riding. Rather than being tools that we use to control our horse's movement through simple cues, our aids become part of the vocabulary of the wordless communication with our horse.

We very rarely use our aids individually. Most of the time, we are communicating with our horses through all our aids (fig. 4.2). Talking about the aids one at a time is like discussing the alphabet letter by letter to understand a new language. We will discuss them here one at a time for simplicity, but understand that individually the aids exist almost without function—however, when delivered as a sentence, we can begin to craft a story in function and form. The more subtly we use the aids together, the prettier the picture and the words change from a list of commands to poetry or musical lyrics. Let's discuss the pieces of our language with our horses that allow horse and rider to create art.

4.3 – *The rider's hands can directly affect the carriage of the horse's head. The horse should be rewarded and encouraged for following the feel of the rider's hands. In this way, too, you can help the horse to define the frame and shift the weight farther back toward the hindquarters. The lower a horse carries his head, the more weight he is going to carry on his front feet. In the interest of keeping the horse sound and diminishing weight and concussion on the front feet, you encourage the horse to lift his head and shift his weight backward. Your hands do not force or hold the head up; instead the horse learns to come to the rider's hands when there is softness as a reward.*

The Hands

We'll begin our discussion with the simplest of the aids. The hands are like the vowels of our alphabet in this language we are creating. In the beginning, when starting a young horse, instruction can hardly exist without them. The hands provide a direct communication to one of the most sensitive parts of the horse. Because the hands are the first aid used on most occasions, they are almost always the most overused. Speaking only with your hands to your horse is the equivalent of addressing an audience using caveman-like grunts and rough gestures. The consonants that create the intricacies of language are missing and we can only drag our horses around in basic maneuvers. But, though they are very basic, they are also very important.

The hands function to initiate direction in the horse as well as head placement. The hands can directly affect lateral flexion and vertical flexion through contact with the middle of the bit. In raising and lowering the hand, the rider can raise and lower the head by changing the rein weight on the bit, to the top or bottom of the snaffle. (See the section on the snaffle bit for a refresher on the function of the top, middle, and bottom of the bit, p. 14.) It is the change in rein weight rather than bit pressure that eventually creates the desired head placement and carriage within the frame (figs. 4.3 and 4.4). Each hand should

4.4 – Here is a good example of the horse's frame and head following the rider's hands. You can also see how Eitan's back and head mirror what the horse is doing, as well.

4.5 – Eitan asks Cheyenne to flex laterally through pressure on the inside rein. The outside rein must have enough slack to allow the horse to bend without running into tension on the outside rein. Here, Eitan's hand is back toward the hip but often, he will open the hand into the bend so the horse is looking toward the hand.

act independently of the other until refinement of cues has taken place.

Lateral flexion is the beginning of bend and should be initiated and taught to the horse from the ground before ever being in the saddle. Even flexion through the cervical vertebrae without rotation of the atlas initiates bend and shortening of the inside of the horse, and lengthening of the outside of the horse. The rider encourages the horse to look to the hand by creating contact outward toward the inside of the bend (fig. 4.5). While an open hand initiates lateral flexion, the hand must not stay open into the circle once the bend is initiated or the rider's weight will fall to the inside of the circle. The rider initiates the lateral bend, then the hand is brought into closer proximity to the shoulder, as it is the shoulder you ultimately wish to communicate with.

As the horse and rider advance in the understanding of their communication, your hands will speak directly to the front feet through the horse's shoulders. You can influence the direction and flight of the forehand through proper application of the rein aids with the timing of the front feet.

Independent use of the hands can prove to

be quite as challenging for new riders as rubbing your stomach and patting your head. The hands need to communicate with the horse one side at a time to help the horse learn balance and bend. When you create contact on the middle of the bit asking the horse to bend, the outside hand must release rein, allowing the horse the freedom to bend without running into the bit.

Effective use of the hands on the reins is essential for the development of Soft Feel. Light and soft hands are the goal of each rider. When riding two-handed in a snaffle bit, your hands provide a direct connection to the bit. Tension in your hands, arms, neck, or torso can be transferred inadvertently to the horse. Keeping your arms and shoulders free of tension is imperative to effective communication. The hands and fingers should have a firm but soft hold on the reins. Giving the horse release from a command or directive may be conveyed by simply relaxing the fingers on the rein. The fingers need to remain alive and in constant minute conversation with the horse. Therefore, soft contact with the horse is essential for the development of Soft Feel through the bit. If we ride on a too long and loose rein, we give up the subtle communication between horse and rider, making all the adjustments through the bit conveyed unclearly, kind of like the child's game of "String Telephone"— the horse with a "cup" on one end and you with a "cup" on the other. Much of the conversation is lost in the transfer. While we want to develop softness through our contact, we do not want to give all that important contact away.

4.6 – *Every rider should strive for soft, quiet, effective contact. Soft hands make soft horses.*

The position of the rider's hands is entirely dependent on the horse. The rider's hands will raise and lower with the horse's head, frame, and gait. There is no "box" or proper hand position in Cowboy Dressage. Instead, keep your hands soft and light on the reins in a position that allows you the best communication with your horse. The most important thing to remember about your hands in your riding is to use them lightly (fig. 4.6). Remember, the hands are your vowels in this language you are building. Very important and part of every word we use, but too much of a good thing muddles the words and creates white noise. Keep the noise in your hands quiet!

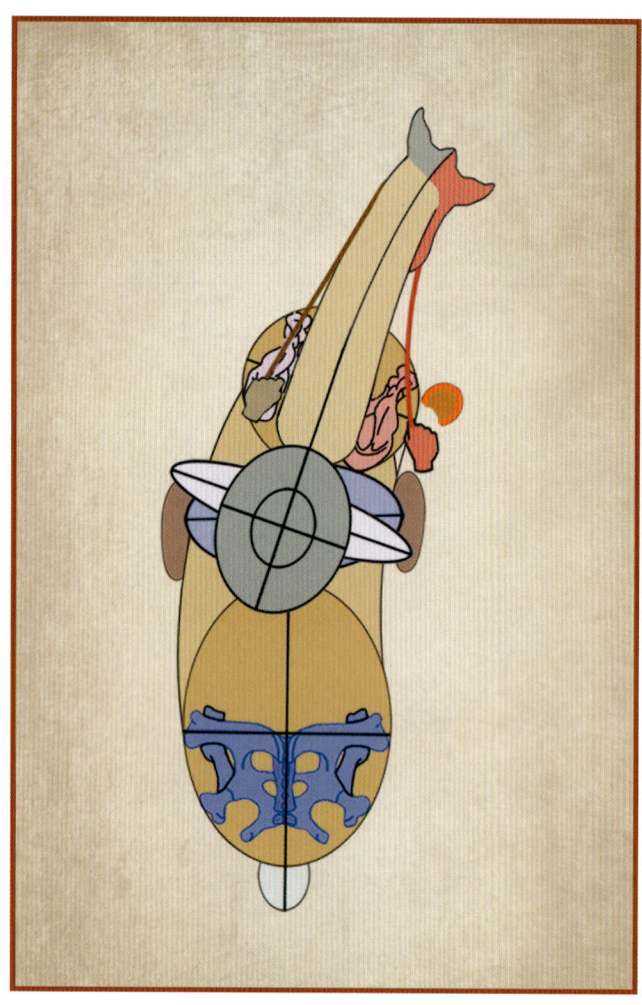

4.7 – *The direct rein aid: Here the horse bends to the right with the right hand/rein speaking directly to the right front leg (areas shaded red).*

Direct Rein

We begin with the simplest of the rein aids, the *direct rein* (fig. 4.7). When we use the term "direct" when talking about rein aids, it refers to the action it exerts on the foot. The *direct rein* communicates *directly* with the front leg on the inside of the horse's bend (so if the horse is being asked to laterally bend to the right, a right direct rein affects the right front leg). By moving the hand to the side ("opening" the hand) the rein will contact the middle of the bit and speak to the corner of the horse's mouth. The horse should follow the rein and look to the hand. When the horse gives to that pressure, he will bend through the neck slightly in the direction of the rein aid and will weight his inside front leg to compensate for his shift in balance through his body as he bends his neck. This is the rein aid used to create lateral flexion.

The Indirect Rein

The *indirect rein aid*, though the same rein as the first example, speaks *not* to the inside front leg directly, but to the *outside* front leg (*outside* the bend), thereby creating an *indirect* effect (fig. 4.8). When using the indirect rein, the hand moves toward the horse's withers without crossing the neck or moving behind the withers. This creates bend through the horse's head and neck but displaces the horse's forward movement toward the

The Five Rein Aids

While I think most of us can visualize how we can affect the horse's front feet through the reins, there are infinite variations in how we can use those reins to effect change in the horse's feet. Here, we will attempt to remove the mystery of the different actions of the reins and how they affect the way the horse's body responds to the rein aids. Consistency with the rein aids leads the horse to seek your hands, creating lightness and balance between horse and rider.

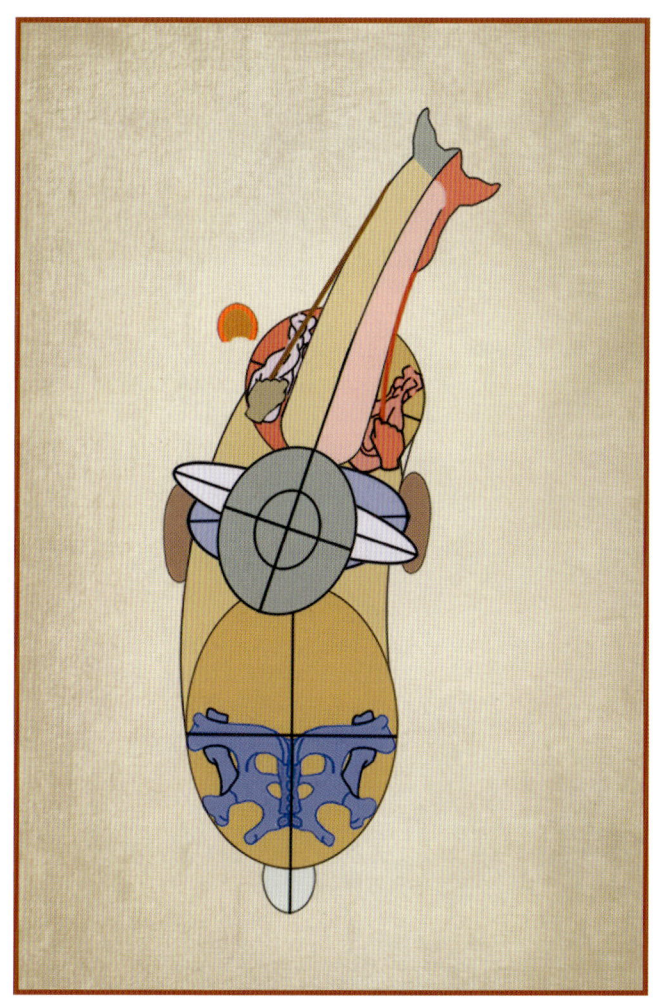

4.8 – *The indirect rein aid: Here the rider's right hand indirectly affects the horse's left front leg (areas shaded red).*

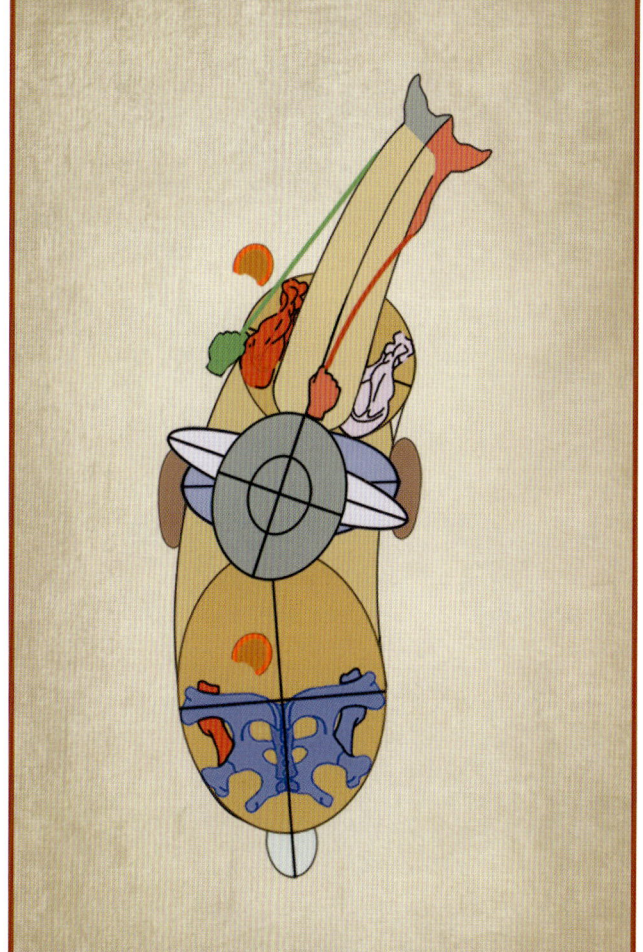

4.9 – *The counter-bend rein aid: Here the rider's right hand shifts the horse's weight to the left hind leg and causes the left front to step over (shaded in red).*

outside shoulder and front leg (outside the bend). This is both a suppling and rebalancing exercise. The indirect rein changes the horse's balance to the outside front leg, causing the horse to lead with that leg.

The indirect rein action comes from "pushing" the inside rein against the inside shoulder and *not* by pulling the outside rein. A good example of when a rider might use the indirect rein is if the horse drops the inside shoulder when riding a circle. You can correct for this loss of balance by shifting the weight back to the outside shoulder. The indirect rein helps to build control on the shoulders of the horse.

The Counter-Bend Rein

The *counter-bend rein* speaks to both the *outside front leg* and *outside hind leg* (fig. 4.9). The inside hand moves behind the withers to the rider's center and toward the horse's opposite hip. This

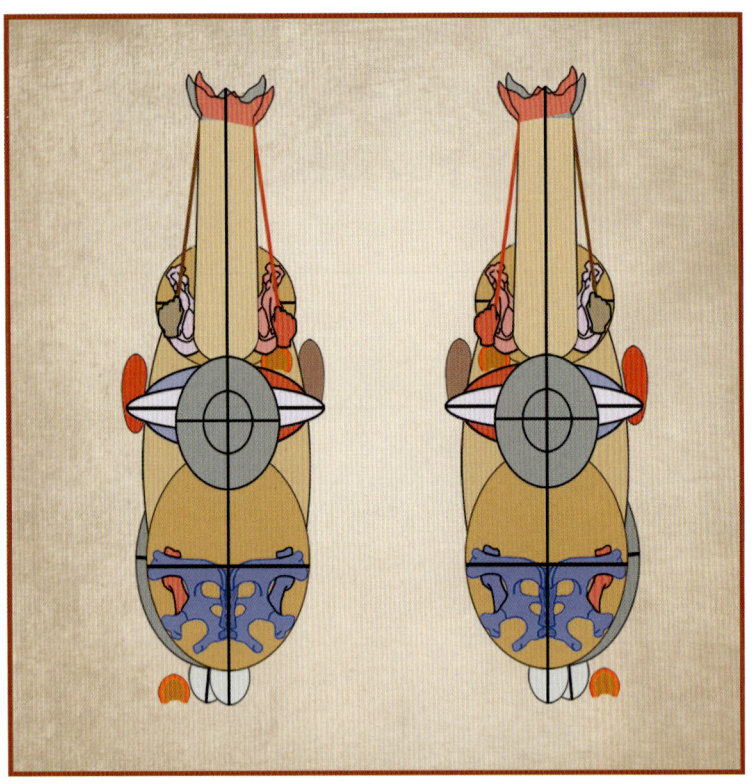

4.10 – *The direct rein of opposition: Here the rider's alternating direct rein aids act on the front leg on the same side as the aid, and the opposite hind leg (shaded in red).*

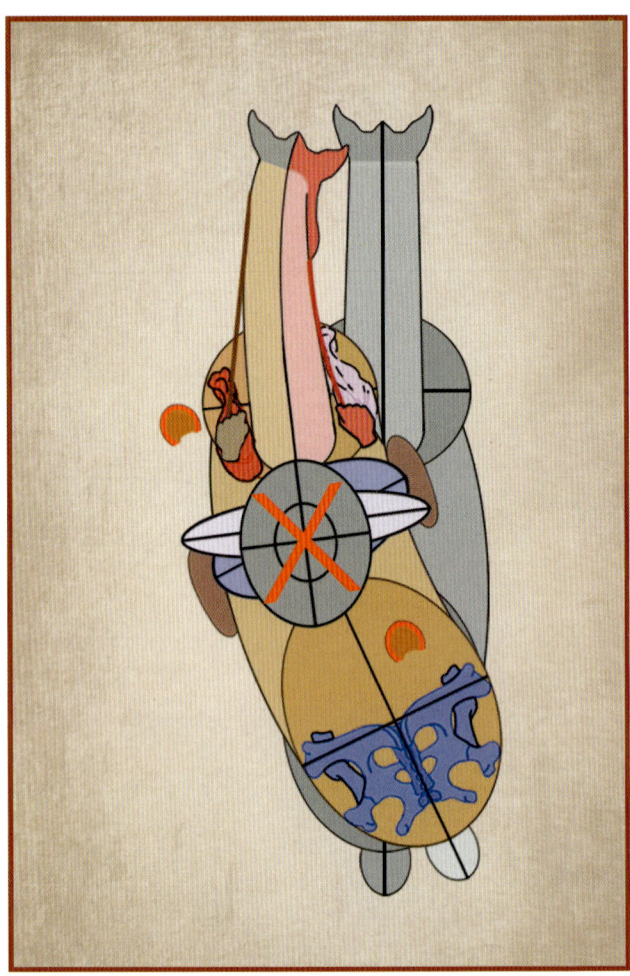

4.11 – *The indirect rein of opposition: Here the rider's right hand indirectly affects the horse's outside front leg and inside hind leg (shaded in red), causing a turn over the horse's center of gravity (red X).*

shortens the inside of the horse and blocks forward movement in the horse, causing the horse to weight the outside hind leg and step back and over with the outside front leg. The outside rein is for balance only and maintains neutral contact with the outside shoulder. It is the inside rein that directs movement. The direction of travel is away from the bend. The horse's balance is shifted to the outside front and back legs. The counter-bend rein is used, of course, in the counter-bend, but also in the leg-yield (with less bend) and to initiate the turn-on-the-forehand.

Direct Rein of Opposition

The *direct rein of opposition* is the rein aid that you use to create a stop or to back up (fig. 4.10). The *direct rein* is acting on the *front leg on the same side as the rein,* and on the *opposite hind leg.* We call it the "rein of opposition" because it *stops* forward movement rather than directs forward movement. You use pressure on the bit in alternating pulses straight back toward your hips. This asks the horse to shift his weight backward, carrying the momentum of the walk or stop backward in alternating diagonal pairs of feet.

Indirect Rein of Opposition

The *indirect rein of opposition* also stops forward momentum, but *indirectly* affects the *outside front leg* and *inside hind leg* (fig. 4.11). The rider's inside hand moves toward the withers, pushing against the shoulder but with opposition to the forward movement. The hand does not cross the neck and stays in front of the withers (as opposed to the hand moving toward the hip in the leg-yield position). The rein blocks the inside impulsion. This brings the horse's head to the inside while pushing the outside shoulder backward. Unlike in "regular" bend, the horse's outside shoulder is back and the inside shoulder is forward. The horse steps out and back with the outside front leg and rotates around the axis in his center. The inside hind leg comes in and forward. This is, essentially, a turn on center with the balance remaining on the center of gravity of the horse. This rein aid can be used to help the horse distinguish between the turn-on-the-forehand and turn-on-the-haunches when he is asked to only move either the forehand or the hindquarters. In this example, he is moving both equally.

The Legs

If the hands are the vowels of our language, the legs are the most commonly used consonants in our equine language (fig. 4.12). The legs help

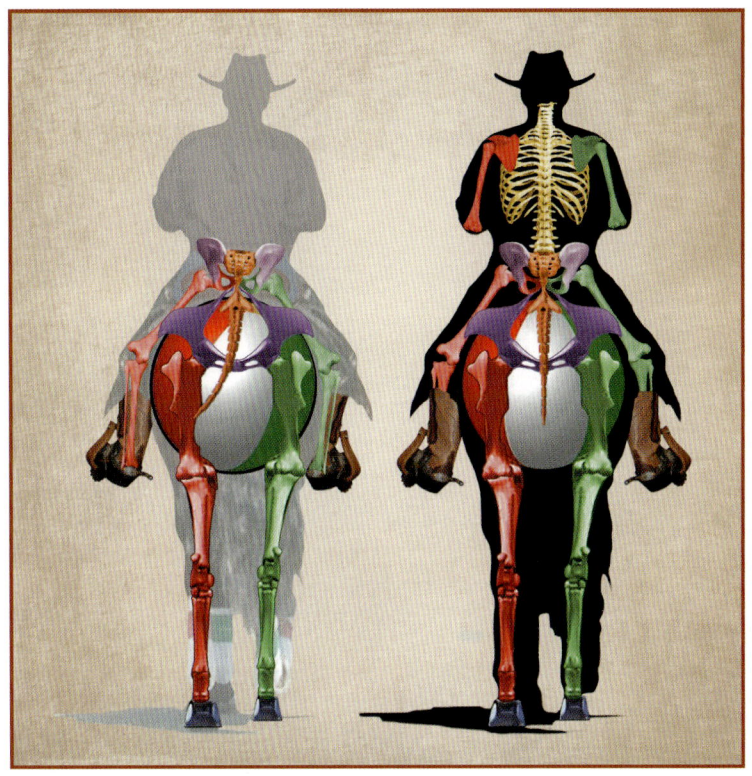

4.12 –*On the right you see the proper positioning of the rider's legs along the sides of the horse's barrel. On the left you see the change to an active right leg-yield: The left leg (red) is not removed from the barrel when the right leg (green) is activated. You can see the horse's barrel rolls to the left and "gives" to the leg pressure. The rider's seat can also be seen to be weighted along with the leg aid.*

give the hands meaning so that *bend* becomes *bend with forward motion*, and the *stop* becomes a *turn-on-the-forehand*. The leg aids applied from the knee down allow you to speak to the horse's rib cage, hindquarters, and hind feet. While the legs should lie against the sides of the horse, they need not dictate every action. If the legs are "on" all the time, we again create "white noise" that the horse learns to tune out.

Unlike the hands that are almost always used

independently, the legs are almost always used in concert. Just as a vowel is generally bracketed by consonants, each leg helps create the communication to the horse. The legs are used to shape and direct the horse's body beneath you. They are essential in the development of bend, and using both legs together helps to maintain balance in both horse and rider. This does not mean that you are applying equal pressure with both legs at the same time. You can have one aid being active while the other is neutral, but in neutrality, still functional. While it isn't exactly a soft image to consider, it is like the iron that is shaped on the anvil. You cannot shape the iron without both the hammer and the anvil. It is the same when considering the leg aids. The hammer is the active aid while the anvil is the neutral aid—yet it gives the active aid the ability to effectively shape the iron (in our case, the horse).

A perfect example of the leg aids being active and neutral is in the lateral movements. In the shoulder-in, the inside leg is active in holding the horse's rib cage in balance and moving forward. The outside leg is in the position to hold the hindquarters from drifting if needed, as well as provide impulsion, if necessary, but is largely neutral in this setting. If the outside leg aid were removed completely, the active inside leg aid may cause the horse to move into a leg-yield rather than a shoulder-in.

The main job of the leg aids is to shape the horse's body. While many people mistakenly believe that the

4.13 – *The rider's legs speak directly to the horse's hind legs: right leg to right hind leg and left leg to left hind leg. The leg aids ask the horse to lift the foot via gentle contact with the calf. As the horse's leg leaves the ground, the seat takes over, riding in rhythm with the horse, telling the leg how quickly to move forward and how far. ASK the hind foot to move, RIDE the hind foot forward, then ASK the other hind foot and RIDE it forward. ASK RIDE ASK in time with the horse's feet is how we ride each stride. This sounds like an awful lot of work but is really a very subtle communication between horse and rider.*

legs are responsible for moving the horse forward, that is not the case. The legs provide the cue to pick up a foot and move the rib cage, but it's the *seat* that carries that foot forward (fig. 4.13). Just as the hands, via the reins, communicate directly with the horse's forefeet and shoulders, the rider's legs communicate directly with the hind legs. When using both our hands and legs with good feel and timing, it is as if we are riding our horse one foot at a time.

The position of the leg is very important for conveying to the horse which part of the body you are speaking to, as well as helping the horse to understand if you are asking him for forward movement or for the stop or back. There are three distinct leg positions, though each of those positions may be used in a variety of "shades," depending on the horse and rider (fig. 4.14).

Seat and Weight and Energy

If the hands are the vowels and the legs are the consonants of our equine language, the seat and weight aids become the punctuation and inflection in our conversation with our horse (fig. 4.15). The seat is our stop-and-go command, while the weight in the saddle adds balance and meaning to the words you are speaking to your horse. The energy that you convey is the pace at which your horse reads the commands that you give with your body. It takes these aids working together to write the beautiful music of Soft Feel. It takes years and years of careful guidance for the horse and rider to be playing the same song.

Your seat and weight are essential in main-

4.14 - *The three leg positions: The forward position is the red boot and is used to cue the horse to stop. The neutral position is the tan boot and this is the position that the rider is in during most of the riding maneuvers. It is also the position that will speak to the horse's rib cage. The green boot is the go position and will also speak to the horse's hindquarters. When the rider shifts his weight forward to lighten the seat, the leg is moved into the go position to ask the horse to go forward. Remember the leg initiates the step and the seat carries it forward.*

4.15 – *Here you see the seat and leg positions working together for the stop, ride, and go seat. The green boots and shirt are the go position. The legs are back and the seat is lightened by the rider leaning forward just slightly. When you lean forward in the saddle with your legs slightly back you reduce the weight the horse feels on the seat bones. This is what we mean when we say "lighten the seat." The ride position is the neutral position with the tan boots and shirt. This is the position you are in to maintain forward movement and ride in balance with the horse. The red boots and shirt are the stop position. You move the legs forward and the upper body back slightly to add weight to the seat.*

taining momentum, rhythm, and balance with your horse. Your seat bones are placed in such a way that they are easily weighted individually, and can apply pressure to the horse's back that he can easily learn to interpret. Unlike in the smaller classical dressage saddles, our Western saddles are built to minimize and distribute back pressure. The Western rider compensates for this not through less use of the seat and weight aids, but through use of weight in the stirrups *as well* as the seat. Through your seat, you can create a metronome that the horse learns to come to for the tempo of the gait.

Center of gravity is defined as the point around which the resultant torque of gravity vanishes. This is a fancy way of saying that center of gravity is the reason we don't all fall flat on our faces when we bend over. It's our internal balance point and it is located right below our rib cage. When our center of gravity is in line with the horse's center of gravity, we are riding in balance with our horse (fig. 4.16). The sacred trinity in horsemanship is feel, timing, and balance and the key to proper balance is good use of your seat and weight aids. Balance is so much more than just the ability to keep from falling off the horse. Riding in balance with the horse has as much to do with not interfering with the horse as it does with guiding or riding the horse.

4.16 – *If you think of the horse's barrel like a big beach ball, you can imagine how your weight and balance through your seat and legs can affect the roll and tilt of the ball. To roll the ball forward, your legs would move backward and you would lighten your seat. To stay perfectly balanced on the ball, you would sit with your legs and seat in alignment in the center of the ball. To stop the forward motion of the ball, you would move your legs forward and add weight to your seat. Rolling along without wobbling takes balance on both a ball and a horse!*

A well-balanced rider will help keep the horse moving in harmony beneath her as well as use her balance to correct form and movement of the horse during maneuvers. The rider should never sit rigid and immobile on the horse but move and adjust with each movement the horse makes. We can use our center of gravity to

4.17 – *The seat is responsible for maintaining the drive in the horse's gait. In this picture, you see how the seat matches the rhythm of the horse to drive the horse forward and upward at the same time. The rhythm of the horse's energy travels in a circular motion, and when the horse's center of gravity shifts to the hindquarters, this circular motion is upward.*

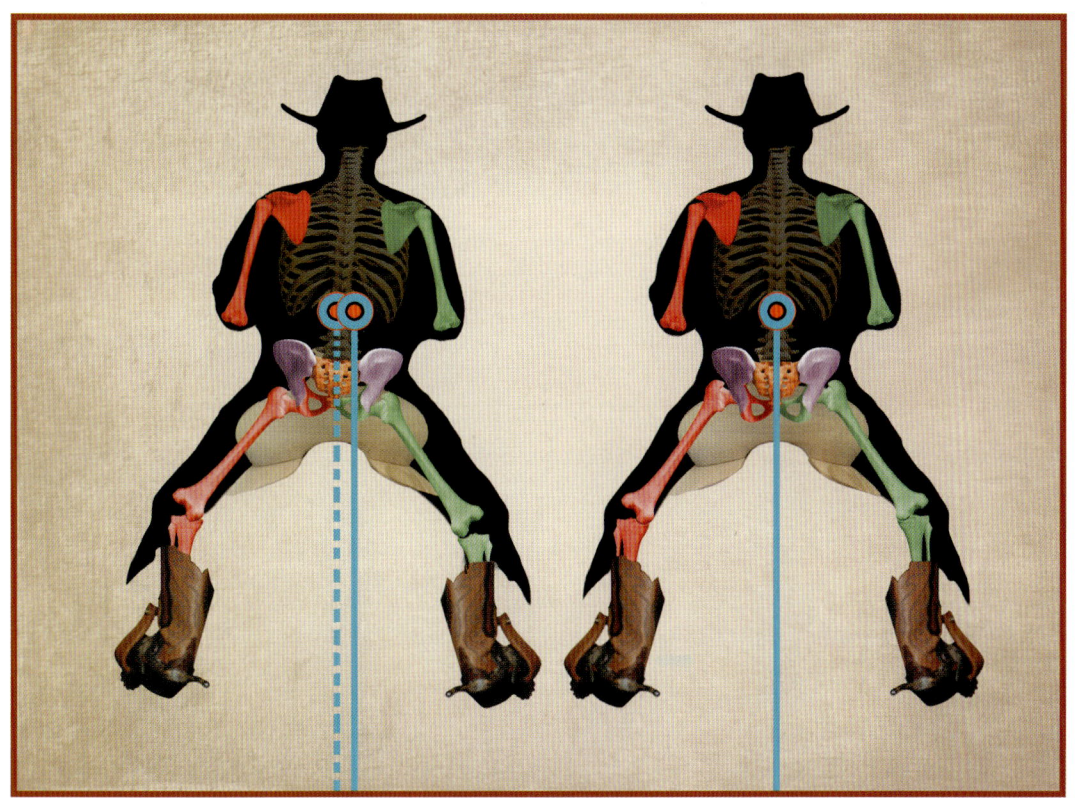

4.18 – *The center of gravity can be changed by the rider shifting slightly one direction or the other, as shown by the rider on the left.*

correct the horse by shifting our weight slightly one direction or the other (fig. 4.17). For example, if our horse is falling to the inside of the circle, shifting our weight to the outside of the circle will encourage the horse to step back into our alignment. It is easier for a horse to move in balance *with* the rider than *against* the rider. These minute changes are easier for the horse to appreciate when the balance of the rider is used intentionally. Most of the time, the horse will move to be back in balance with a rider who has shifted her center of gravity (fig. 4.18). But the horse will learn to ignore the rider who is consistently out of balance.

Energy Core

Your energy core is directly tied to your center of gravity within your body. In humans, the energy core and center of gravity lie just below the diaphragm. You can ramp up or dial down your own personal energy centers in a way that is easily interpreted by the horse. The energy of the rider's body becomes the emotional and steadfast energy that the horse responds to. Control of this energy center is why some people's horses are always nervous and active, while others are sedate and quiet. Being able to tap into that energy core to communicate with any horse, either from the saddle or the ground, is part of that "special something" that great horsemen have that allows them to instantly be "read" by the horse. Many people can "read" the energy center within the horse, as well—it is often said to be that elusive quality called "presence." It is an innate greatness and undercurrent of vitality that speaks to all of us if we allow it to.

The Voice

While the horse is certainly smart enough to understand some basic language and can acquire a small vocabulary, we believe the value in using the voice as an aid lies largely on the way language affects our own body language. Horses may not understand the lyrics of the voice, but they can understand the emotional music. We are so attuned to the spoken word as humans that you can induce the physical expression of a yawn through the mere use of the word. Horses respond to being spoken to quietly because it calms us down. Somebody uttering soft soothing words to a frightened horse when she is deeply frightened herself has little effect on the horse. If horses responded well to voice commands, no rider would have to worry about a bolting horse because they would all stop when we screamed, "WHOA!" Voice cues like clucking or kissing, which are sharper noises, seem to be the most effective in conversation with horses. These are remote cues that horses can learn to associate with a specific command or function to redirect their attention so that they are prepared for the cue that will follow.

Generally voice aids can be the least effective of our available aids. This in no way means we need to enter a silent relationship with our horses. But, in our effective riding we need to be aware that voice commands really are mostly for our own sake and not for the horses. If your horse is responding just to voice cues you are missing the innate beauty of the aids being used together.

How the Horse Communicates with Us

When we began to discuss the language that we use to speak to our horses, we mentioned that it is a two-way communication. Your horses speak to you through body language just as you speak to them. The astute horseman learns to read the basics of horse body language and can evaluate the mood and intention in the horses she meets. Because you are building Soft Feel and partnership with your horse, it is essential that you allow him to communicate with you, just as you communicate with him. While most of the time, you are the leading partner in the dance, your horse will tell you if you are a good dancer or not. Reading the horse's body language is not only often a matter of safety, it is a very important part of effective timing of communication. Neither horse nor human can effectively learn when scared or frustrated. Knowing when to continue the lesson of the day and when to allow the horse the space and time to process is a direct product of properly reading his body language. The good horseman is always looking for that "golden spot" in the lesson to stop for the day. Understanding what your horse is saying to you helps you find that place.

The Mouth

With the advent and subsequent popularity of natural horsemanship, most of today's horsemen understand the importance of "licking and chewing." Horses, as grazing animals, have very active mouths. Indeed, the masseter muscles and the temporomandibular joint are the most used of the skeletal muscles and joints in the entire body. Because a horse in the wild must eat almost constantly to survive, he is nearly always chewing and grinding and working his mouth. Anyone who has peacefully listened to the rhythmic grinding of a horse grazing knows that it creates quite a racket. At the first sign of trouble, the horse stops chewing so he can listen.

The horse is also an obligate nasal breather. The horse cannot breathe through the mouth and does not need to clear his mouth or swallow to facilitate breathing. Therefore, a grazing animal, suddenly spooked by a lion, will clamp its mouth, stop chewing, and prepare to run—even with a mouth full of grass—as quickly as possible. Once the coast is clear and the horse relaxes, he will also relax his mouth and work the jaw that was previously tightened, and resume chewing the grass that was left.

We can see this in our horses during an interaction in which the horse is "stressed" or asked to work. Even a horse willingly working is stressed to a degree as he complies with our requests. Often, as soon as the stress is released, he will lick and chew to resume an age-old normal function. A horse that has relaxed his mouth to lick and chew can be said to be processing or "soaking

4.19 – *The relaxed horse has a relaxed mouth. Licking and chewing are normal equine behaviors and are indicative of a relaxed mind.*

in" the lesson or exercise that was just completed.

The horse that chomps and mouths the bit repetitively is engaging in a different activity entirely from licking and chewing. The horse that continually mouths the bit is generally expressing discomfort, distaste, or insecurity with the bit. While a wet mouth dripping foam has traditionally been a positive thing, especially in the dressage world, it is better interpreted as the horse expressing tension and a degree of displeasure. For some horses, this becomes such an aversion to the bit that even when ridden with light hands, he still foams and chews out of habit. A calm, relaxed horse is much more likely to be licking and chewing and swallowing rather than foaming at the mouth (fig. 4.19).

The Eyes

The large eyes of the grazing prey animal allow it to see almost 360 degrees (fig. 4.20). Horses did not need to evolve with large expressive eyes to survive on the plains. It seems the expressive eyes of the horse are more directly related to the complex social structure and high level of communication in the equine. Horses will show worry and stress in the eyes by dropping the lower lid away from the globe, as well as the formation of "worry wrinkles" in the corner of the eye. These can also be a sign of submission and are commonly observed as part of the "baby face" that a foal will use to convey his lower social status to an adult horse.

A horse that is scared or threatened will widen the eye, often showing the white sclera. While

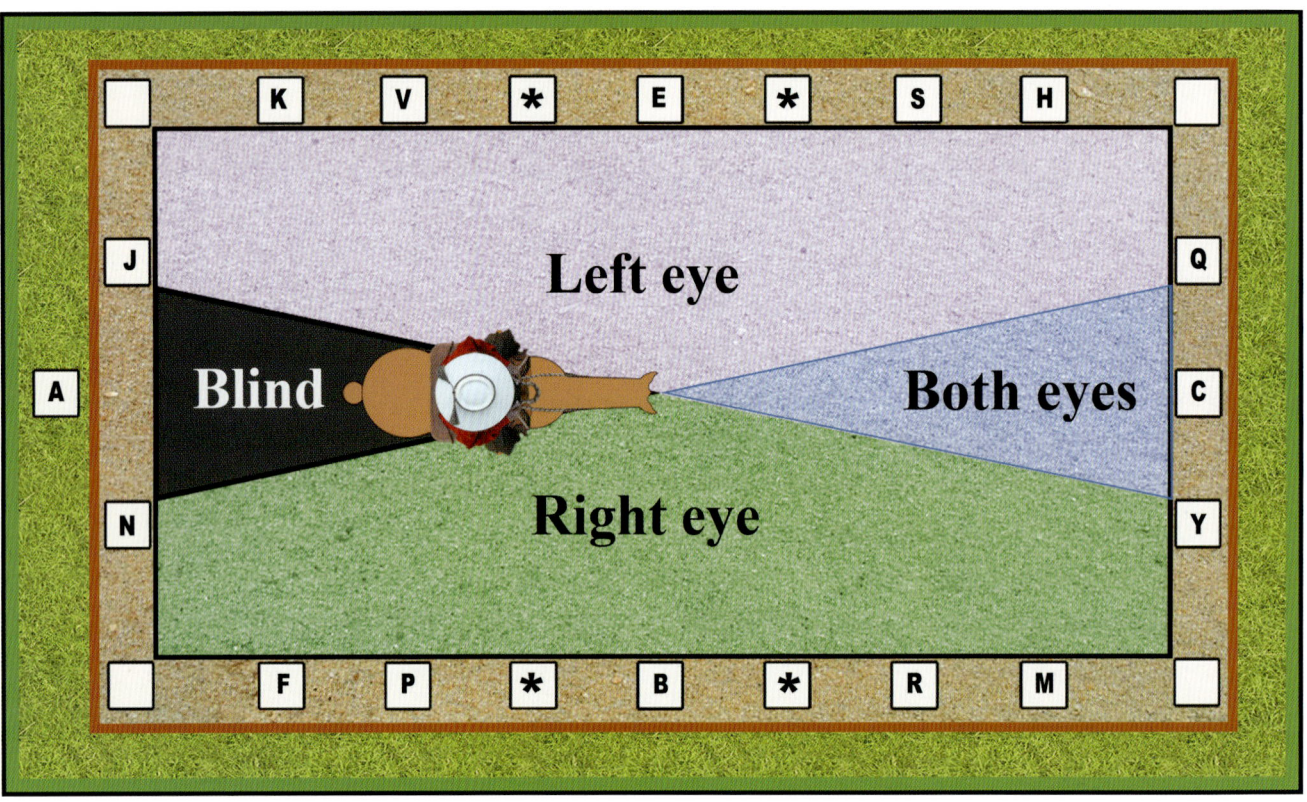

4.20 – *This illustration demonstrates both the monocular vision of the horse (labeled "left eye" and "right eye"), which has limited depth perception but a wide field of view, and the binocular vision (labeled "both eyes") that is narrow and limited to a small area in front of the horse. The blind spot is directly in back of the horse. While the horse can see things almost all around his body, the monocular vision is best for detecting movement and strange shapes. The horse will then turn to look at the object with both eyes to assess whether it is a threat. This is why a spooked horse often stops and spins to face a perceived danger.*

this varies quite a bit by breed and individual, showing a lot of white around the eye is a good indication that the horse is afraid. A horse that is showing signs of outright fear is not able to learn, and if pressed, will have to choose between flight or fight. Knowing the difference between fear and worry and the variations in that scale will keep the horseman from pushing a horse too far in his instruction.

Body Tension and the Tail

The willing and supple horse will remain willing and supple through his entire body. When you are speaking to your horse with Soft Feel, you can feel the way his body is responding below you. As you release your aids when indicating a proper response, your horse should also "release" beneath you. When the horse remains tense, he has likely not appreciated the release or understood the conversation that just occurred. The horse exhibits tension in the body by over-flexion of the neck, dropping of the withers, hollowing of the back, and swishing of the tail.

You need to be able to interpret these signs of tension and not release the aids until the tension in the horse has relaxed. Recognizing tension in the horse is just another tool for you to understand when the horse is having difficulty deciphering the aids. If the horse is showing signs of tension and not responding to your aids, increasing pressure of the aids will only increase tension in the horse. But, if you instead soften the aids (but don't release) until the horse calms and shows signs of released tension before applying the aids again, the horse is more likely to be in a frame of mind to understand the aids being used.

Your aids are not simply just the application of pressure you use to direct the horse. Your aids are a vast and complicated language through which you speak to your horse. Consider your aids individually, but use them in entirety to communicate with your horse in the fullness of language.

5

THE COWBOY DRESSAGE COURTS

"Dressage is just a French word for training. We can dressage a parrot, dressage a cat, dressage a monkey. Don't be worried about the word 'dressage.' Worry about riding your horse."

EITAN BETH-HALACHMY

In Cowboy Dressage, we have three "Courts," 20 by 40 meters, that we ride in competition settings: the Cowboy Dressage Court, the Cowboy Dressage Challenge Court, and the Partnership Court (fig. 5.1). Each of the three Courts has a specific purpose in training our horses from the ground up. All three of the Courts are designed to be user-friendly for optimum success and accuracy in riding. A big part of building softness and responsiveness in our horses is the ability to softly guide them through the Court with accuracy. The Cowboy Dressage Courts give us a framework for building that accuracy.

The Cowboy Dressage Court is the same size as the traditional small dressage arena but has the added benefit of having a marker every 5 meters all the way around (fig. 5.2). This makes the entire Court able to be read and ridden on a simple 5-meter grid pattern. Once a rider

5.1 – *The Cowboy Dressage Court is our classroom and our playground. We use the Court to educate our horses and build partnership to help our horses and ourselves be the very best we can be.*

is familiar with the concept of the 5-meter grid, riding maneuvers and patterns become much simpler, taking the guesswork out of the ride and allowing horse and rider to focus on softness, partnership, and harmony. Cowboy Dressage added four letters to the traditional Court that mark the quarterlines: Q and Y at the C end of the Court, and J and N at the A end of the Court.

Setting Up Your Court

Familiarizing yourself with the lay of the land and the seemingly random assortment of alphabet soup that is the Cowboy Dressage Court is essential when you begin to use the Court to school your horse and ride tests. Going through the steps of setting up your Court at home can be a great way to learn where the letters are and

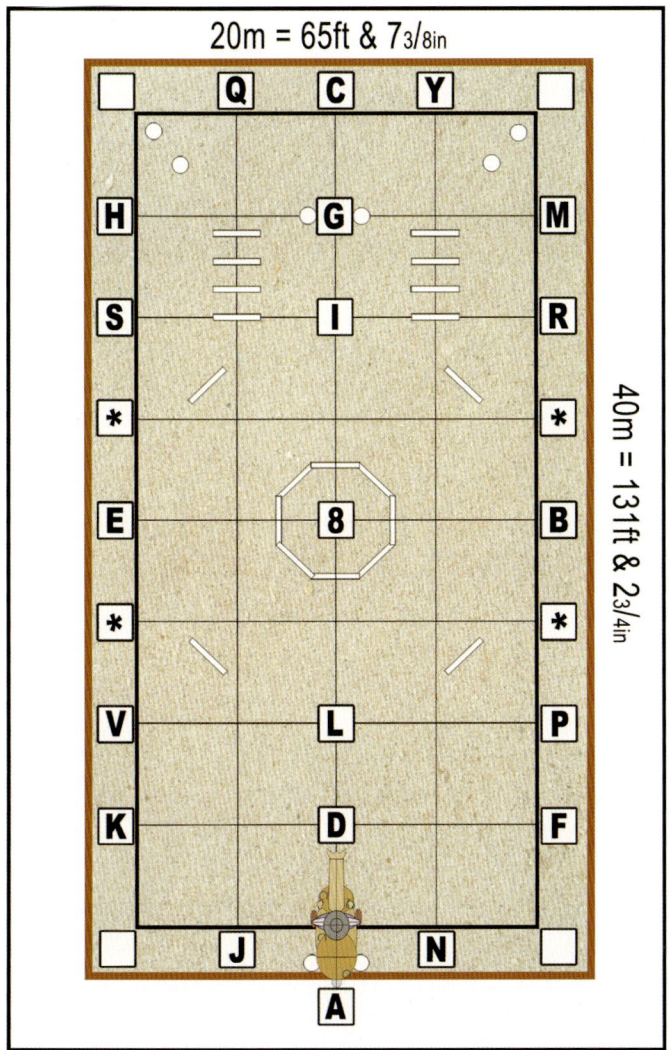

5.2 – *The Cowboy Dressage Challenge Court, showing the 5-meter grid pattern and all the markers, including the midline markers.*

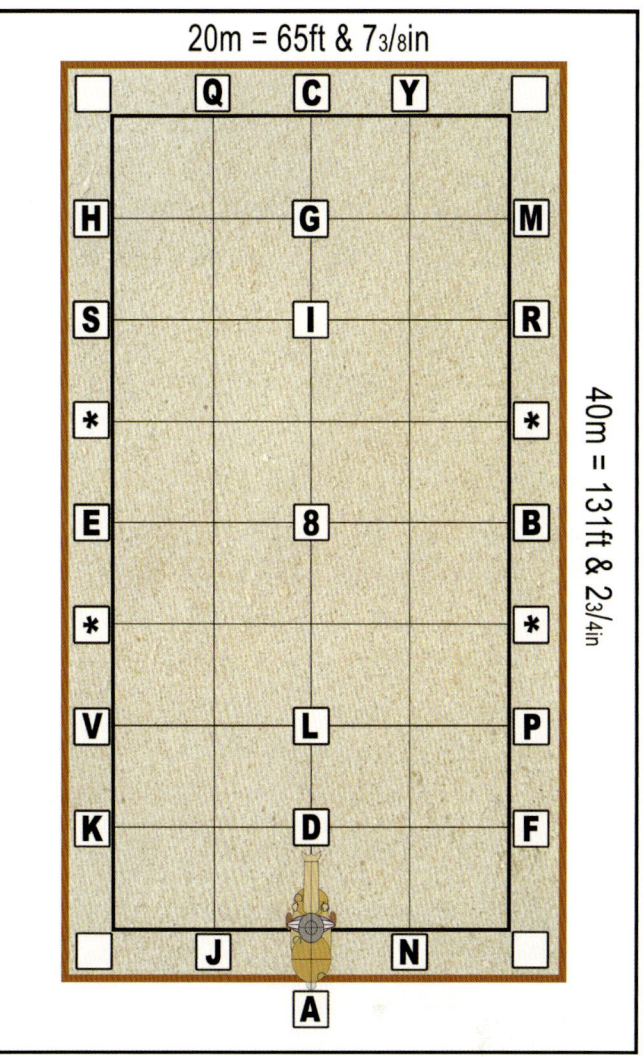

5.3 – *The Cowboy Dressage Court: How to set up the letters.*

how they are paired on the Court in the common maneuvers (fig. 5.3).

In order to begin to set up your Cowboy Dressage Court, it is useful to have a 40-meter tape measure. Because the Court is set up using a 5-meter grid, the meter tape measure does make things simpler, but it is not essential. A 100-foot tape measure can also be used. Because the measurements in feet can be a little more intricate to keep track of, some Cowboy Dressage enthusiasts will mark their 100-foot tape with a permanent marker to correspond to the 5-meter marks, rather than do the math or repetitively measure out the 16 feet, 4⅞ inches between each marker.

There are many different ways to set up your Court, and people will have their own surefire way to make sure the Court is square and correct. Some choose to begin with the centerline (A–C line) and the midline (B–E line) at "8" (the center of the Court, marked in recognition of Eitan). You may choose to set up the Court as two 20-meter boxes. However you set up your Court, it is very helpful to have at least one helper to aid in keeping your lines nice and straight. If you start with your centerline and midline, it is useful to then set your letters by using your long and short diagonals. The long diagonals are F–H and K–M. The short diagonals are P–S and V–R. Then you are only left with your blank cones on either side of B and E and your quarterline letters on either side of A and C. The quarterlines are Q–J and Y–N. Setting up the letters as you would be using them on the Court can be easier than just memorizing their order around the Court (fig. 5.4).

Aside from the standard letters on the periphery of the Court and the 8 that marks the center of our Cowboy Dressage Court, there are also some "invisible letters" that mark the grid line up the centerline. From A, traveling up the centerline to C, those letters are D, L, 8, I, G. In some of the more advanced tests, these letters become more important but though they are "invisible," they are easily located because of the grid lines. D is on the K–F line. L is on the V–P line, I is on the S–R line, and G is on the H–M line. You may find it useful to develop your own tricks to making these letters make sense to you and helping you remember them. One of the ones we use for the centerline

5.4 – *The Cowboy Dressage Challenge Court set up in preparation for the Final Gathering at Murieta Equestrian Center in Rancho Murieta, California.*

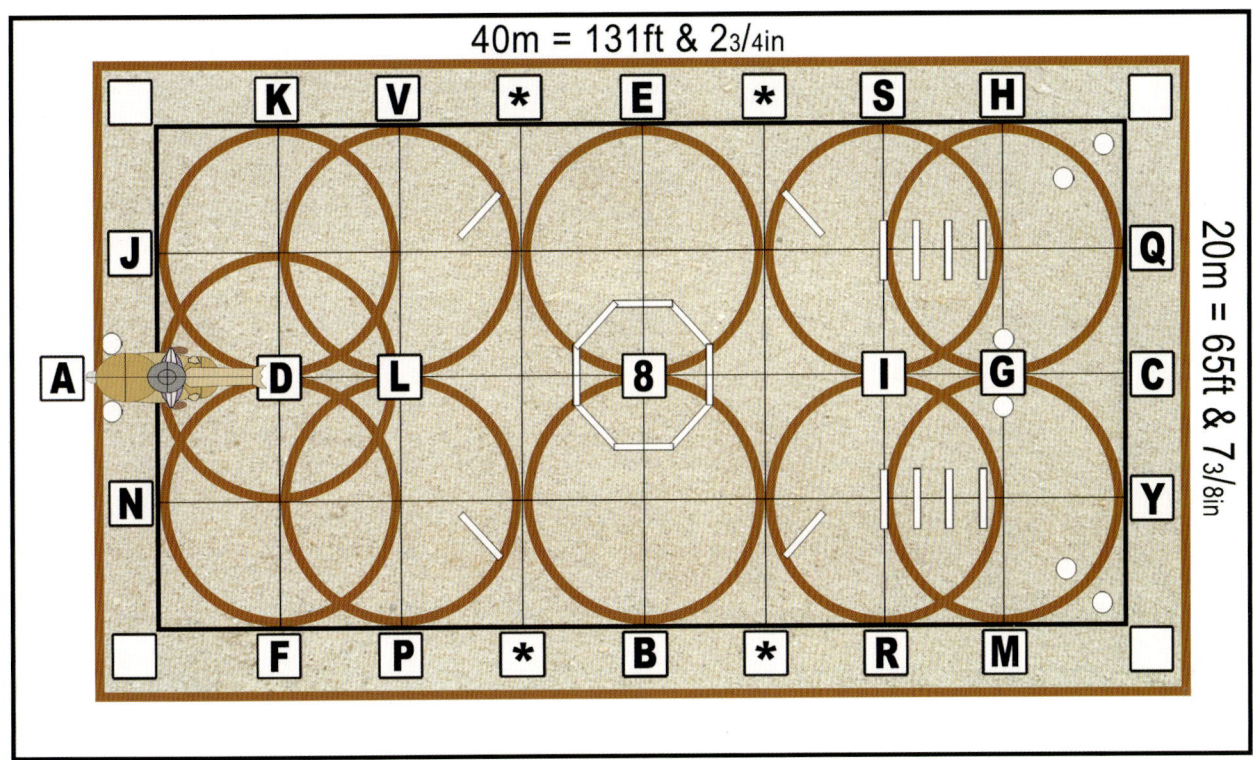

5.5 – *The 10-meter circles on the Cowboy Dressage Challenge Court. There are twelve 10-meter circles (the circle at C is not shown on this Court and cannot be ridden on the Challenge Court due to the ground poles) that may be used in a Cowboy Dressage test.*

letters is All Dogs Love Eitan (8) In Grass County. We remember the quarterlines as the New York line and the Quirky Jenni line. The point is, familiarize yourself with the letters in any way that ensures they make sense. The Court is there to help you and your horse, not intimidate you.

Circles

The 5-meter grid pattern is perfectly set up for riding circles with ease. When learning the geometric layout of the Court, it is helpful to first visually establish circle touch points by riding the circles as diamonds. For instance, the 10-meter circle at Q is ridden from Q to H to the intersection of S and Q, and then to G and back to Q. The 20-meter circle is ridden similarly, with four touch points in a diamond pattern. A 20-meter circle at C will touch at C, S, 8, R and back to C. As you are learning to navigate the Court and the geometry of the circles around the Court, riding them from point to point to point helps you and the horse to feel where the circles should exist in space, allowing for the pattern to help both you and the horse to learn bend and accuracy in your riding.

On the Cowboy Dressage Court there are twelve 10-meter circles and three 20-meter circles to be ridden (figs. 5.5 & 5.6). The various

5.6 – The 20-meter circles on the Cowboy Challenge Court. The three circles may be called at any of their touch points. For example, the 20-meter circle at A is the same as the 20-meter circle at P or V.

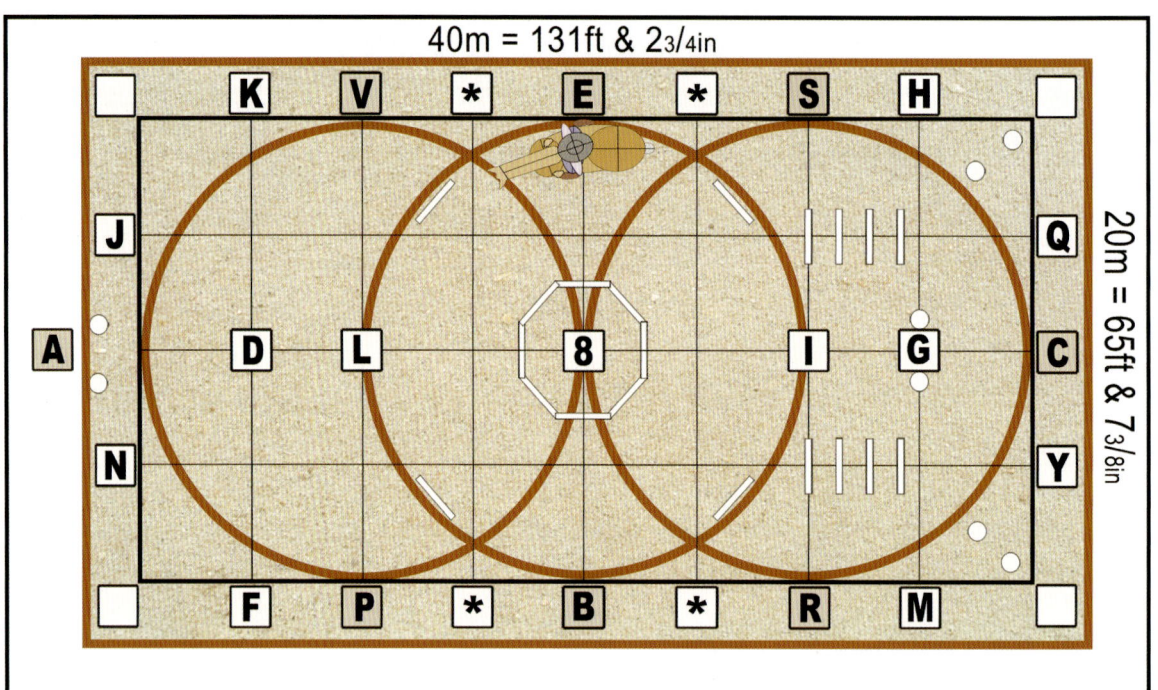

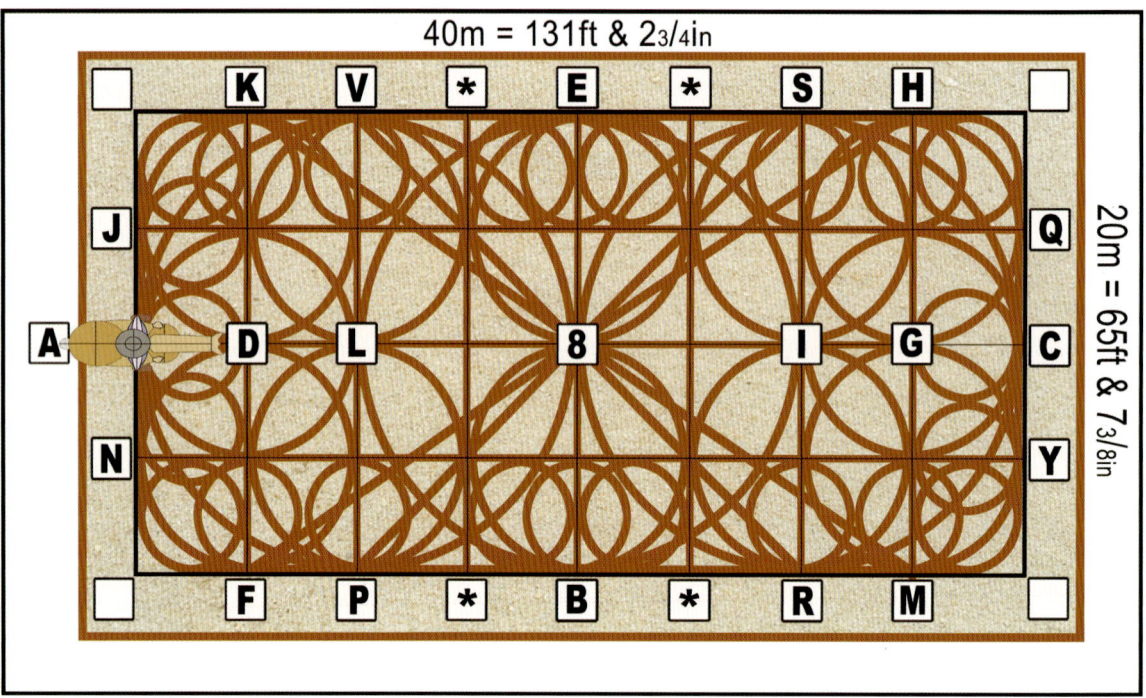

5.7 – This busy diagram shows all of the circles and straight lines that are possible on the Cowboy Dressage Court and that are currently included in our Cowboy Dressage Tests. There are infinite possibilities and the maneuvers are as limitless as the rider's imagination. For riders who say they get bored in the arena, we challenge you to get bored riding on the Cowboy Dressage Court—there is enough here to keep horse and rider busy for an entire afternoon!

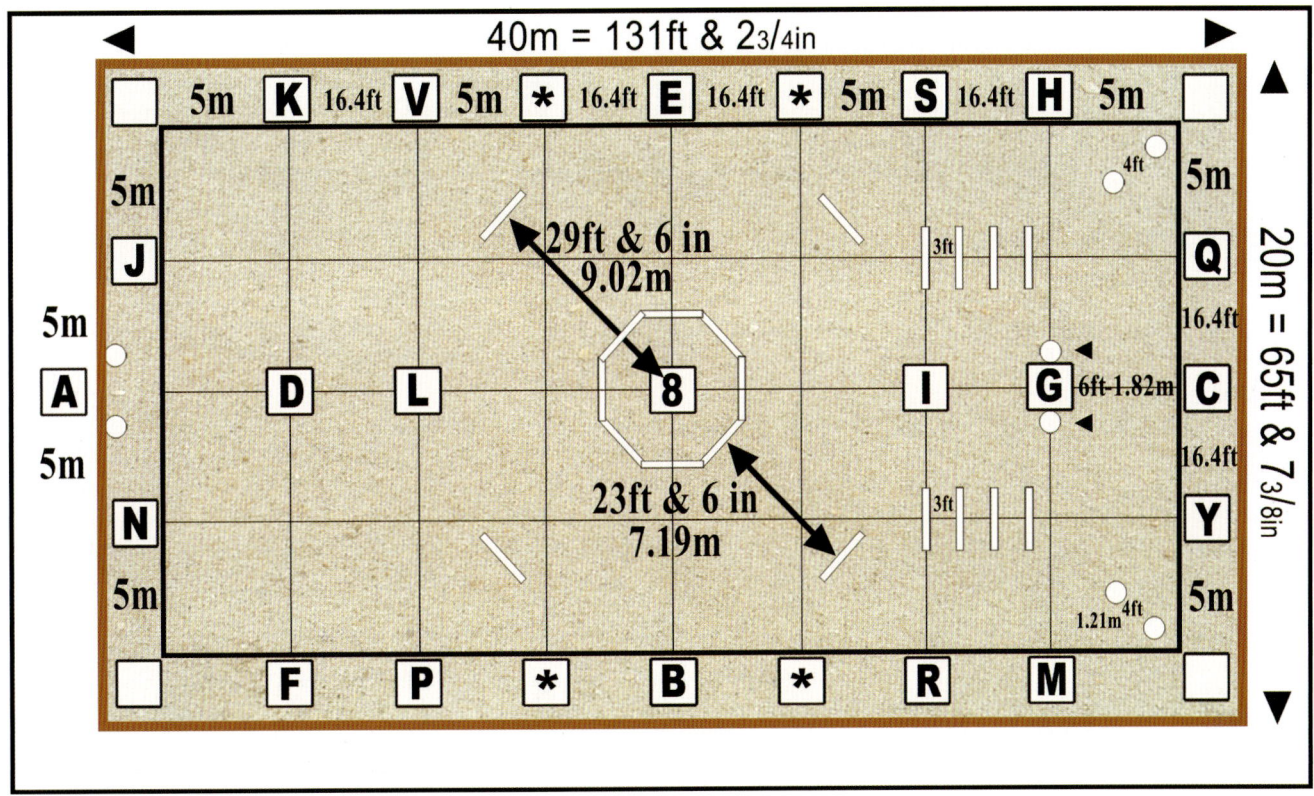

5.8 – *The Cowboy Dressage Challenge Court: How to set up the letters, ground poles, cones, and octagon.*

opportunities to use the grid to ride so many different circles allow for an almost unlimited combination of maneuvers on the Court to keep the horse's mind engaged and actively communicating with you. Because the circles can be initiated in so many different locations on the Court, the horse learns to wait for you and to listen rather than anticipate the maneuver to be performed (fig. 5.7).

Challenge Court

The Challenge Court is a product of Cowboy Dressage that is meant to not only provide even more visual markers for you to learn the geometry of the Court but also gives you ground poles to incorporate in your riding (fig. 5.8).

As mentioned earlier when we discussed groundwork (see p. 45), ground poles provide a valuable function in training our Western horses. The ground poles will encourage the horse to lift his feet and his back and promote rounding through the topline. They also help stretch muscles and ligaments by asking the horse to pick his feet up just a little more than he is likely to do on his own. This helps your horse to increase strength and flexibility. It is also good for you to learn the placement of the horse's feet for maximum success while navigating the course. As the tests on the Challenge Court become more advanced, you have to shorten and lengthen stride appropriately to navigate poles at the walk, jog, and eventually, the lope.

5.9 – *The Cowboy Dressage Challenge Court showing the quarterline ground poles, octagon, diagonal ground poles, and cones in the upper corners on the 10-meter bend line as at G.*

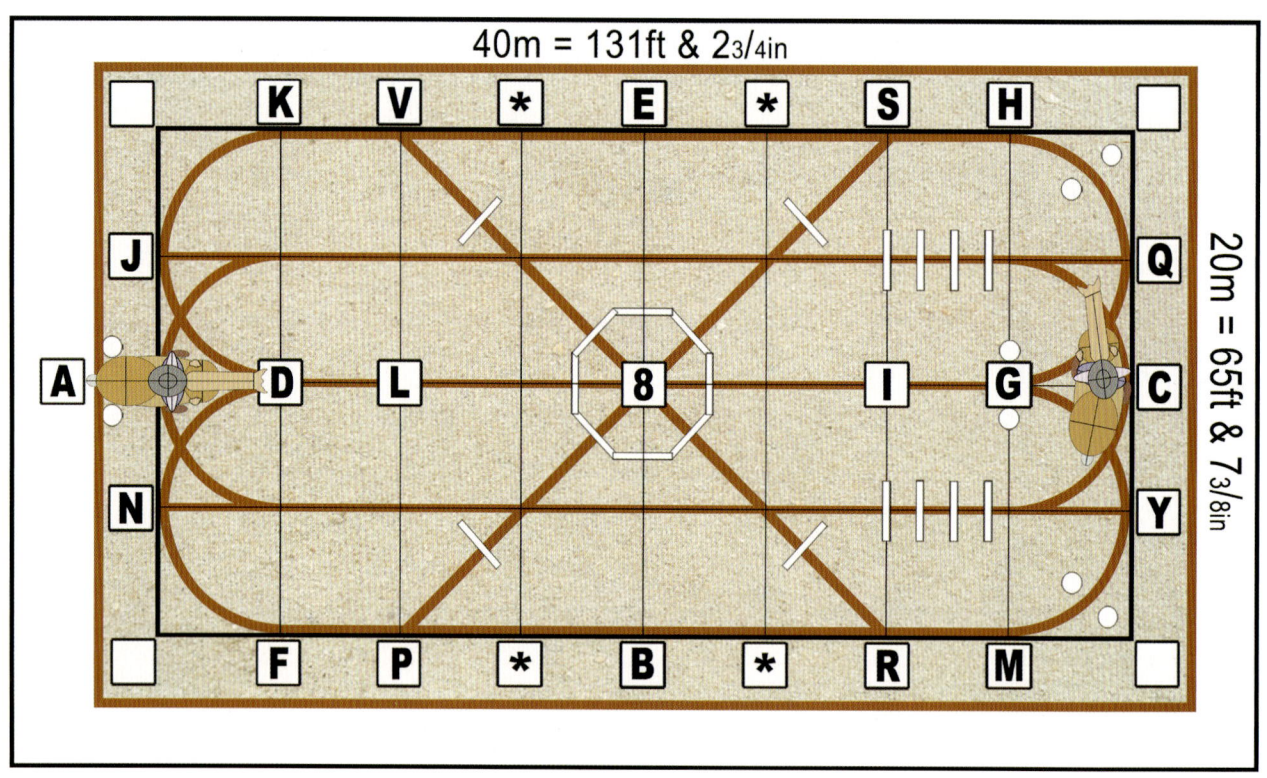

5.10 – *The Cowboy Dressage Challenge Court provides visual aids to help perform specific exercises, such as the 10-meter circle at Q or H.*

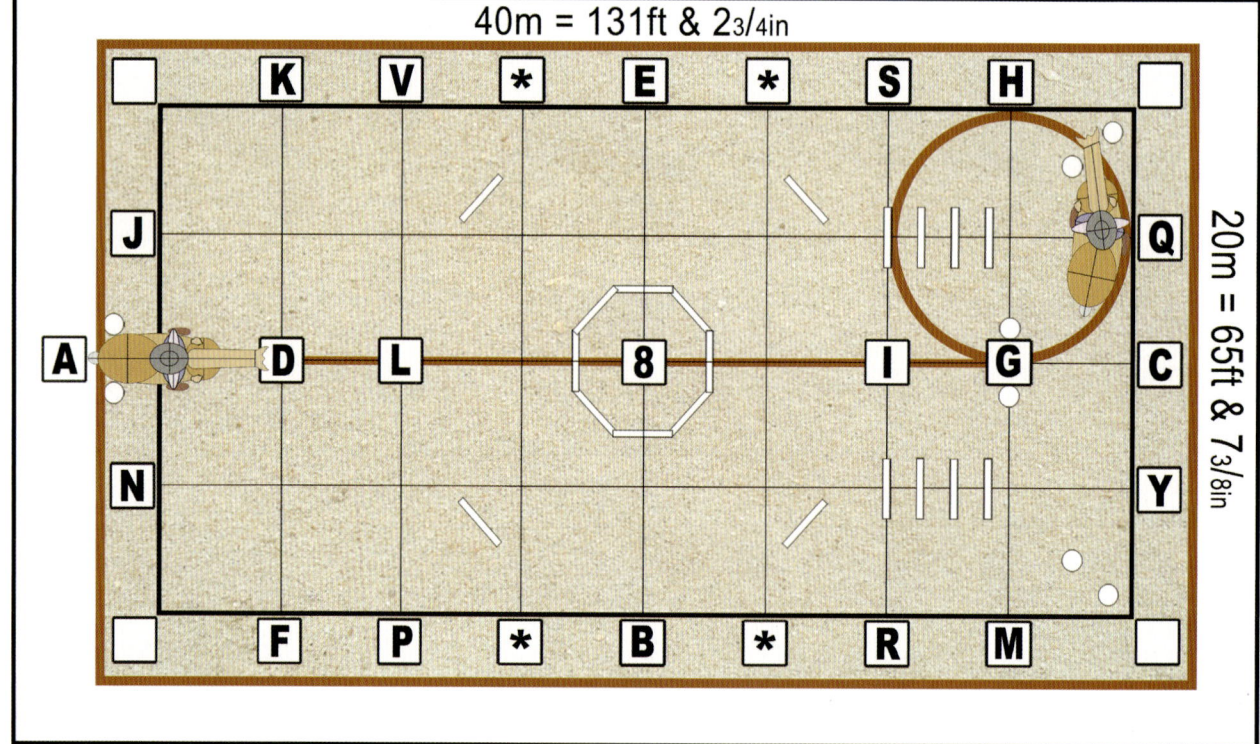

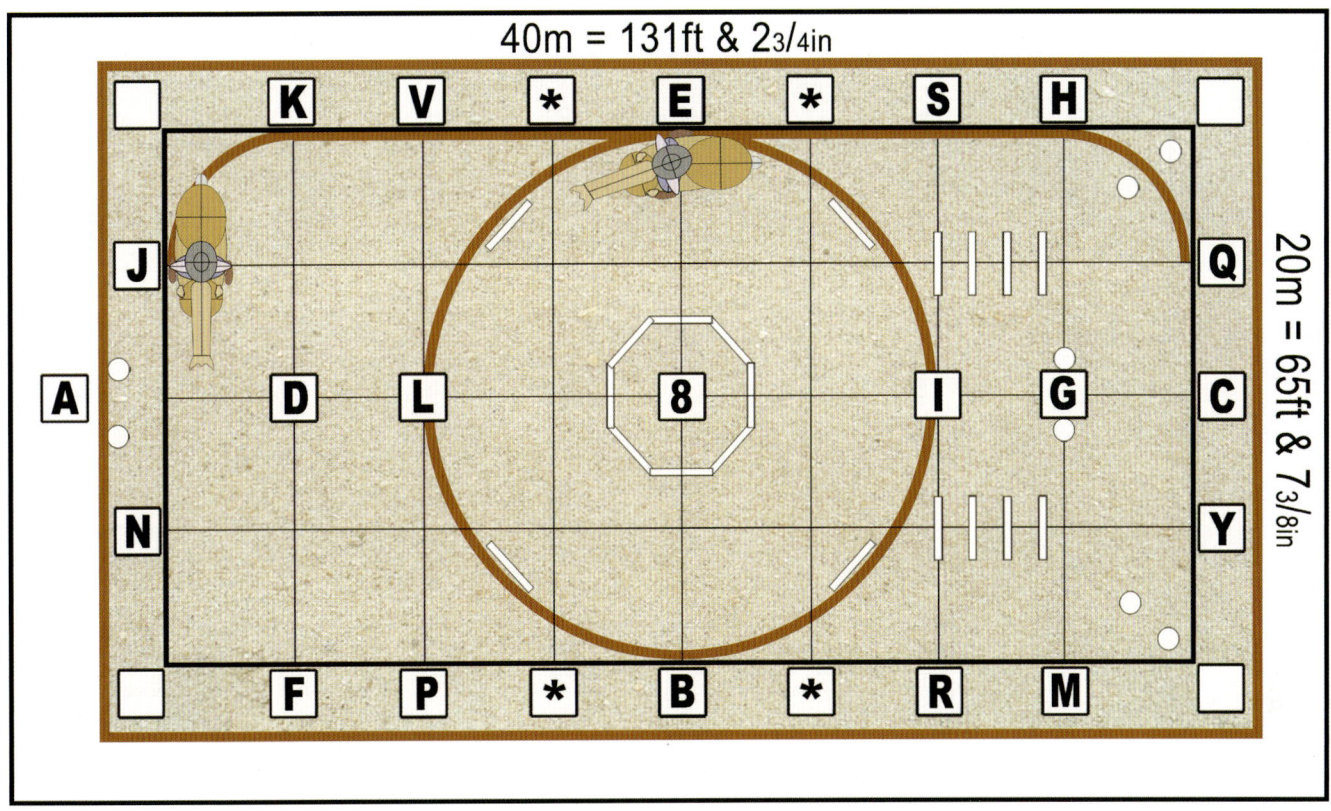

5.11 – *Diagonal ground poles are placed on the Cowboy Dressage Challenge Court to help horses and riders perform the 20-meter circle at E or B.*

For many riders, the Challenge Court provides an important visual aid when learning the geometry of the Court (fig. 5.9). At the C end of the Challenge Court, the ground poles and cones provide solid markers for the creation of the 10-meter circles at Q and Y, or H and M. A 10-meter circle performed at H on the Challenge Court will travel from H between the third and fourth ground pole, between the cones at G to Q, through the cones on the 10-meter bend line, and back to H (fig. 5.10). The 20-meter circle at B and E in the center of the Court is also easier to visualize on the Challenge Court as the diagonal poles at the corners serve as additional markers for the geometry of the 20-meter circle (fig. 5.11). The diagonal poles of the 20-meter circle are also used in riding the short diagonal lines of the Challenge Court on the P–S diagonal and the V–R diagonal, which also travel through the octagon (fig. 5.12).

There are several additional maneuvers that are incorporated in the Challenge tests that are not part of the other Courts. First, for the upper-level Challenge tests, you are required to enter the Court through a gate. The gate is a simple rope gate that is opened either right- or left-handed, then the rider must enter the Court. In addition, you must be sure you are directly on

5.12 – *The diagonal ground poles and octagon provide visual markers when traveling across the short diagonal, as well.*

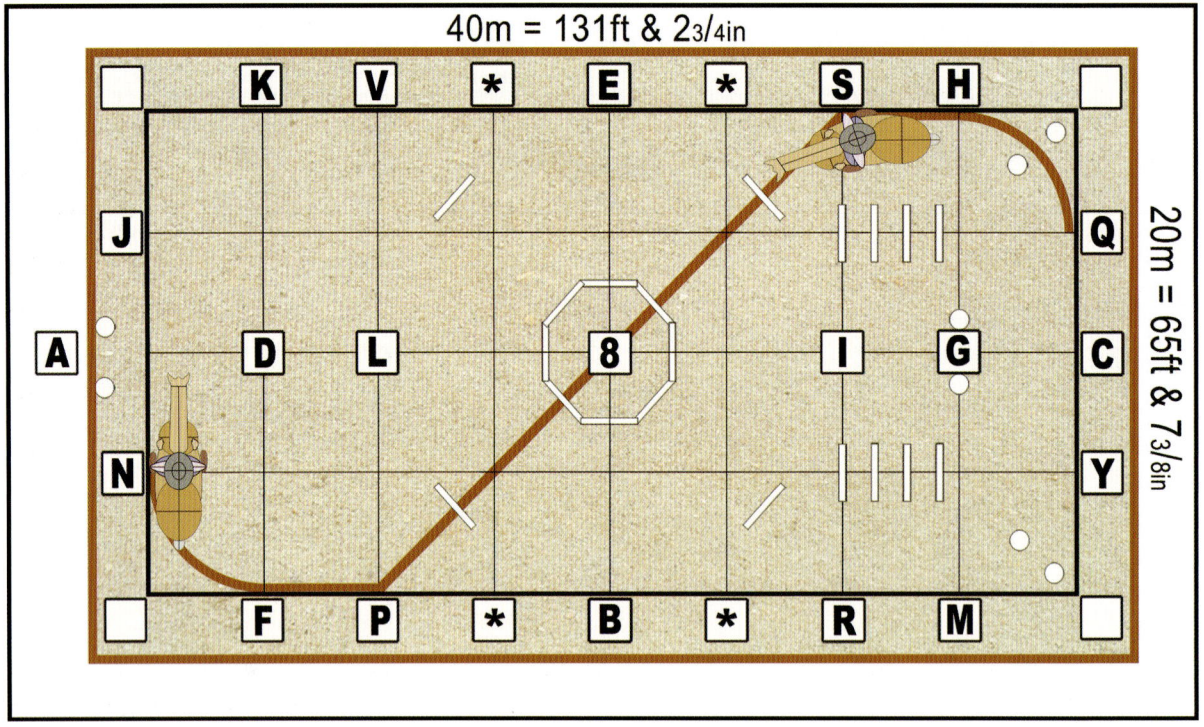

5.13 – *The C end of the Challenge Court provides the structure for the Partnership division, as well as the Walk/Walk challenge tests. You still enter the Court at A, but all the maneuvers are condensed to just one end of the Court.*

the centerline and can initiate the required gait as you step onto the Court (rather than entering the Court already in that gait, as is more common on the standard Court).

As mentioned, the Challenge Court is where you find the useful octagon (see p. 81). The octagon, while providing a visual marker for your halt at 8, also creates a challenge for many horses as they are required to step into the box and stop square. The octagon makes it quite easy for the judge at C to see if you are square or not! For most maneuvers besides the halt, you will move through the octagon (or "box," as it is often referred to on the test call sheets) during a maneuver. There are also required maneuvers within the box on some of the more advanced Challenge Tests, calling for both a circle and later, a full turn-on-the-haunches within the box.

Half-Court

The Partnership on the Ground and Under Saddle tests, as well as the tests in the Cowboy Dressage Walk/Walk division (see chapter 10 for a description of divisions), are performed on *half* the Challenge Court: 20 by 20 meters (fig. 5.8). For the ground tests, this simplifies the pattern while also keeping the handler from having to jog all the way around the track! The other great thing about the small Half-Court is that it provides a viable training option for the Cowboy Dressage enthusiast with limited space. The Half-Court allows for practicing 10- and 20-meter circles, straight lines, as well as the ground-pole maneuvers of the Challenge Court.

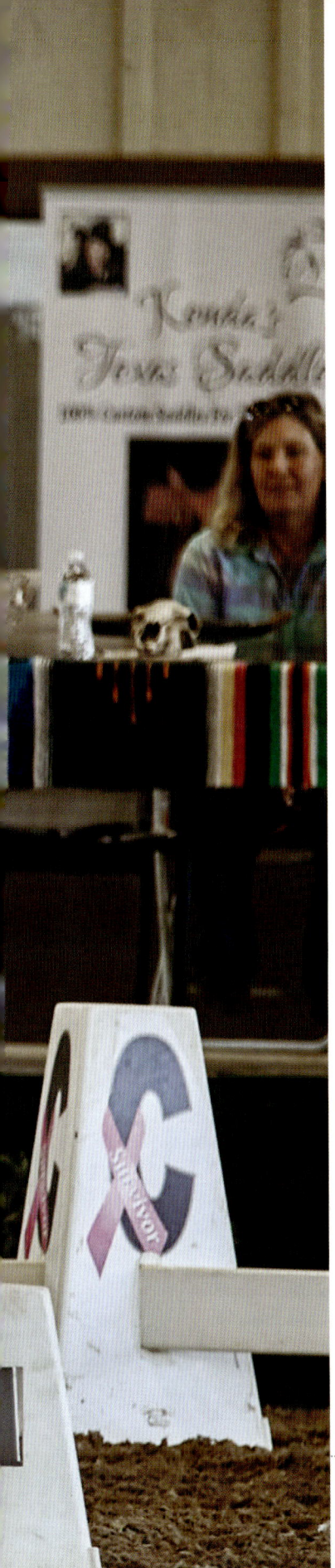

6

CADENCE AND GAITS OF THE COWBOY DRESSAGE HORSE

"The secret is to ride the stride that hasn't happened yet."

EITAN BETH-HALACHMY

We often say that the Cowboy Dressage horse is defined by his gaits, and indeed, in the competition arena the gaits of the Cowboy Dressage horse are quite different from the gaits that we see in Western Dressage, as well as in most traditional rail classes. Cowboy Dressage attempts to create in the horse a gait that is pure to the movement of the individual horse, while cultivating a shortness of gait and handiness unique to the traditional Western working horse. The gaits showcase softness, cadence, and make the Cowboy Dressage horse a pleasure to ride all day, whether on the Court or on the trail of a herd of "doggies."

The walk, trot, and canter, or gallop, are the natural gaits of the horse. The Cowboy Dressage jog and lope are cultivated gaits that were born on the ranches of the West. Instead of a fast ground-covering long trot, the shorter jog is better for slipping from pen to pen without spooking the cattle. The rocking-chair lope that is comfort

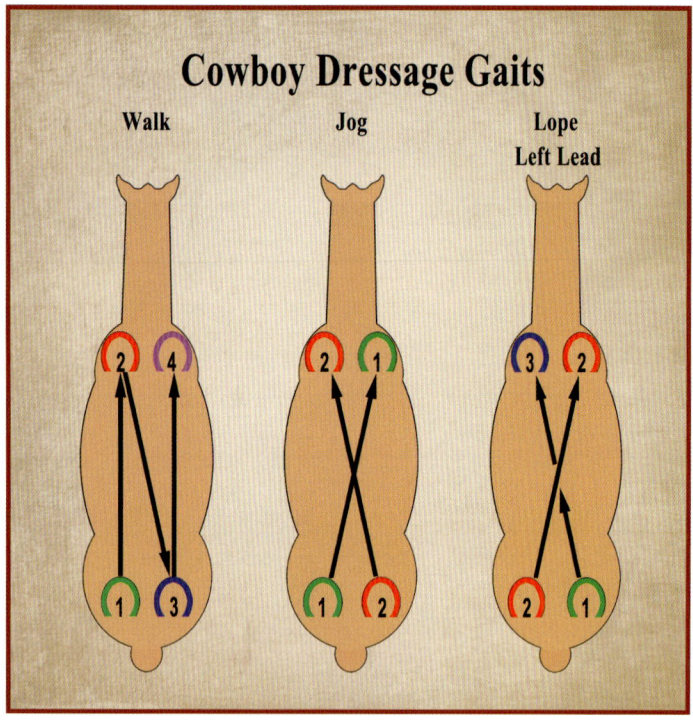

6.1 - *The footfall pattern of each of the natural gaits of the horse.*

able to sit all day is the shortened form of the rougher and faster canter. Many Western horses are now bred to more naturally move in these slower gaits but it is much more than just a change in nomenclature from traditional dressage. The Cowboy Dressage gaits are as unique as the discipline, and we believe, when done correctly, will help to build balance and harmony in the horse.

While only the jog is considered a true diagonal gait, all of the gaits share a diagonal component pattern in the footfalls (fig. 6.1). In the walk, the diagonal movement happens once in each stride as the weight is shifted from the front with the second beat to the opposite back leg. As the stride is completed, the diagonal weight is transferred again from the fourth beat back to the first beat. In the jog, each stride has two diagonal components as the diagonal feet move as a pair. In the lope, that component is split into a broken diagonal. The second beat is the movement of the diagonal pairs, and it splits the diagonal movement of the first and third beat. Aside from just academic curiosity, this principle is important to understand because it directly affects your balance and timing in all three gaits. As you cue for the next gait, you should be thinking not about going faster or more forward, but about how it will change the movement of the diagonal pairs of feet.

Cadence

Cadence can be defined as the rhythm of the ride. It is the musical beat that is the background of the gait and it should remain consistent throughout the gait. When the cadence speeds up, this is a change in *tempo*. The same 2/4 rhythm common to both soft rock and hard rock varies not in cadence but in tempo. Cadence is one of the things that makes a well-balanced horse a pleasure to ride because it is easy for the horse and rider to get in time with each other. Green horses often have poor cadence under saddle as they attempt to adjust to the awkward feel of the rider on their back. The gait is irregular and it's difficult for the rider to maintain a balanced seat because the horse is moving forward with uneven steps. Cultivating good cadence in your horse's gaits is an important part of building a willing and soft partner.

Forward and Frames

We cannot speak of gaits without first speaking of *forward*. While cadence is the rhythm of the individual gaits, forward is required for the cadence to occur in the first place. Forward is that quality within the horse that is always asking to go. A forward horse is one that is ready and willing to get something done. If you are consistently begging the horse to go forward, you are already behind the game. While the desire to move forward will vary by horse, it is our job as riders to always encourage the forward because the loss of it affects everything you try to do with your horse.

In each of the gaits we will also be talking about the separate frames and how they affect the gait and cadence. There are three frames of the Cowboy Dressage horse: the *short (collected) frame*, the *medium (working) frame*, and the *long (free) frame* (fig. 6.2). In the Cowboy Dressage tests, you will be asked to perform in the working and the free frame. We use the short frame primarily as a frame of preparation and transition, though many advanced dressage maneuvers

6.2 - *The three frames of the Cowboy Dressage gaits are the short frame (collected frame), medium frame (working frame) and long frame (free frame). Notice not only the shortened stride length but also the horse's head position in each of the frames. With each shortening of the frame from the lengthened frame, the center of gravity shifts farther back toward the hindquarters. The only thing missing from this illustration is the adjustment in the rider's position as was discussed in chapter 4 on the aids. The rider's hands would mirror the horse's head position and the rider's seat would rock backward slightly as the center of gravity is shifted toward the hindquarters.*

are performed in the short frame. We will discuss the working and free frames in each of the gaits in this chapter, while the short frame is covered separately in chapter 9 (see p. 155).

The Queen of Gaits: The Walk

The most important of all the gaits—and the gait most often neglected in the training of our Western horses or show and working horses—is the walk. The balanced walk is a four-beat gait requiring even distribution of the horse's weight between all four feet as he carries his weight forward. The footfall pattern of the walk is left hind, left front, right hind, right front. A single stride of the walk includes movement of all four feet beginning with the left hind and ending with the right front (fig. 6.3). Because the rider's body moves side to side in a two-count rhythm as her horse is moving in a four-count rhythm below, the walk is often counted with the steps of either the front or the hind feet. While technically incorrect to count steps rather than strides of the walk, it can be useful to begin to both get in time with the horse, as well as learn where the horse's feet are as he steps.

An elemental exercise performed in riding schools across disciplines is to call out the steps of the horse's front feet until the rider can successfully feel when the right front foot is traveling and when the left front foot is traveling. Learning to

6.3 - *The four-beat gait of the walk, beginning from the left hind: The footfall pattern is left hind, left front, right hind, right front. If the horse has stopped square he will always initiate the walk from the hindquarters, pushing himself forward into the gait. The first foot to move is the front foot to catch the balance as the horse moves forward. Therefore, the hindquarters drive the horse forward in the walk, and the forehand balances him.*

become attuned to the movement in *your* body as you feel *the horse's* body moving below you is essential in developing feel and timing to cue the horse's feet as they are preparing to travel, rather than when the horse's feet are on the ground. The walk is the most important gait for the rider to cultivate to successfully get those cues working for the horse. You can only influence the movement of the horse's foot *when it is moving.* When the foot is weighted the horse cannot immediately respond to your cues. While this is a simple enough concept to understand, the execution of the cues in time with the feet is one of the secrets that separates the good horsemen from the great.

Most instructors of horsemanship and equitation have their own methods of helping the rider to feel where the feet are as the horse moves. For some riders, it is helpful to first watch the shoulders of the horse to determine which of the front feet is moving. You can also look at the horse's poll in front of you.

Engagement and Disengagement

Understanding the walk by its essential parts of the stride can help you learn to identify, and thereby feel, where the feet are at any given time during the motion of the stride. The stride is composed of weight-bearing and non weight-bearing (flight) phases, which at the walk happen independently for each foot. Both the horse's head and hip shift in balance with the weight-carrying phase of the hind feet.

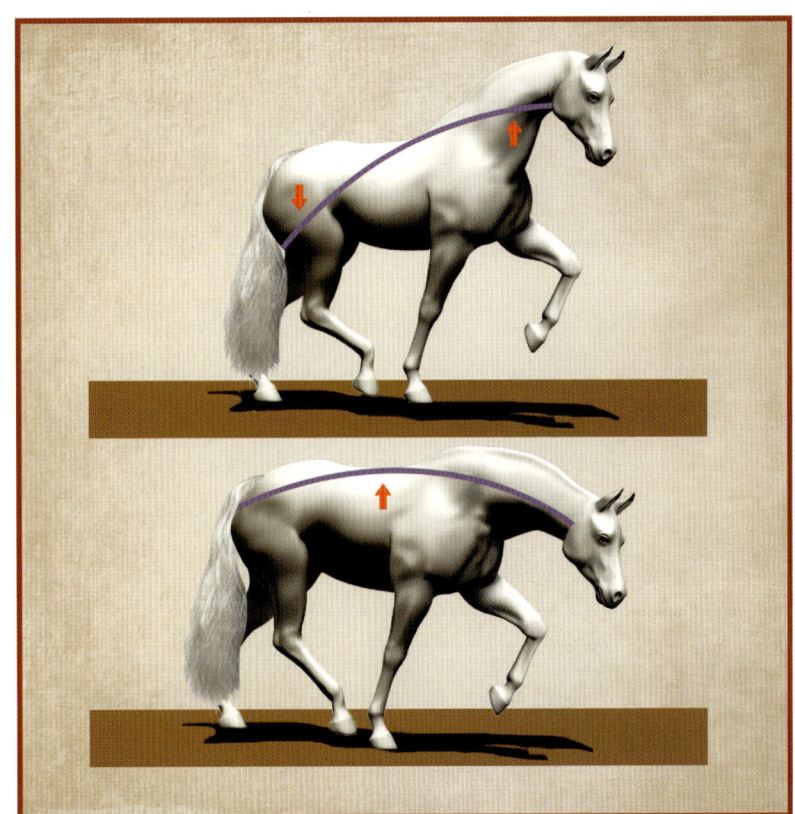

6.4 - *Engagement is the phase of the stride that is actively pushing the horse forward (in red). The engaged phase of the stride happens under the horse's body. By increasing engagement in the stride, you are improving the quality of movement, the balance, and forward drive of the stride.*

We define *engagement* in the stride as the forward weight-bearing phase. In the hindquarters this phase happens from the moment the horse's foot becomes weight-bearing under the body of the horse to the moment it passes under the hip of the horse on its way to the flight phase. As the horse steps into engagement in the hindquarters, the horse pushes forward and the head goes up (fig. 6.4).

Disengagement is defined as the portion of the gait when the horse's leg is behind the hip as it enters the flight portion of the stride. As the horse shifts the weight of the hindquarters to the forehand, the head goes down. Therefore, as the left hind leg pushes forward, the head is up until the left hind is at the end of its weight-bearing phase, and then in its disengagement phase, shifts the weight to the horse's left foreleg, causing the head to go down.

This all takes far longer to write about and think about than it does to happen. As you study the horse's walk and learn to identify both the weight-bearing and non weight-bearing phases of the stride, as well as the engaged and disengaged portions of the stride, you can better learn to be in time with the feet.

Another technique for getting into time with the horse's hind feet is to feel the rolling of his barrel underneath you. When your legs are lying

6.5 - *The movement of the horse's head can tell the rider where the feet are. The head bobs like a counterweight as the horse's weight shifts from the front to back in time with the footfall. The horse's head will rise as the horse shifts his weight to the hindquarters, driving forward in engagement with the left hind foot. This is also the point at which the left front foot strikes the ground. The head will bob down as the horse shifts his weight to the forehand and the left front foot is in weight-bearing engagement. This is also the time when the right hind foot strikes the ground.*

along the horse's sides in gentle connection with the horse, you can feel the horse's barrel moving between your calves. As the horse lifts the hind end and steps with the left hind foot, the barrel will roll to the right. The rider riding in time with the horse will also feel the rhythm of the walk on the seat bones.

So, if you put this cadence together:
- The horse's hindquarters will lift as the horse begins to step with the left hind foot.
- The barrel will roll to the right against your right calf.
- Your left seat bone will follow that roll, then your left shoulder will roll backward slightly as the horse's poll lifts.
- The hindquarters drop and the horse's left front foot moves forward.
- Then the horse's hindquarters lift again, and as the right hind foot moves forward, the barrel moves to the left as your right seat bone follows.
- The horse's head lifts and your right shoulder rolls as the horse lifts the right front, completing the stride (fig. 6.5).

All that is happening at the walk, on a regular frame in a straight line! Obviously, it's way too fast for anybody to think about. Play with each of the pieces as you ride, experimenting by concentrating on the horse's poll and the timing of the feet, and then your seat with the timing of the feet. When you can put each of these pieces together to help you find the feel, you are reaching the ultimate goal. Until you can feel the horse's feet moving with your body without thinking about it, it is difficult to master riding in time with your horse. Development of feel is a lifelong cultivation.

Working Walk

The *working walk* is the very foundation of all the work that we do in Cowboy Dressage and is the framework for introducing Soft Feel and self-carriage (fig. 6.6). In the working walk, the horse moves with the rider in a softened and slightly shortened frame. It is important to carry the energy of the walk into the working frame so that the gait retains a snappy energy without becoming sluggish. In the working frame, the horse carries his head and neck in a position to encourage shifting of the center of gravity backward toward the hindquarters with softening of the poll, relaxation of the jaw, and elevation of the withers from the shoulder.

It is important to note that there isn't a "headset" in the Cowboy Dressage horse. The balanced carriage of the horse will depend in a large part on the conformation of the horse being ridden. An up-headed light horse such as a Morgan or Saddlebred will have a higher head and neck carriage in the working frame than a more levelly built traditional Western stock horse like the Quarter Horse or the Paint. The horse must be encouraged and rewarded for the carriage that best suits his individual build.

The *working frame* is developed in the horse by encouraging the horse to relax into light contact through the reins while engagement of the

6.6 - *The working walk is a soft, medium-frame walk with light contact.*

hindquarters carries the propulsion forward into the gait. The working gait is an unhurried yet snappy gait. It is the gait from which the horse is ridden one stride at a time in partnership with the rider, ready for the next maneuver or command. It is a frame of readiness for the execution of the next step. In the working frame, you should be intimately connected to the feet of the horse through the aids. You communicate with the front feet through the reins and to the hind feet through the legs and seat. When the horse is going with Soft Feel, partnership, and in harmony with the rider, the slightest cue or change in signal from the rider communicated in time with the horse's feet should be met with immediate response from the horse. With this intimate connection, you are able to properly execute commands and guidance via a series of communications often referred to as *PERR*—Preparation, Execution, Release, Relaxation (fig. 6.7).

Because you are riding with the horse in readiness and Soft Feel in the working gait, you can first *prepare* the horse by a subtle shifting of your energy to tell him a command or cue is about to be given. Then, assured that the horse is ready for that cue, you *execute* the command in time with the horse's natural movement. As the horse executes the desired movement, you release the command, then relax your body and energy as the final reward. The communication of PERR is a subtle conversation between horse and rider. When a horse and rider are operating with Soft Feel, the observer should not be able to see the *preparation*, the cue for *execution*, or the *relaxation* and *release*. Instead the horse and rider appear to be riding as if of one mind. That is Soft Feel at its best.

Teaching the horse to develop a good walk begins on the ground. You can teach the horse to respond to the energy in your body language through your groundwork—lengthening and shortening the stride at the walk. Groundwork exercises are a very important part of creating a good walk once the rider is aboard. The walk is also one of the best gaits to warm up the horse's joints and muscles before moving up to faster gaits.

Use your walk wisely in your schooling because failing to build a good walk as a fundamental gait in your horse is something that is difficult to rebuild later down the road in your training. The walk is the alphabet in learning to read. You have to know each piece of your horse's walk before moving on to the jog or the lope.

Encourage your horse to walk with energy and forward propulsion during groundwork

6.7 - *Soft connection in the working frame allows for proper use of PERR—Preparation, Execution, Release, and Relaxation.*

exercises. By allowing your horse to drag his feet or sedately walk around you during groundwork, you are encouraging the lack of *forward* that will also plague you under saddle. Remember that in groundwork you are always working toward riding your horse—from the ground up. Quality of gaits on the ground builds quality of gaits under saddle. Cultivate that quality by rewarding a snappy, productive walk on the ground.

6.9 - *The free gait is long and low with extension of the topline and lengthening of the frame.*

6.8 - *The relaxed frame of the free walk demonstrated on the long diagonal.*

Free Walk

The free walk is the four-beat walk in the horse's lengthened frame (fig. 6.8). It can be used as a reward to the horse after periods of working or time spent in a short frame, or when the horse has been asked to do something difficult mentally or physically. Because the muscles of balance are smaller and weaker than the muscles of extension in the topline, those muscles become fatigued more quickly and require periods of rest and stretching in order to be developed to their maximum potential. The free gaits, especially the free walk, allow the horse the opportunity to relax and stretch the muscles of extension and allow for a recovery period for the muscles of flexion (fig. 6.9 and see sidebar for discussion of muscles of balance).

Muscles of Balance

The horse evolved for one purpose on the plains of this earth. He evolved to survive. He became fleet of foot with a long neck that was able to get to the often sparse grasses on the plains. The eyes of early equines were large and set wide apart to allow for greater vision while in the grazing position. The skeletal frame was designed to effortlessly carry the horse across miles and miles of ground without tiring in the pursuit of food, water, shelter, and safety. To that end, the basic equine frame is one in which the topline is level. In a grazing stance or at periods of rest, the center of gravity shifts forward, but in movement, the center of gravity shifts more toward the midline to even the distribution of weight and concussion of the forelimbs. Forelimb performance lameness as we know it in the domestic horse, including navicular, laminitis, pastern arthrosis (ringbone), and pedal osteoarthritis are largely unknown in the wild horse population despite the 15 to 20 miles the average wild horse travels in a day. As horsemen, we must ask ourselves *why*.

We must be careful when comparing our domestic horse to the wild horse in all ways but form to function because we are making demands on our horses that are completely unnatural. Sure, horses in the wild can perform rollbacks, spins, canter pirouettes, sliding stops, and lofty extended trots. They do not, however, perform them with a large weight in the middle of their spinal column, nor do they sustain those movements for long periods of time. Most of us in decent physical health could perform a burpee. How many of us could perform 10 of them in a row without extreme fatigue? It takes conditioning, muscle strengthening, and suppling to correctly perform athletic maneuvers without causing undue stress, strain, and wear and tear on normal joints.

Our goal as we ride and condition our horses in the hopes of developing a sound, athletic body is to create balance and suppleness through the entire frame. Like any good athletic coach will tell you, this starts with a good working knowledge of how the body is put together.

The equine spinal column is composed of three "arches" (fig. 6.10). Unlike the human skeleton that is designed to carry weight in a mostly upright position on a bipedal frame, the equine skeleton obviously distributes the weight along the spinal column over all four feet. As already discussed, in a grazing position, that balance shifts to carrying the weight more on the front feet, but in times of athletic movement, that weight shifts back to the "business end" of the horse, allowing for rapid acceleration and quicker turns.

In an athletic stance, you would like for all three of these arches to be evenly engaged, effectively rounding out the entire horse. In neutral, the arches form one long, low arc. It is interesting and instructive to note that the lateral mobility of the equine spine is largely limited to the first and last arch. The lateral movement through the thoracic vertebrae is limited at best, and the loin and fused sacral vertebrae allow for virtually no lateral movement at all. The only direction the lumbar-sacral joint can move is vertically, allowing for coiling of the pelvis and flexion of the hip. Because the lumbosacral joint has dorsal (topside)/ventral (underside) flexion of only 6.5 degrees, most of the flexion in the back of the horse occurs with flexion of the hip.

Not only are we attempting to develop a frame on the horse capable of athletic movement, we also must build the muscles responsible for carrying our weight without causing injury or excessive wear and tear on the horse's frame, as well. When the horse is first mounted, he will drop his back away from the weight of the saddle and the rider, as you might expect. The horse does this by extending his spine, contracting the *longissimus dorsi*. This is also the longest muscle in the horse's body and runs from the

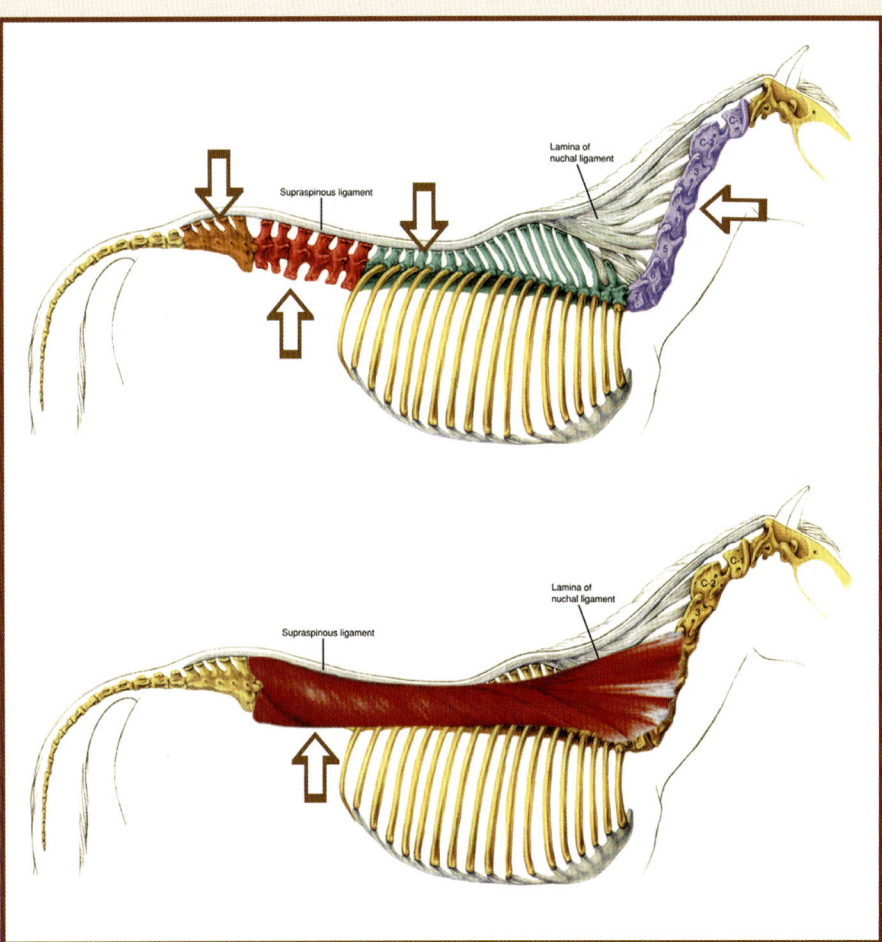

6.10 - *In the top image, you see the equine spine. The three arches of the spine are: 1. Cervical vertebrae (in blue). 2. Thoracic and lumbar vertebrae (in green and red). 3. Sacrum and caudal vertebrae of the tail (in brown and tan). In the second image, you see the long muscle of the topline—the* longissimus dorsi. *You can imagine if that muscle was contracted how the back would hollow as it pulls each of the points of attachment closer to each other.*

transverse processes of the last four cervical vertebrae along the transverse processes of the thoracic vertebrae, and it inserts on the dorsal processes of the lumbar vertebrae. This causes a "reverse arch" through the thoracic vertebrae under the saddle and a general flattening of the first and third arch, as well. Stiffening of this long muscle due to fatigue or pain impairs the ability of the horse to round underneath the saddle. Obviously, this is not ideal, and as riders, it's our job to help the horse learn to deal with the weight and build the muscles that will allow him to carry the weight in a balanced frame.

The muscles that are responsible for initiating coiling of the loins and the beginnings of balance through the topline are the hip flexors. They are the muscles responsible for the thrust that drives the equine body forward. When these muscles contract, they lower the croup and loin, which "loads" the hip in preparation for the thrusting phase of the movement. This spring-like action carries forward into the second and first arches like loading a spring. When the hindquarters are not brought into play first and you attempt to create an arch through the horse's body by compressing or flexing just the head and neck, this drives the neck down into the thorax, flattens the back, and pushes the hindquarters out behind the horse.

There are several ways to help your horse begin to develop the muscles that flex the hips. Hills, going both up and down, work these muscles efficiently. Backing your horse (as long as he is correctly stepping back using diagonal pairs) will develop the muscles of the hip flexors. Lateral movements such as shoulder-in, haunches-in, and leg-yield also cause the horse to work the muscles of the hip flexors. Any movement that asks the horse to step deeper underneath himself while still maintaining propulsion will improve the strength and flexibility of these flexor muscles (fig. 6.11).

The muscles that are responsible for flexing the hip and coiling the loin may not be the muscles you think of when you look at the back of your horse. The Western horse is often prized for big, beefy hip muscles that extend well beyond the point of the hip. Those are the *semimembranosus* and *semitendinosus* muscles, and they are responsible for extension of the limb and help to propel the horse forward in the stride. These are the very muscles that helped give the American Quarter Horse his name, as they are responsible for the quick burst of speed for which the breed is known.

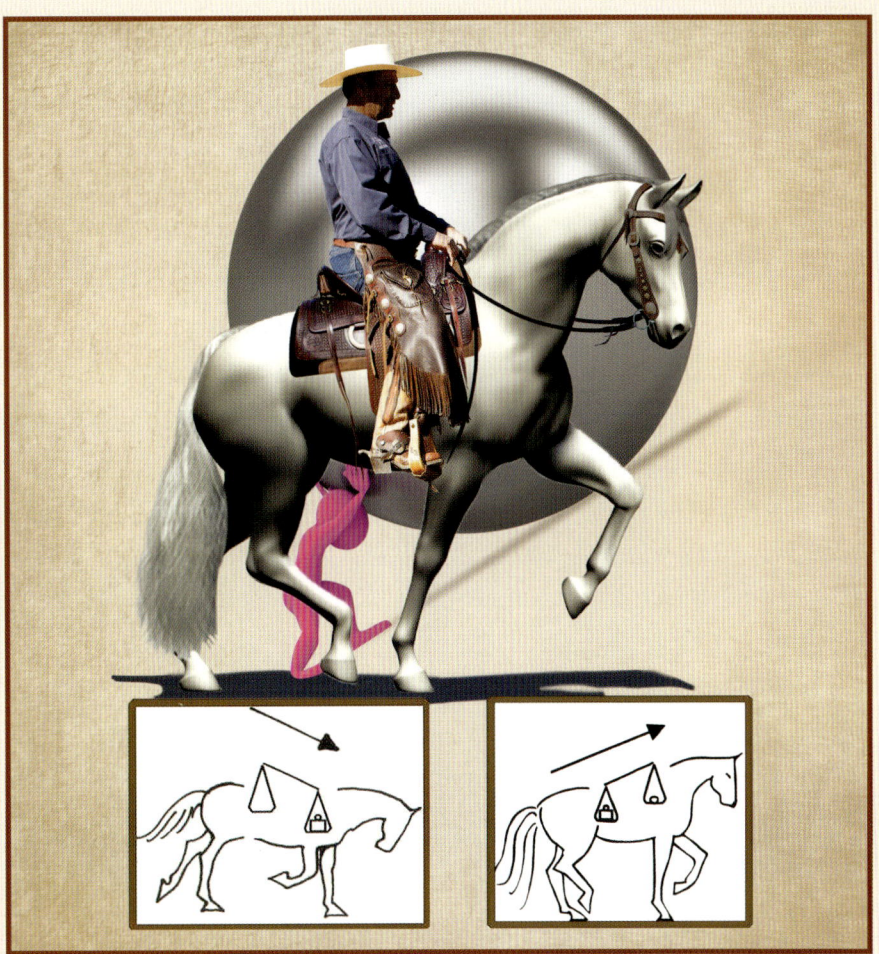

6.11 - *As the withers lift and rise out of the shoulders, the back is lengthened. The poll is raised and the weight shifts to the back end of the horse as the hip flexors lower the croup. Contraction of the abdominal muscles lifts the back.*

They are not, however, the muscles that coil and flex the hip. The hip flexors live deeper and include the *psoas major* and *minor*, *tensor fascia latae*, and *gluteus superficialis*. These muscles work in opposition to the large *semimembranosus* and *semitendinosus* muscles on the back of the leg. In fact, suppleness through these muscles is as important as strength in the flexor muscles when allowing the horse to coil the loins. Some even suggest that the long muscles of the hip are equivalent to a second topline that enables the horse to stretch forward and step underneath himself, allowing the balance of the horse to shift farther back toward the loin.

The second arch of the spine is the thoracic vertebrae and loin. We wish to develop muscles that lie *below* the transverse processes of the vertebrae rather than *above* them. So while we, as horse owners, spend a lot of time talking about developing a horse's topline, it is not building the muscles of the topline that concerns us as much as it is making sure those muscles remain soft, supple, and flexible. While we need good muscle tone along the top of the back for strength when carrying weight, these are not the muscles that are most effective in creating an arch and loading the spring of the spine.

If you have ever seen a sway-backed horse that is also in good flesh, you will note that the dorsal processes (bony projections at the top of the spine) are not very evident. This is because a sway back is not due to lack of muscles along the top of the spine; contraction of muscles dorsal to the transverse processes causes the spine to hollow. Horses that are worked in this hollowed frame (park horses, harness horses, and often gaited horses) will have well-developed muscle tone along the upper spine, and poor muscle tone below the spine.

In order to cause the spine to round up and load the arch, you need to work the muscles that lie below the transverse processes. These muscles are involved, not only in elevation of the spine, but in lateral movements as well. This is why lateral movements through the rib cage help to build strength and suppling in the muscles responsible for rounding of the spine. *Bend* is the key to lateral strengthening, as well as balancing and rounding the mid-section of the horse through loading of the muscles below the spine. You need all the muscles working together to strengthen and balance the horse.

The muscle groups responsible for lifting and rounding the back are smaller than the muscle that extends the back. Like in the third arch, it is important for the muscles of opposition to remain supple and loose in order for the smaller muscles flexing the spine to act. These muscles include the *rectus abdominus, iliopsoas complex,* and *longus colli scalenus.*

The *rectus abdominus* is a large thin muscle that lies along the abdominal wall and slings the abdominal contents like a hammock. It attaches at the fourth, fifth, and ninth rib, and inserts at the pubis by means of a large tendon. This muscle acts to create an arch in the back, largely by flexion at the lumbosacral joint. Therefore, when engaging the abdominal muscles, you aren't lifting the back so much as flexing the loin, which then acts on the vertebrae of the back to arch it slightly.

If you look at the horse's body as if it's a suspension bridge, you can see how the first and third arch in the spine anchor the span of second arch (fig. 6.12). The muscles of the abdomen and back below the vertebrae help lift the back into the securing arches of the neck and loin. If either the arch in the neck or the arch in the loin is lost, the roundness in the back drops, as well. It takes each piece of the horse's body working together to maximize the poten-

6.12 - *The muscles of balance that act together to raise and round the back act like a suspension bridge.*

tial in all body parts. The whole horse is stronger if each of the body parts is doing its job and working in harmony with others. Think of the tail end of the horse as the end of the bridge that has all of the supplies for building the rest of the bridge. You start there, then you create a base on the opposite side, and then you link the two sides together.

The greatest part the head and neck play in the overall balance of the horse is in shifting the weight of the horse backward, toward the second and third arch, allowing the horse's center of gravity to shift more toward the hindquarters, thus freeing the forehand for lofty movement and lessening the concussion on the front feet and legs. Too often, people start to "balance" a horse by worrying about the "headset" before worrying about engaging the horse properly.

In order for the horse to correctly soften and arch the neck from spine to head, he must first lift the base of the neck where it meets the withers. As these vertebrae lift, you can see the engagement of the muscles just to the front of the withers and just in front of the saddle. This sets the horse up for proper head and neck carriage. If you attempt to create an arch through the neck by only flexing the poll, this compresses the vertebrae, as well as causing bracing at the third and fourth vertebrae.

A properly engaged head and neck should appear larger at the base of the neck than at the mid-thoracic vertebrae. It is easy to tell if your horse has been developing the wrong neck muscles because he will bulge behind the poll. Think of the head and neck as lifting from the chest and extending upward and then downward. Some suggest it's the action a horse makes when he is looking into a bucket—he must first lift, then stretch, then "give" at the poll. This makes "giving" at the poll the very last action involved in the engagement of the muscles of balance and softening of the horse from tail to head.

What about the muscles at the base of the neck? Those should also be loose and stretchy, allowing for the "telescoping" of the neck. Thickening or tightening of these muscles shortens the cervical spine and creates the "ewe-necked appearance." The muscles at the top of the neck responsible for stretch and lateral flexion are the only muscles that should enlarge in the properly worked and balanced horse. Those muscles should be toned and even from the poll to the withers.

When the poll is flexed or braced without proper engagement of the remainder of the neck, you get thickening of the *rectus capitis*. This becomes the widest part of the horse's neck and is especially noticeable when viewed from the saddle.

The well-developed and balanced horse will have even muscle development through his entire upper body with soft, supple, stretchy muscles along the topline. Obviously, not every horse needs to be an elite athlete, just like not every rider is an elite athlete, but knowing which muscles are the "wrong" muscles and which are the "right" ones for balance may help you spot trouble areas in your riding and keep your horse sound and healthy well into his later years.

It is important to note, as touched on earlier, that the free walk is *not* a quickening of the gait but a *lengthening*. The horse will stretch and lengthen the topline as he is reaching down and forward to stretch. The stride will lengthen so that it takes fewer steps to cover the same amount of ground as in the previous working or shortened frame. Schooling the horse to relax in the free gait is as important as teaching him to soften in the working gait. When properly performed, the free gait should feel like you might imagine it would feel to sit at the top of a rainbow. You should be able to feel your horse's back rise beneath you as he stretches his head and neck down, lengthening all the muscles of extension in the back (fig. 6.13).

With the lowering of the horse's head and neck, the center of gravity moves forward from the rib cage to the front half of the horse. However, even with the change in the center of gravity, it is important not to "dump" the horse onto the forehand. To properly engage the horse

6.13 - *In the free walk the horse lengthens and lowers the head, and lengthens the frame.*

6.14 - *This concept is easy enough to understand but more challenging to accomplish under saddle. From the working frame, riding with forward energy and light contact with Soft Feel, you should lengthen and lower the reins, allowing the rein weight to fall to the bottom of the bit. As the horse's head lowers, you continue to ride in time with the hind feet, riding them toward the horse's head. Your legs will cue each hind foot as it leaves the ground and your seat directs that energy forward.*

in the free walk, the rider must continue to ride the horse forward so that propulsion through the hindquarters will keep the horse engaged and driving from behind, helping to lift his back—like the top of that rainbow (fig. 6.14).

Once the horse learns that this frame is a sort of release from the working gait, he will seek this release and may even gently pull the reins through your hands when he feels the signal to enter into the free gait. It is not uncommon for a horse to lick and chew, sigh, and sneeze as he is released into this frame. These are all signs that the horse has relaxed into the frame and is using it as the reward and relaxation phase it is intended to be.

One of the challenges that riders and horses new to Cowboy Dressage face is that the release into the free walk is often met with the horse speeding up into the jog, and taking over the ride. This common frustration makes riders fearful of releasing the reins while still riding the horse forward with propulsion in the seat. As the horse learns to listen to your seat and the energy that is created there, as well as trust that your hands aren't going to "hold" him in a gait or frame, it becomes less of a problem. There are many ways to help build the connection between you and your horse in the free walk.

Because horses are social creatures whose herd communication and social structure is based almost completely on body language, they are astute observers of what we say with our body—whether or not we are aware of it. Learning how to channel our inner energy and breathe our excess energy out is especially important for those horses that feel the need to speed up in the free gait. We absolutely cannot execute a free gait if we are holding the horse back with the reins. They have to learn to maintain the cadence of the gait *without* undue rein pressure.

The next time you are in the saddle, take a minute to just sit and be on the horse, allowing the horse to feel your energy. As you sit and breathe you may notice that you begin to sit more heavily in the saddle. You may feel your pelvis roll back slightly into a deeper seat. Your legs and feet should relax on either side of your horse with the pressure released off your feet so that you can easily lift the ball of each foot upward off the stirrups. Your leg should lie along the side of the horse softly, like a hand resting on a shoulder. The legs are there as soft guidance in their neutral position. Breathing in concert with your horse and teaching him that it is a cue for relaxation helps to build the connection between you both and is invaluable in managing the energy in your ride.

For many riders, learning how to channel their own personal energy is as important a step in advancing their riding as learning how to properly saddle the horse. It is an elemental piece of Soft Feel and partnership, and is best accomplished as you and your horse learn how to transition from the working walk to the free walk on a long, relaxed rein.

On the Cowboy Dressage Court, just traveling the track at a walk can introduce the concept of lengthening and shortening the frame through use of a 10-meter bend through the corners. As the horse moves around the Court, transitioning from a 10-meter bend to a straight line, he is learning to lengthen and shorten his stride by shortening and softening one side of his body at a time. As you move out of the 10-meter bend onto the long diagonal and allow the horse to lengthen his walk across the diagonal and then shorten it through the 10-meter bend on the other side of the Court, you are teaching the concept of frame and stride length to the horse.

Ground Poles for Adjusting Stride

Working the horse over the quarterline ground poles of the Challenge Court can also aid in teaching the horse to lengthen and shorten his stride (fig. 6.15). Note that the distance between the quarterline ground poles never changes. The poles are always 3 feet apart, whether the horse is walking or jogging through the poles. For some horses to properly step evenly through these poles at the walk, they will have to lengthen their stride, while others will have to shorten it. The same applies to the jog. The horse (with support from the rider) learns to adjust his stride accordingly to navigate the ground poles.

If the horse is "splitting" his stride over the ground poles rather than shortening and lengthening, it will interfere with his natural cadence and rhythm, causing him to strike the poles with his feet. Through repetition, the horse can learn to adjust his stride to cleanly carry himself over the poles at the free walk. You can assist him by guiding him down the middle of the poles rather than drifting across the poles at random places. This assures that the strides must remain consistent through each pass. You can also help the horse to place his feet so that his steps completely pass over the poles rather than landing on top of them, which causes the horse to either jump the poles or trip.

As the horse approaches the ground poles, guide him directly to the center of the first pole. Make slight contact through the reins to tell the horse to place the front foot just in front of the first pole. Then release the horse to ride forward over the remaining poles, lengthening the stride.

6.15 - *Through the use of ground poles, you can help the horse learn to lengthen and shorten his stride in all three gaits.*

If the horse doesn't lengthen the stride to carry himself over the poles, he will take two steps between the poles and the cadence of the gait will be altered.

The Jog

In classical dressage, the two-beat diagonal gait of the horse is called the trot. The trot is characterized not only by its two-beat diagonal movement but by the suspension desired between the foot placement of the diagonal pairs. It is this suspension that gives the trot its animated jaunty appearance. The Cowboy Dressage horse's jog, while also being a two-beat diagonal gait, is quite different from the dressage trot in more than just nomenclature (fig. 6.16).

The jog should be very comfortable—for both the horse and the rider. While retaining the propulsion of the classical dressage trot, it lacks suspension in both the working and the free frame. By discouraging suspension but retaining the forward momentum, the concussion to both horse and rider is removed from this two-beat gait. A Cowboy Dressage horse in a working-frame jog should be smooth and comfortable to ride seated. The jog has its origin

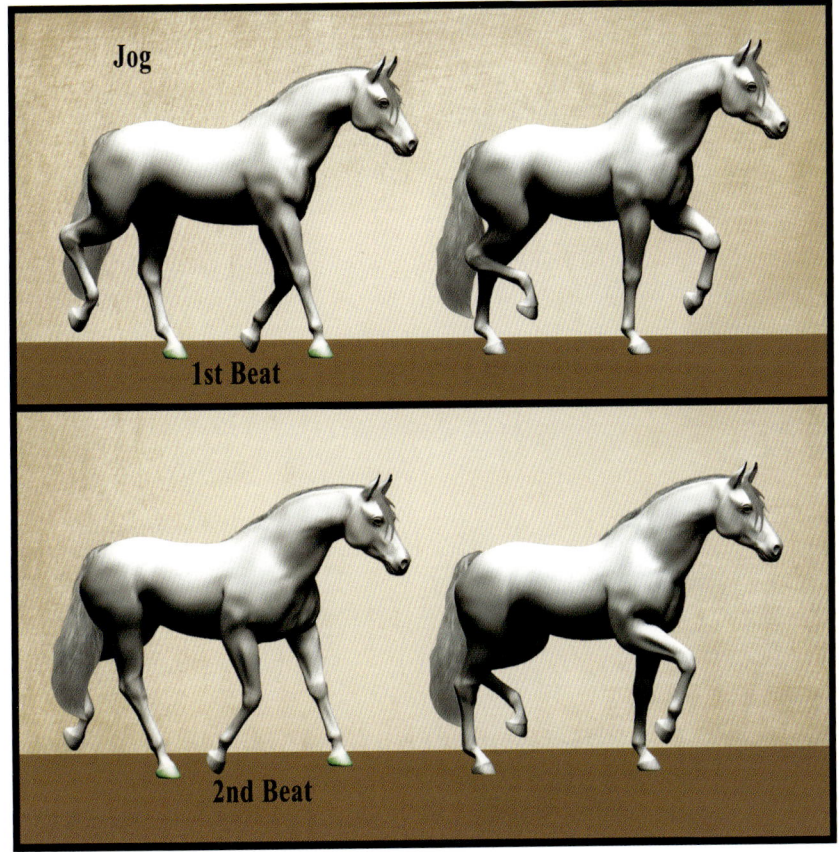

6.16 - *The two-beat jog features the feet moving in diagonal pairs. The two feet should hit the ground at the same time. A horse that is heavy on the front will have a split beat as the front foot hits the ground slightly ahead of the hind foot. Conversely, a horse that is weighted back onto his hindquarters may strike the ground with his hind foot slightly ahead of the forefoot. This is considered advantageous movement and is referred to as diagonal advanced displacement.*

6.17 - *The working jog is a nice, medium-frame jog that should have snappy forward movement without suspension. A good Cowboy Dressage working jog is one you should be able to sit all day.*

in the working cowboy who spent hours in the saddle. Like the working walk, it is a gait of preparation for the execution of further maneuvers and commands. You may wish to jog over to a gate, stop to turn back a cow, or skirt around a rodear (tight group of cattle); the point being that the gait should be one of practicality—a calm, relaxed jog that doesn't jar you and has cadence and softness in a ready frame for the next task required.

Working Jog

The frame of the horse when transitioning from working walk to working jog shouldn't change noticeably (fig. 6.17). The compression and shortening of the frame in Soft Feel that occurs at the walk should be carried into the jog with the same soft contact. This is why correctness, cadence, and Soft Feel at the working walk need to be accomplished before the horse will find success with the working jog.

The transition from the working walk into the working jog should be thought of as an *upward* transition, not a forward transition (fig. 6.18). If you think back to the diagram of all three gaits (see fig. 6.1), the difference between a walk and a jog is that the diagonal pairs are working together. To transition from the walk to the jog, you simply ask those feet to move together. A perfectly executed transition from the working walk to the working jog means the horse does not change his frame. From the working walk, you prepare the horse for the transition by making soft contact with the reins, asking the horse to first compress slightly. Then you cue for the upward transition—not by urging the horse forward or faster but by asking the horse to "lift up" into the jog. You accomplish this by lifting and tightening your core, driving with your seat, and if needed, a gentle nudge with the calf. As the horse transitions up into the working frame, hold the horse until he is balanced in Soft Feel, then lightly release the light contact and ask him to hold the gait and cadence on a soft rein.

The downward transition from working jog to working walk should be accomplished much the same way. The frame of the horse and forward momentum shouldn't change. Instead of stepping up into the jog, the horse "melts" down into the walk. By carrying the frame forward in the downward transition, the horse will not bounce to a stop or land on the forehand. A properly executed downward transition maintains the engagement from behind but allows the energy of the jog to melt down into the walk.

6.18 - *The working jog features a medium frame with soft contact on the bit. The horse is relaxed through the poll and the center of gravity is directly under the rider with the horse stepping up underneath himself.*

Free Jog

Like the free walk, the free jog is performed in a lengthened frame (fig. 6.19). From the working jog the horse is asked to maintain cadence while driving from the hindquarters. On a lengthened rein, the horse reaches outward and downward, stretching the long muscles of the topline. The free jog can be one of the more difficult gaits to teach both horse and rider to execute correctly. The most commonly seen pitfall in the free jog is that the horse hollows the back instead of stretching the topline down and out.

To facilitate the transition into the free jog from the working jog, it is important that the horse has learned to stretch in the free walk.

6.19 - *The free jog is the lengthened frame of the working jog. The cadence of footfall should ideally be the same but with longer strides. The horse should use his back well, rounding evenly from head to tail in a nice soft arc.*

Because the free jog requires the horse to drive from the hindquarters while shifting the center of gravity forward from the working frame, it is more difficult for many horses to do in the two-beat diagonal gait. Teaching the horse to follow the feel forward and reach for the stretch is of the utmost importance (fig. 6.20).

As when transitioning from working walk to free walk, you make a small contact with the horse before lowering the hand and releasing the rein, thus allowing the horse to carry the rein forward and downward through your hands. While not required, the Cowboy Dressage rider is encouraged to post the free jog to additionally help the horse understand the transition between the gaits. Posting is also a very helpful way to encourage the horse to lengthen the stride and drive from the hindquarters into the gait. Posting from the back of the saddle to the front of the saddle—rather than posting up and down—encourages a longer stride. It is important to not speed the horse through the free jog by over-posting, posting too quickly, or dumping the horse forward on the forehand by throwing the reins away.

While the free jog is ridden on a long rein, there is still light soft contact through the bit to the rider. The reins are long enough and free of

6.20 - *The free jog frame has a lengthened stride and soft relaxed contact that is low and long.*

undue pressure so as to allow the horse to reach forward and open the throatlatch, but not so loose that they are flapping in the wind. A soft "float" in the reins is generally the desired result of Soft Feel in all the gaits, including the free gaits.

The Lope

The lope is the three-beat rocking-horse gait for which the Western horse is so widely known. It is soft in its cadence and also without suspension. The lope may be either right- or left-"leaded" with the lead of the gait being assigned to the front limb moving without a paired back leg. For instance, the right-lead lope is initiated with the horse's left hind foot, followed by the diagonal pair of the right hind and left front, and followed by the right front foot (fig. 6.21).

It is often argued that the lope without suspension must be a four-beat gait, but it is the impact of the feet striking the ground that is responsible for the beats of the gait. A true three-beat Western lope has three distinct beats as the diagonal pair is impacting the ground at the same time as a single beat. The suspension phase of the gait that occurs at faster speeds occurs between the leading front foot at the completion of the stride and the initiating hind foot at the beginning of the next stride. In a three-beat lope, the hind foot is striking the ground as the leading front foot is leaving the ground so that there is no suspension in the stride.

The four-beat lope that is often found in an incorrectly moving Western horse is caused by slowing the feet down to the point that the

6.21 - *The footfalls of the lope in the right lead are: left hind, the diagonal pair of right hind and left front, then right front. The left hind strikes the ground as the right front is leaving, thus eliminating the suspension phase.*

horse splits the diagonal pair of the front and hind limbs moving together. This will appear to create a horse that is trotting in the hind end and loping in the front end. Often called the "trot-a-lope," this is an undesirable gait, showing limited propulsion, and is not the goal of a Cowboy Dressage lope.

Like the walk and the jog, the lope is performed in Cowboy Dressage in two frames: working and free. Also, like the walk and the jog, it is the difference in the length of the stride rather than the speed of the gait that distinguishes the frame of the gait.

Working Lope

The working lope is a soft three-beat gait executed in a working frame with Soft Feel (fig. 6.22). The horse should initiate the lope from the hindquarters and step up into the lope in the upward transition without speeding up the working jog or walk into the transition. Again, once the frame has been established in the previous gait, it can be carried upward into the next gait.

Just as success of the working jog is dependent on success of the balance and softness of the working walk, so too is the working lope dependent on balance and softness of the working jog. Preparing the horse for the upward transition into the working lope from the working jog is accomplished through slight compression of the horse through soft contact, asking him to shift the weight just slightly backward, thus "creating a space" for the horse to step up into. The young horse is best prepared for the transition through use of bend as this establishes direction for the lead as well as shortens the horse laterally, facilitating the upward transition. You sit up and back through the slight compression with soft contact and use a little inside leg and inside rein to emphasize the bend and direction required in the next gait.

Transitioning Between the Working Jog and the Working Lope

Because the lope stride is initiated by the outside rear leg, the cue must be given as that leg is preparing to move forward. This again is another reason for the rider to be in time with the horse's feet (fig. 6.23). The cue for lope can only be immediately executed as that hind foot is about to come forward. Because the jog is a two-beat gait moving in diagonal pairs, we know that the outside rear foot is about to move forward in flight as the outside front foot strikes the ground. At that instant, the rider can switch leg aids from the inside leg holding bend to the outside leg, which cues the upward lope transition. With proper conditioning the horse can learn to "hold" the preparation for the lope transition for several strides, waiting for the rider to cue the transition at precisely the right time.

Once the stride is initiated, hold the working frame, releasing just slightly between strides

6.22 - *The soft working lope is a joy to ride and beautiful to watch.*

6.23 - *The three phases of the lope in the left lead: right hind, diagonal pair of the left hind and right front, followed by the left front. Notice how the hindquarters and forehand rise and fall in the rocking-horse motion. As a rider, you must follow that motion, helping to lift the horse in the stride as the hindquarters drop, and ride the motion forward with your seat as the horse's hindquarters are lifted and the horse's head is down.*

(fig. 6.24). The lope should be ridden one stride at a time to help maintain balance and frame. Because the working lope is a shorter frame than the free lope, most horses will require the balance and drive from the rider to help them maintain the gait through a circle or maneuver without dropping to the jog or falling out of frame (fig. 6.25).

The downward transition from the lope to the jog is more difficult still than the downward transition from the jog to the walk. The lope requires the horse to hold his center of gravity back toward the hindquarters to be executed correctly, but many horses want to fall forward through the downward transition from lope to jog, dropping their balance onto the forehand, causing loss of Soft Feel, loss of propulsion, and making the transition anything but smooth.

6.24 - *The working lope demonstrated on the Challenge Court.*

6.25 - *The working lope is a medium-frame lope with soft contact through the reins and the horse driving from behind.*

The working lope to working jog transition is made similarly to the working jog to lope transition upward. Slight contact with the reins tells the horse to stay in the frame on Soft Feel. Breathing out or dropping your seat bones down and slightly back as the diagonal pair of feet strikes the ground allows the horse to step directly into the two-beat diagonal gait of the jog, without creating the "jog-a-lope" transition, *if* the gait change occurs when the leading front foot or leading hind foot are cued.

Free Lope

The free lope, like the free jog and the free walk, is a change in frame within the gait that is the result of *lengthening* and *not* quickening the stride (fig. 6.26). The transition between working lope and free lope, as in the other working gaits, allows the horse to stretch forward in the head and neck, reaching out and slightly down, thereby stretching the muscles of the topline. As the horse advances from walk to jog to lope, the balance of the gait gets harder to maintain, and rushing and dropping of the weight onto the forehand becomes harder and harder to avoid.

This is exactly why it is essential to school the gaits carefully. You don't teach a horse to lope by going in endless circles on a loose rein. The gaits are natural to the horse. He understands the mechanics of a gait without instruction. It is the balance of the rider and the elevation needed for the working frame that requires muscles that the horse is not used to using. Teaching the horse to engage those small muscles and to hold that

6.26 - *The free lope has a lengthened frame without adding speed.*

position in increasingly difficult gaits, transitions, and maneuvers is the very essence of schooling the horse in Cowboy Dressage.

The free lope, therefore, is not asked for in the advancement of the Cowboy Dressage tests until the horse has been adequately schooled through the other gaits and is proficient at maintaining balance and Soft Feel long enough to hold those gaits successfully in self-carriage. Then you can begin to introduce the free frame of the lope to the horse.

From the working lope, lengthen and lower the hands, signaling to the horse that he may lower and extend the head and neck (fig. 6.27). It is important not to tip the horse too far forward onto the forehand. This is accomplished by continuing to ride the hindquarters forward, up under the horse. Soft contact needs to be maintained in the free lope on the lengthened rein, especially to prevent the long reins from flopping and interfering with the balance of the horse within the gait.

Final Thoughts on the Free Frame

It is so important for the Cowboy Dressage rider to completely understand the difference between the free frame and just riding on a long, loose rein (fig. 6.28). The free frame is an *engaged*

6.27 - *The free lope has a long soft rein with a lengthened stride, head, and neck.*

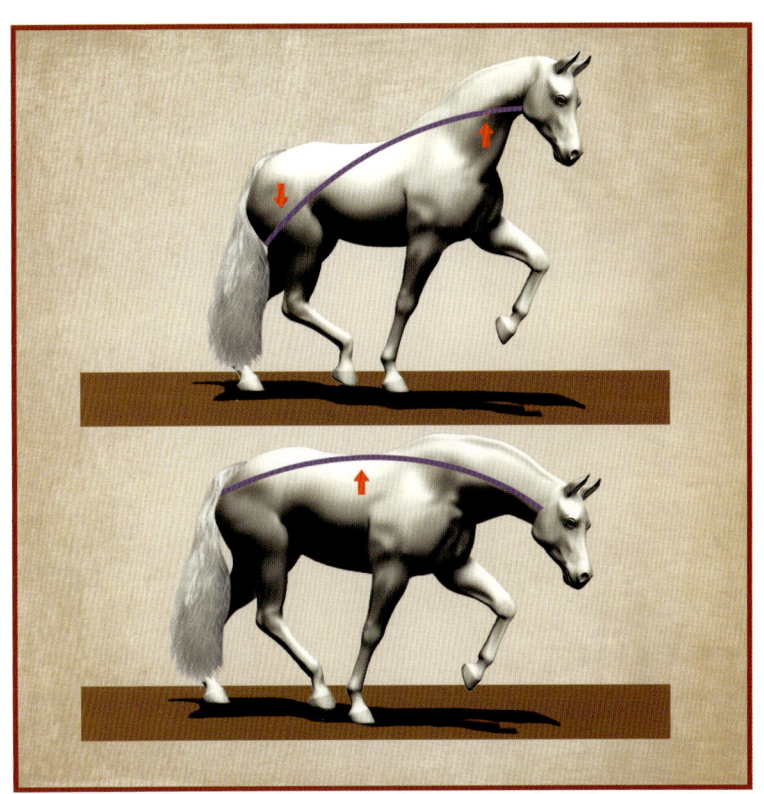

6.28 - *Both the working frame and the free frame feature a rounded topline and an arch. The working frame shifts that arch more upward, with the horse's center of gravity farther back (above), while the free frame has a longer arch (below).*

frame in all of the gaits. While it is a frame of relaxation for the horse and can be used as a "reset" and reward following either mental or physical fatigue, it is not a slouching or hollowing gait—especially at walk.

For all but the luckiest among us, correct posture and optimum bone alignment do not, in fact, come naturally. Because we are constructed of muscles that work in opposition, one set or the other of those muscles is generally working harder than the other at any given time. In all cases, the muscles of extension tend to be stronger than the muscles of flexion. This means that, at rest, we tend to be in a state of spinal extension. For the horse, this means that he holds himself at rest in a posture with the spine curving downward. This is part of the reason that horses become swaybacked with age rather than humpbacked. Gravity would, of course, be the other side of that aging coin.

When you ask the horse to stretch down and out into the free frame, while it is supposed to feel relaxing to the horse, it is not meant to create hollowing, as this is counterproductive to the building of the muscles of balance (fig. 6.29). The majority of horses walking along on a trail ride are not in fact in a free walk. When left to their own devices, they are most likely to be in a hollowed walk with the center of gravity moved forward to the front feet and the hind legs trailing the front end rather than driving from behind. If you watch that horse's stride, you will notice that most of the swing in the pendulum that is the hind leg takes place *behind* the tail. That's because the pelvis is tipped forward, the hind limbs are dragging behind the horse, and his back is dropped under the saddle with the head and neck extended forward.

When you look at the stride of the horse, the phase of the stride in the hind limb that takes place behind the tail is the *disengaged* portion. The weight-bearing phase of the stride, taking place under the horse's body, is the *engaged* portion of the stride. If you can take the part of the stride that is behind the tail and add it to the part of the stride that is under the body, you can lengthen the stride in engagement (fig. 6.30). This is counter to the disengagement that occurs

6.29 - *The free jog, showing extension and engagement from behind.*

when the horse hollows and leaves the hind legs trailing behind his body.

Recognizing the difference between a hollow, relaxed frame and an engaged, free frame will enable you to cultivate athletic strength and a long, strong, and elastic topline in the horse.

6.30 - *The free jog, showing stretch over the topline and extension of gait. The appropriate head position will be determined by a horse's conformation.*

7

STRAIGHTNESS AND BEND

"We bend our horses to ride them straight."

EITAN BETH-HALACHMY

Straightness

You might not necessarily think of *straightness* and *bend* belonging in the same chapter, but they are inseparable in the education of our horses. It is the rare horse that is perfectly straight in his movements. The ability to travel perfectly straight is a fairly advanced skill, and the ability to go from bend to straightness and back again is even more challenging.

In Cowboy Dressage, we value straightness in the horse every bit as much as bend. There are several straight lines on the Court and each test begins and ends with a straight line. Horses are judged on their ability to travel square and straight through their bodies in several gaits and frames. Many find that the long straight diagonal in the free walk is the most challenging maneuver in the test.

Straightness in the horse can be adversely affected by the rider (fig. 7.1). It is imperative that you find the straightness in your own body before you can adequately school the horse. Your balance, weight, and aids must be even through your body as you communicate with your mount. If you find yourself stronger on one side of the body, you will have to learn to condition the other side to improve the transmission of information between you and your horse and to prevent the horse from drifting off course (fig. 7.2).

Straightness in the horse is much more than just the ability to travel in a straight line across the track. Straightness also means that the horse

7.2 - *Straightness in the horse requires straightness and balance in the rider, as well as careful development of the horse's strength and balance. The horse is constantly adjusting to or compensating for our balance as riders. When we ride with intention and balance and the horse is strong and balanced below us, we become straight together.*

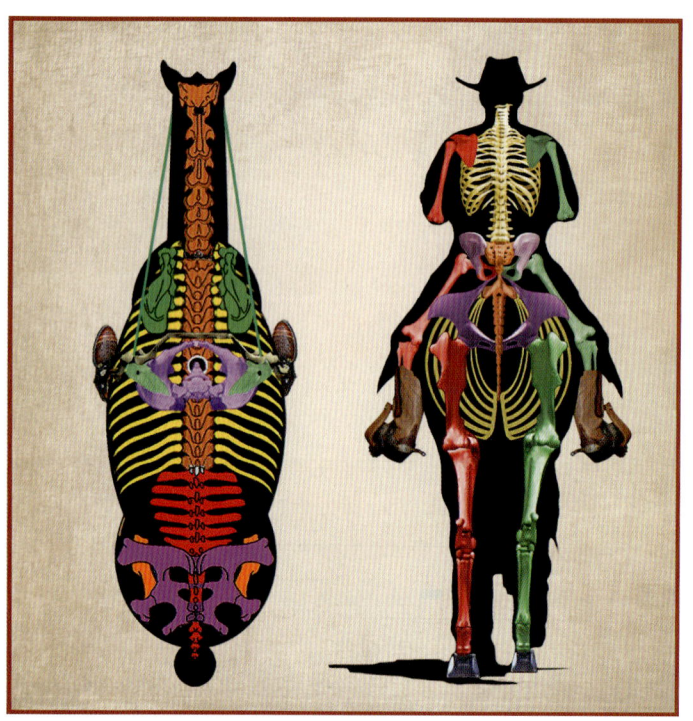

7.1 - *Straightness starts with the rider. The horse is a reflection of our body position and how we communicate through our aids.*

can travel straight and even on his vertical axis as he travels through a bend. When you ride a young horse in a round pen, you may feel like the horse is leaning over at an acute angle as he travels around it. This is because the horse has not developed the ability to remain straight through his body. This requires strength and dexterity in the horse. How do you build that strength in the horse to go straight and true and even? You teach him to bend. *Bend* is the key to keeping the horse straight (fig. 7.3).

Bend

Creating bend in the horse and rider is the equivalent of equine yoga. It strengthens and supples the horse throughout his core. It allows for the horse to evenly develop his spine and engage his frame, creating strength and making the horse travel straighter underneath you—once he has a firm concept of bend (fig. 7.3).

Like you, most horses are naturally either right- or left-sided, to a degree. This phenomenon can be exaggerated in the horse due to our proclivity for handling and leading the horse primarily on the left side. Other natural tendencies can contribute to the "handedness" of the horse. Many horsemen will tell you that a horse will be stiffer on the side on which the mane falls. (Perhaps selecting horses with a split mane is an indicator of athletic evenness?) Others will avow that the swirl on the forehead will tell you which side the horse is most likely to bolt toward when the flight reaction is triggered.

Whichever theory you subscribe to, it is hard to ignore that some things will come more easily to a horse in one direction than the other. Through the teaching and practice of bend, you can help to even out this natural crookedness in your horse for better athletic and more correct movement.

When considering bend in the horse, you need to keep in mind that the horse, unlike you,

7.3 - *Bend is the key for all of the things you work to build in your horse including suppleness, straightness, a shortened frame, and self-carriage. It all starts with bend.*

is a quadruped. The horse moving on a perfectly straight line moves on two even tracks (fig. 7.4). The left front and hind step on one track, while the right front and hind step on another track. Ideally, this is the same when moving on a straight line as it is in a circle. If you view the horse on a 10-meter circle from above, you can appreciate the anatomic changes that occur when the horse enters into a bend.

The outside track is obviously longer than the inside track on a circle. This means that when the horse is perfectly bent from head to tail and evenly arced through the body, the outside legs will take longer steps than the inside legs. This also means that the muscles of bend on the inside are in flexion, while the muscles of the bend on the outside are being stretched and lengthened.

Keeping balance and forward movement through the bend will help ensure that the horse continues to engage the entire body without just bending the head and neck, which is a common pitfall. When the head and neck are the only parts of the horse that are bent, it is easy to imagine the hindquarters and rib cage drifting out of the circle so that the inside hind leg is on the outside track instead of the inside track.

This shortening of the horse one side at a time is an elemental exercise in developing collection in the frames and gaits of the horse.

The Skeleton Presents Itself

Rider posture and aids are the keys to building proper bend in the horse. When you ride in unison with your horse, your balance and posture help the horse to understand the position that his body is being asked to take below you. This concept of your skeleton "presenting itself" to the horse is vital in the discussion of body position in the rider, in all the lateral movements, as well as in the development of bend.

While you are not a quadruped, the horse is such a natural student of body language, reader of energy and nuances of balance, that when you are consistent, the horse can learn to follow the lead of your body. Giving the horse guidance and

7.4 - *The railroad track is a great way to visualize the shortening required of the inside of the horse when he enters onto a bending line. The inside legs (in green) must take shorter steps than the outside legs (in red) for the horse to remain traveling on two tracks around the bend.*

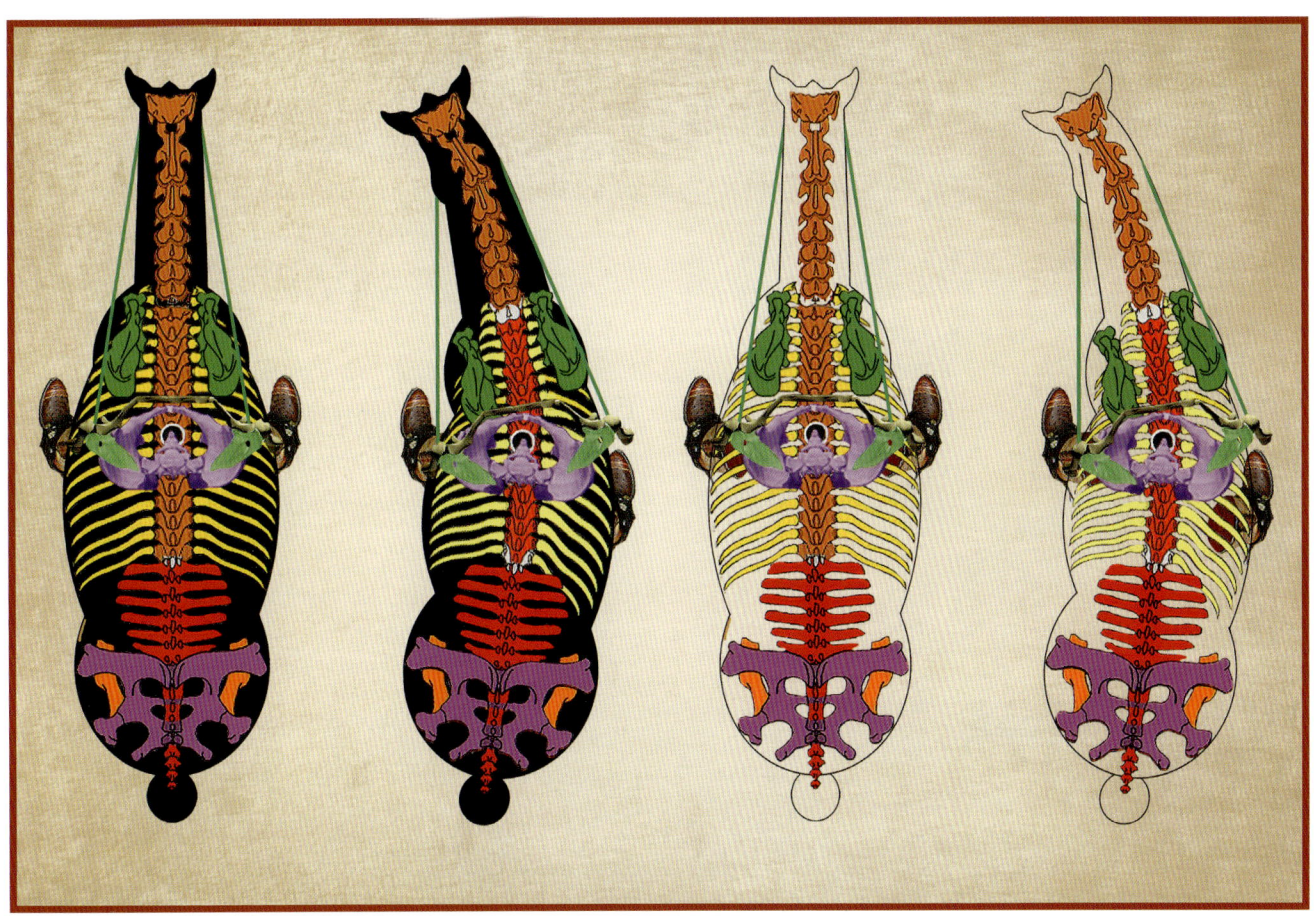

7.5 - *Visualization of the bend in both equine and human skeletons: When the horse is bent, his pelvis tilts to the outside of the bend while his shoulders tilt inside the bend. Your skeleton does the same. Your shoulders point into the bend while your pelvis points out.*

instruction through the skeleton goes beyond aids and cues and is more like a direct connection to the horse at his very core. While it all sounds very Zen and New Age, equitation and balanced riding has long been recognized as an art.

If you can visualize the corresponding piece of the equine skeleton in your own body, it becomes a matter of habit to "talk to the horse" through your skeleton. When you ride in cadence and time with the horse beneath you, it also becomes easier to feel how your body moves with the horse's skeleton below you. You can influence each of the sections of the horse through your aids and individual body parts.

Now, instead of Maneuver A requiring Cue B, you can learn to talk to your horse through body position and energy. Riding becomes less and less about mechanics and more and more about art: a dance between horse and rider moving fluidly through space.

The position of your skeleton in relation to the horse's skeleton is especially crucial in the development of bend (fig. 7.5). When the horse enters into a 10-meter circle, the head and neck

7.6 - Bend is important in all the gaits. Here, you see 20-meter bend in the working lope.

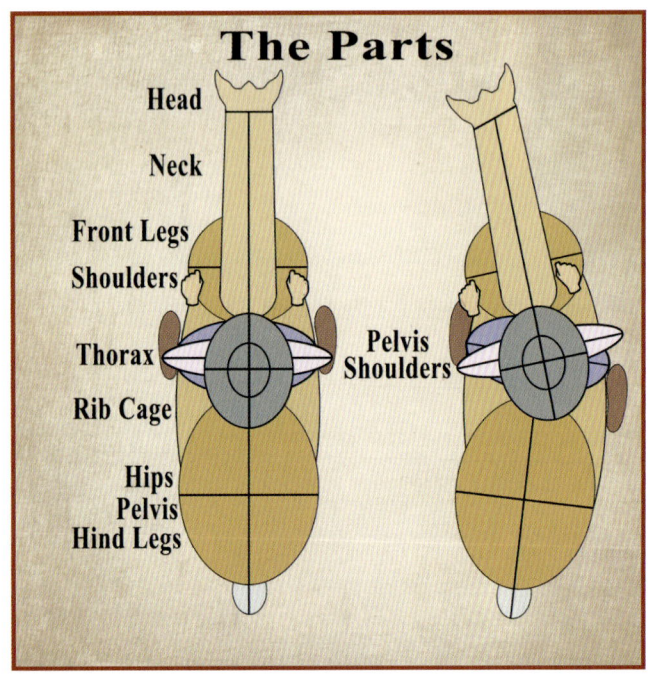

turn to look into the bend so that just the corner of the eye is visible. If the entire neck is bent evenly from withers to atlas, the neck telescopes slightly, filling the bend evenly through each of the vertebrae, and allowing the head to remain vertical. The mandible tucks slightly under the wing of the atlas. If there is rotation of the head and neck in the bend, either the nose will come first or the jaw will stick out, and the head will be rotated into the bend on the vertical plane. This is incorrect and will, typically, result in the horse's inside shoulder "falling into" the bend while the outside hip drifts outward.

The inside shoulder should move back slightly into the bend, while the outside shoulder moves forward slightly, holding the horse onto the outside track (fig. 7.6). The rib cage, which has minimal lateral flexion, does move slightly *away* from the bend. The pelvis moves slightly forward to the inside of the bend, allowing the inside hind leg to step deeper under the body, while the outside hind leg makes a slightly longer step on the outside track.

How does this translate to your skeleton? Your skeleton needs to mirror the horse's skeleton in the bend, and vice versa (fig. 7.7). This means that as the horse's shoulders look to the inside of the bend, so must *your* shoulders look to the inside of the bend. Your inside shoulder is back slightly as your outside shoulder

7.7 - Another way to visualize your body mirroring your horse's body through the bend.

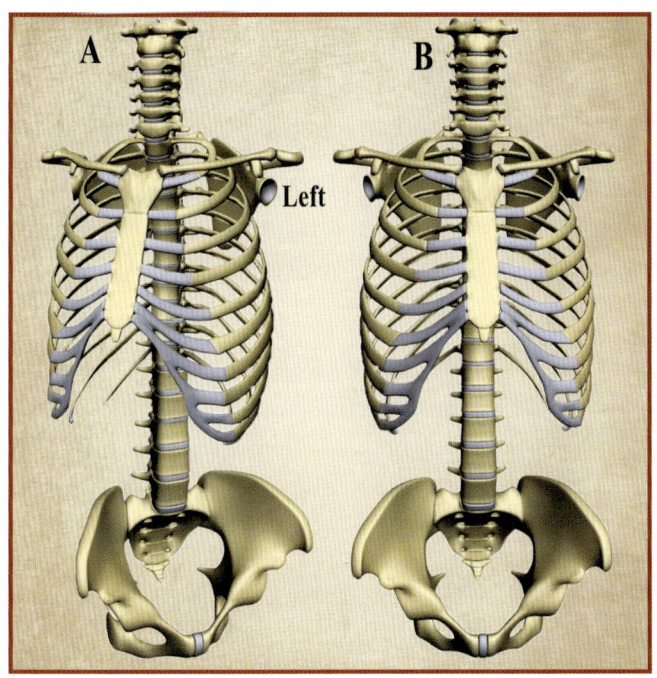

7.8 - *Left bend: The shoulders turn left while the pelvis turns right.*

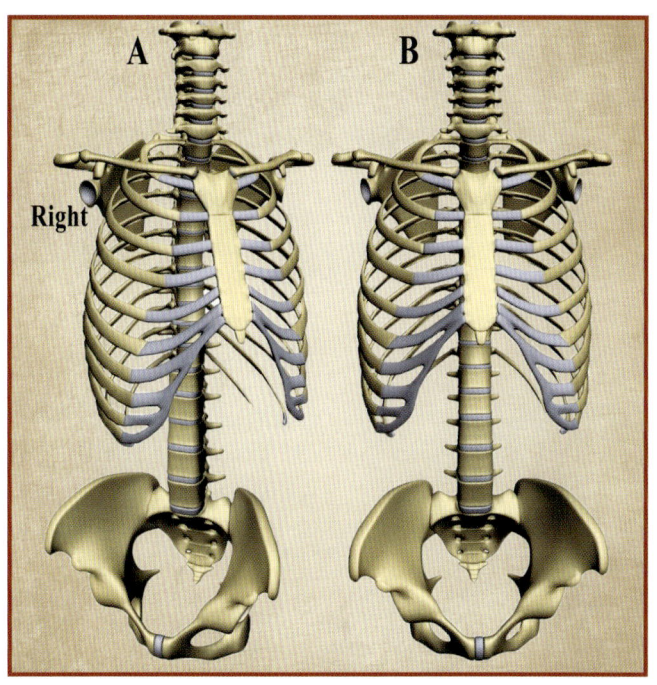

7.9 - *Right bend: The shoulders turn right while the pelvis turns left.*

is forward slightly. Your rib cage shortens and moves slightly to the outside of the bend. Your inside leg is positioned at the area of the greatest flexibility of the rib cage in the proximity of the girth. Your pelvis is rocked slightly forward to the inside and slightly back to the outside of the bend, while the outside leg is back slightly to encourage the bend in the horse's skeleton to continue (figs. 7.8 & 7.9).

Because we are bipeds and not quadrupeds, our skeletons are not normally experiencing a twist like this as we walk in bend. When a human walks in a circle, the shoulders and the hips will, by necessity, follow in the same alignment. This is not true in the horse. You need to remember that the horse's body moves through space differently than yours does. While initially this position will feel awkward to the rider, with practice, the horse will read the body position of the skeleton in the absence of the application of aids to establish bend just through body positioning. This is the essence of good Soft Feel and riding the horse from the feet up.

Beginning of Bend: Lateral Flexion

Bend in the young horse begins as you teach the horse lateral flexion, following the direction of the rein, and looking to the hand. Here is where you establish the correctness of bend through the head and the neck, with softness at the poll and engagement of the entire cervical process. Indeed this can and should be taught from the ground before the horse is even introduced to the bit.

Standing at the horse's side, you pick up soft

7.10 - An excellent example of 10-meter bend straight up in the bridle.

contact on the lead rope or the side of the halter and ask the horse to "give" by bringing the head and neck over while remaining perpendicular to the ground and soft through the poll. There are some schools of thought that encourage the horse to reach all the way around to his girth area in a full lateral flexion from the ground in a halter. While there is merit to this exercise, this is different than beginning to establish bend. A Cowboy Dressage horse should learn to come to the bend that is asked of him through the reins or hands of the rider. If any small pressure says to the horse to bend all the way to the girth, you will get over-flexion of the neck and stiffness through the ribs and pelvis. Instead, it is helpful to teach the horse to follow the feel of lateral flexion in increments, coming as far as you request but no farther, and holding that flexion with slack in the rein or the lead rope. When release and reward are given for proper flexion rather than extreme or rapid flexion, the horse is taught form to function and it paves the way for correctness of bend (fig. 7.10).

From the saddle, you can introduce bend similarly. By opening the inside hand and making contact on the middle of the bit, the horse can learn to look to the hand into the bend. Looking into the bend and following that direction helps to soften and open the bend through the head and the neck. The outside rein is as important

7.11 - A nice, soft, 10-meter bend through the corner of the track.

when initiating bend through the head and neck. The outside rein needs to lengthen, allowing the horse the space to lengthen the muscles on the outside of the neck. Soft rein pressure laid against the outside shoulder keeps the shoulder from drifting outward in the bend.

Your hand position in the 10-meter bend is open, allowing the horse to bend within the aids without leaning on them (fig. 7.11). Imagine holding a handlebar while riding in a straight line. If you turn the handlebar to initiate the bend, the inside hand will come back and slightly down, while the outside hand will move forward and slightly up to hold the bend consistently throughout the circle. Consider how your skeleton presents itself in bend, the hands through the reins communicating with the horse's head, neck, and shoulders, and through the shoulders to the front feet. The hands have no practical effect on the body of the horse. If the horse's body drifts to the inside of the circle in the bend, it is not corrected by the hands. Discrepancies in the movement of the horse's body must be corrected through your body (fig. 7.12).

Riding Not Guiding

One of the keys to successfully riding bend and correct 10-meter circles is to realize that you don't steer the horse through the circle. This is a common misconception in new riders,

7.12 - *The inside leg is essential in creating bend through the rib cage of the horse. While there is minimal lateral flexion in the thoracolumbar spine, the rib cage can "roll," "giving" to the inside leg, which aids in shortening the inside of the horse's body, while making room for the inside hind leg to step deeper under it. You can see that the pelvis also affects this roll in the rib cage, and in a more advanced horse, the pelvis plays a stronger role in this aid than the leg does.*

and micromanagement of the horse through over-correcting through the hands is a sure way to end up riding an "amoeba" rather than a circle, and he will not cultivate self-carriage or Soft Feel.

You create the bend and ride it forward. If you get the correct bend through the horse's body by establishing the bend in *your own* body, the only thing required to make the circle work is forward momentum. But, that of course, is in a perfect world where mechanics are more at work than two living, breathing beings trying to dance as one. So, to help correct the horse's circle and bend through riding rather than guiding, it is first important to think about balance.

With each step the horse takes, his balance adjusts to compensate for the movement and shifting of weight-bearing feet. In a four-beat gait like the walk, the balance is shifting with the movement of each foot in the stride. Therefore, in a single walk stride, the balance of the horse and rider will shift four times. If the balance shifts too drastically in a step one direction or the other, suddenly your perfect circle is out of whack. When we spoke of feeling the horse move underneath us and being in tune with the movement of all four feet, the balance of the horse and rider is part of that program.

When you have properly established bend through the horse's head and the neck, communicating through your hands to the horse's front feet, but the horse falls to the inside of the circle, you can respond in two ways: If the horse has fallen to the inside of the circle just from loss of balance and not loss of bend, correcting that balance by weighting the outside hip asks the horse to step back onto the outside track and back onto bend. If the horse has fallen to the inside of the circle due to loss of bend through the rib cage, the inside leg can become active to remind the horse to bend around it. If the horse is falling to the outside of the circle through the rib cage because of loss of bend in the hindquarters, the outside leg can ask the horse to step back into bend, while the inside hip is weighted to encourage the horse to step up and underneath himself into the circle.

You may have to adjust your balance to help the horse maintain bend through each step of the circle. These changes in balance are minimal in most cases and not easily observed from the outside. If you dwell on any of these changes for too long, it becomes an over-correction. Like a dancer who stays light on her feet, you must stay light and balanced on your aids to prevent the horse from becoming desensitized to the subtle nuances of riding with the body rather than guiding with the hands.

Exercises in Bend

Like the runner who does toe touches and lunges before heading out for a jog, bend becomes a stretching and suppling exercise as important to the warming up of the horse's muscles as a good walk. Warming the horse up by moving through 10-meter bend at the walk serves as a checklist of sorts to ensure the horse is moving well and evenly beneath you.

All riders will utilize the Cowboy Dressage Court in their own way to help warm the horse up using bend (fig. 7.13). For a young or green horse in need of repetition, working through all 12 of the 10-meter circles on the Court in one direction and then the other direction is one option (see p. 80). For the older schooled horse or one that tires with repetition, this may prove too many circles at once. For those horses, combining 10-meter circles at the working walk with

7.13 - *The 5-meter grid of the Court means there is a wealth of opportunity for practicing the 10-meter bend. Let your imagination be your guide.*

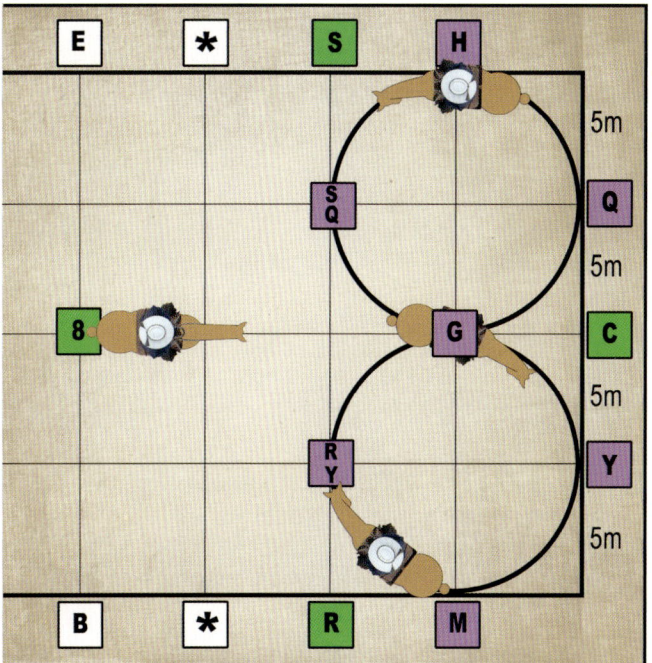

7.14 - *The figure-eight exercise with a change of bend at G. You can see that the figure eight is essentially two circles meeting. The change of bend must happen at the intersection of the two circles.*

long periods of free walk across the long diagonals is a valuable exercise.

Changing Bend

Changing bend from one direction to the other is also a valuable suppling exercise that helps to build balance in the horse. The ability of the horse and rider to smoothly change from bend in one direction to the other is very important. When changing from a right bend to a left bend, the change in bend is initiated through your skeleton before the change of direction is established with the hands. You initiate the change in bend by changing hips and legs and essentially leg-yielding the horse into the change of direction and bend. The hands follow just a beat behind the change in the body, making the transition seem to occur smoothly over just a step or two within the stride.

If you picture a 10-meter figure eight at G, the change of bend in the body happens just a step before your stirrups pass over G (fig. 7.14). At G, your hands follow the change in bend through the horse's body to establish the new direction. As you are on a left bend approaching G, your *inside* leg is the *left* leg. A step before G, change legs, making contact with the right leg, guiding the rib cage over into the new bend, weighting the left hip, and then changing the bend through the hands. When done correctly and smoothly as viewed from above, the horse will smoothly go from left bend to right bend exactly over G, mak-

7.15 - A tool for building bend at your disposal is the garrocha pole. You can use the pole just as you use the octagon as a focus for the bend. By keeping the horse's bend constant around the pole, you can concentrate on creating the bend and riding it forward. It becomes much harder to micromanage the horse when you are holding onto the reins with one hand and a pole with the other. The combination of the garrocha pole and the octagon just means you have even more ways to help you and your horse develop bend.

ing the two 10-meter circles touch at that point.

Another way to work on variations of bend is to change through the inside of a circle, as if you are inscribing the Yin Yang symbol on the ground. Practicing smoothly shifting bend through the rib cage, then changing direction with the hands while maintaining the same circle, is a challenging and useful exercise.

The Octagon for Bend

The octagon on the Challenge Court is like having your own gymnastic bend tool right in your arena. Using the octagon—or using the octagon with the *garrocha* pole—is an excellent way to teach the horse to bend, and hold the bend, while carrying it forward (fig. 7.15). The physical presence of the ground poles gives purpose to the horse, more so than he experiences on the Open Court. The octagon is more than a 10-meter bend, even when going around the outside of the poles, so it is more difficult.

The octagon can be used both to teach and to warm up the horse in bend. Riding around the outside of the octagon, ask the horse for bend at each junction of the ground poles by making contact with the inside rein and inside leg at the same time. This is done with rhythm. Once the horse feels good around the *outside* of the octagon, you can ask the horse to step to the *inside* and ride him in the smaller circle (fig. 7.16).

Rather than physically pushing the horse into and out of the octagon, think of it as switching your intention from the inside of the poles to the outside. This is a great way to get the horse feeling your weight and center of gravity. When you are on the inside of the octagon, you can shift your weight to the outside of the octagon, allowing the horse to step over with you. You can tell if the horse is following your seat because he will step out with the outside foot and step in with the inside foot. Often, when riders push their horse out of the octagon with the inside rein or leg instead, the horse steps over first with the inside leg. Neither is wrong per se, it is just a useful exercise to help the rider be aware of how the aids are affecting the horse's feet.

Remember not to spend too much time working on bend in or around the octagon as too much bend kills "forward." If you feel your horse is beginning to drag or lose the forward impulse, take a break, and allow him to free walk for a time before returning to work on bending the opposite direction.

20-Meter Bend

While the 10-meter bend is the bread and butter of the Cowboy Dressage Court, the 20-meter bend, especially in the free jog and working lope, is also an important element (figs. 7.17 & 7.18). The 20-meter circle is easier in some ways and

7.16 - *The octagon can be used to help a horse develop bend. You can work around the inside or the outside.*

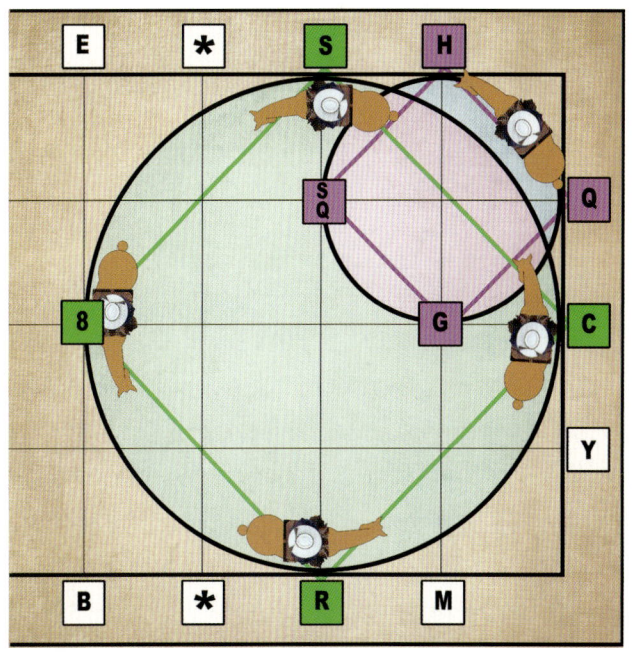

7.17 - *Changing from 10- to 20-meter bend is one of the most elemental of the Cowboy Dressage exercises. There are several different places to work on this maneuver on the Court.*

7.18 - *Here you see 20-meter bend in the working lope.*

to a lesser degree (fig. 7.19). There is less bend through the head, neck, body, and pelvis; however, you should be careful not to let the horse become too straight.

Balance and drift in the horse's body as well as loss of bend become an even greater challenge in the 20-meter circle as it is performed generally in the free frame with longer rein contact. Also, the rider in the free jog is posting, which removes consistent seat aids in the bend. The leg and weight aids, therefore, become even more important in the maintenance of bend in the free gaits (fig. 7.20).

For the horse and rider that find the 20-meter circle a challenge to navigate, beginning by riding that circle as a diamond can be helpful to make sure you are establishing and meeting more difficult in others. The 20-meter circle at the lower-level tests is generally an unwinding exercise used as a break between 10-meter circles to reestablish "forward" while maintaining bend in the horse. The over-application of 10-meter bend, while great for suppleness, can inhibit forward in most horses. And so enter the 20-meter circle, which allows the horse more freedom in forward movement by encouraging stretching of the muscles of bend in the free frame, as well as "greasing the wheels," so to speak, to keep the horse interested in moving forward. The elements of bend established in the 10-meter bend are the same in the 20-meter bend but applied

7.19 - *An excellent example of 20-meter bend in the free frame.*

7.20 - *A nice 20-meter bend in the free jog.*

the touch points on the circle. Physical markers such as cones or barrels at the top and bottom of the 20-meter circle (at B and E) are useful on the Cowboy Dressage Court and Challenge Court, though the Challenge Court does provide the added guides of the diagonal ground poles. By riding the circle first as a diamond, then by thinking about the bend in short one-quarter-circle arcs, many riders have found the 20-meter circle much simpler to achieve.

Counter-Bend

Once the horse has a firm understanding of bend and Soft Feel within the bend, the concept of counter-bend can be introduced to the horse. Counter-bend is a useful suppling exercise and is generally used to gain more control of the horse's shoulders and strengthen the response to the inside leg and seat aids. Counter-bend is simply a change in direction of travel without a change in bend.

7.21 - *In counter-bend, the horse is bent opposite the direction of travel. Here the horse is in left bend and the rider looks to the new direction of travel. Ideally, the rider's body will still mirror the horse's body in bend except for the head looking into the new direction. Eitan's slightly dropped shoulder is the shift in intention and center of gravity in the body. Notice the inside hand has come back toward his belt buckle and toward the horse's withers, while the outside rein still has light contact to frame the bend.*

Just as in a regular 10-meter circle in which bend is created and then ridden forward, counter-bend is best taught in much the same way. From a 10-meter circle with right bend, the horse is ridden to the left holding the 10-meter bend already established to the right. The only thing that changes in either horse or rider is the direction of travel maintained by forward drive in the seat, as well as support through the right leg, which is what helps the horse hold the bend.

Forward drive in the counter-bend is established much the same way as was discussed earlier when we described generating energy and direction through the rider's energy center (fig. 7.21). Your skeleton mirrors the skeleton of the horse but you look into the new direction of travel, casting your energy in that direction. An active inside leg (note that the leg inside the bend becomes the outside leg in the direction of travel in the counter-bend) helps to guide the horse through the new circle in the counter-bend.

For the horse and rider new to schooling the

counter-bend, there are several pitfalls to avoid. First of all, the horse is *ridden into* the counter-bend and not dragged through the new bend with the hands. Many riders, in an attempt to force the horse over into the new direction, will pull both reins over toward the desired direction of travel. This causes problems for the horse. First, if the horse is in right bend and the rider pulls the right rein over the withers and across the neck to the left in an attempt to steer the horse that direction, the horse will become over-bent and will lock up the right shoulder. For the horse to step lightly through the counter-bend in Soft Feel and forward movement, the left leg needs to reach out into the new direction, while the right leg steps forward and across the chest in travel. If the right shoulder is locked up by the head and neck being pulled too far backward and to the left (while still bending to the right) by the right rein across the withers, the right shoulder will not be free to step across the chest.

Therefore, as when establishing a regular 10-meter bend, the right hand (when bending to the right) should remain open to allow the horse to look toward the hand. The left hand that was holding the outside rein in gentle contact with the left shoulder can open outward into the direction of travel, without creating backward pressure on the bit and counteracting the right bend. By opening the left hand, you allow room for the horse's left front leg to move into the new direction through the counter-bend.

Initially, this change of direction without change of bend will confuse the horse, as you have likely worked hard to establish the concept of "where the nose goes, so shall you," by always asking the horse to look into the direction of travel. Therefore, as this more physically difficult task is introduced, the horse should only be asked for a few steps of counter-bend before being released and praised so that he can build on small incremental steps. When releasing the counter-bend, you should wait until the horse has moved at least one step correctly, and also be sure that the horse is in Soft Feel and not pulling on your hands. This will be an easier goal to meet if you are not trying to do too much with the reins.

The counter-bend exercise is most easily introduced to horse and rider in the 10-meter figure eight. If using the Challenge Court, it is easier to place your figure eight at D instead of G because the ground poles are unnecessary obstacles during this exercise. Depending on your arena and your horse, you may find that asking for the counter-bend as you are traveling up the centerline at D toward "8" is easier for the horse than when you are traveling down the centerline at D toward the rail. For some horses, the rail can be an aid to understanding counter-bend but for others, it seems to create a sense of claustrophobia, which can cause both horse and rider to lock up.

8

LATERAL MANEUVERS

"The shoulder-in is the vitamin C of bend."

EITAN BETH-HALACHMY

In our mission to build better communication with the horse's body parts as well as strength and athleticism, we turn to the gymnastic exercises known as the *lateral movements* (fig. 8.1). These exercises are designed to isolate and strengthen a specific part of the horse's body, as well as help the horse build the muscles necessary for shortening the frame and balancing in self-carriage. You can think of the lateral movements as the Pilates of your Cowboy Dressage program. As discussed earlier in this book, all horses are born crooked with a tendency toward strength and weakness evident on one side or the other, just as people are. The lateral movements help to create straightness in the horse by strengthening one muscle group at a time. They also help you build responsiveness and understanding of your aids, bettering communication with your horse.

As with everything that you do in Cowboy Dressage, Soft Feel must be foremost in your mind as you begin to school and learn

8.1 – *From left to right: 1. Straight. 2. Shoulder-in. 3. Shoulder-out. 4. Haunches-in. 5. Haunches-in on four tracks. 6. Haunches-out.*

these lateral maneuvers. For both horse and rider, developing a feel for when the maneuver has been executed properly and when to release the cue and reward the horse is a journey. The prerequisite to proper performance of the lateral movements is to know where the horse's feet are. As you develop that knowledge, it is very helpful to have a pair of eyes on the ground that can see what your horse's body and your body are doing, and help you figure out when you get it right. If you are riding outside on your own, watching your horse's shadow is a good substitute for another pair of eyes. But, it cannot be overstated that *feeling* your horse's feet is the key to success in these exercises.

As we discuss the position of the legs and hands of the rider or legs of the horse through these maneuvers, the *inside leg* is always the leg on the *inside of the bend*. The *outside leg* is always the leg on the *outside of the bend*. This distinction is irrespective of the rail. The diagrams that accompany the descriptions will make this clearer.

Turn-on-the-Haunches

Begin with the isolation maneuver of the turn-on-the-haunches, which asks the horse to move just the shoulders while the hindquarters remain stationary with limited forward movement (fig. 8.2). Unlike the reining spin, the turn-on-the-haunches is a balanced movement performed one step at a time without speed. In a turn-on-the-haunches, the horse is asked to shift his weight and balance to the hindquarters. Looking slightly into the direction of travel, the horse steps around, reaching with the inside front leg back and out, while crossing over with the outside front leg until he has walked a circle with the shoulders around the hindquarters. The bend is toward the direction of travel in this maneuver.

The turn-on-the-haunches is a common Western maneuver. In dressage, both the turn-on-the-haunches and the walk pirouette are exercises ridden in training and in tests, with the turn-on-the-haunches being the more elementary form of the walk pirouette. You can improve the quality of your turn-on-the-haunches if you think of it as a walk pirouette. Not only does it improve the quality of the maneuver, it makes it more functional for the horse and it helps to avoid some of the mistakes that we often see a rider making on the Court.

In a perfectly executed turn-on-the-haunches the horse will turn around the inside hind leg, but it is acceptable, and indeed desirable from a functionality standpoint, for the inside hind leg to step in place as opposed to pivoting while weighted (fig. 8.3). The only undesirable move-

8.2 – *The turn-on-the-haunches inside the octagon.*

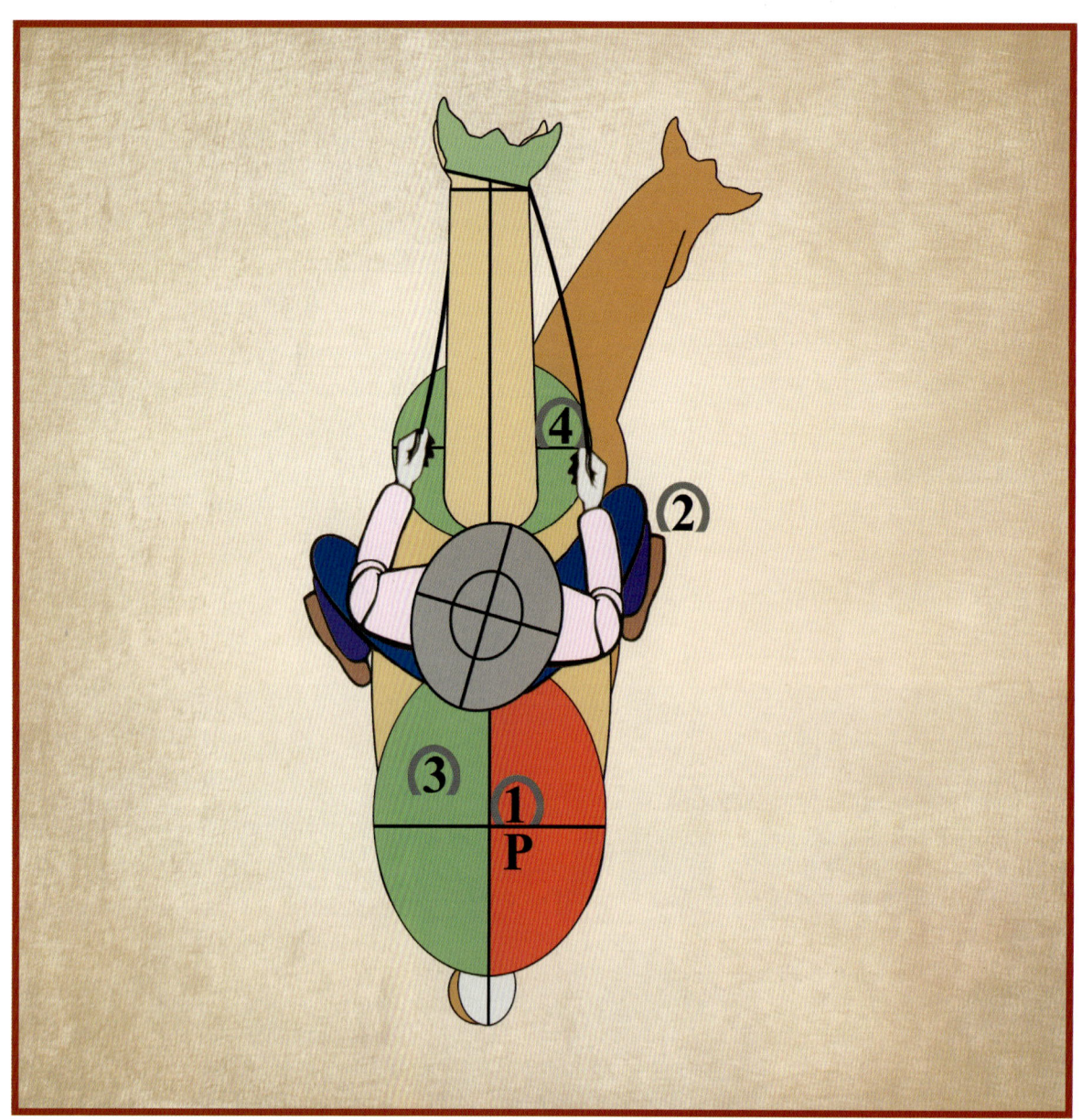

8.3 – Here you can see the footfall pattern of the turn-on-the-haunches. The inside hind foot is the first beat as the weight is shifted to this foot to initiate the turn (in red). When the turn is initiated from walking a small circle, you wait for the horse to step underneath himself with the inside hind leg and then ride the other feet around that leg. So, the footfalls are: 1) Inside hind steps in place and is the weight-bearing leg. 2) Inside front steps outward and slightly back toward the rider's foot. 3) Outside hind must step forward, driving the horse through the turn. 4) Outside front foot steps forward and over, crossing in front of the inside front foot. The inside hind leg then lifts and steps in place as the horse turns. If performed this way, the pivot is eliminated, diminishing the strain on the horse's legs.

ment is for the horse to step backward, losing the forward momentum of the turn. This is usually caused by the pivot foot being placed too deep under the horse, resulting in loss of balance until he is forced to step out of the turn. Loss of forward momentum in the turn can also be due to the horse weighting the wrong foot.

For the rider to cue for the turn-on-the-haunches, you first shift your weight through the seat to the hindquarters (fig. 8.4). You then open your inside hand, creating bend and the direction of travel, asking the horse to look to the inside hand in the turn. The inside leg aid is relaxed at the girth. Momentum through the turn is created by the seat. The outside hand asks the horse's outside leg to step over the inside leg by making contact at the shoulder with the rein. The rider's shoulders should mimic the horse's shoulders by looking into the turn. In the turn, the rider focuses on driving the horse's outside hind leg. The stationary leg will carry more weight in the turn-on-the-haunches and is strengthened through this lateral maneuver.

Ride a Box

Like most other advanced maneuvers under saddle, the turn-on-the-haunches is best built one step at a time (fig. 8.5). A useful exercise for helping the horse to isolate the front shoulders, and begin to reach out and back with the inside

8.4 – *Turn-on-the-haunches asks the horse to turn the forehand around the hindquarters. The direction of the turn is also the direction of the bend. This is a turn-on-the haunches right. You can see how balance through the turn is important for the horse. The horse in this photo starts the turn-on-the-haunches on the inside hind leg then loses forward momentum and the weight shifts to the outside hind leg. This swapping of weight from inside to outside hind leg may be corrected by more drive from the rider's outside leg through the turn.*

8.5 – *The crossing of the front legs in a correct turn-on-the-haunches is an important element and can only be accomplished by forward movement through the turn and engagement of the hindquarters.*

leg and step over with the outside leg, is to ride a box. This can be an imaginary box that you visualize in your arena, or you can use the 10-meter box marked by ground poles on the Court. As the rider approaches the 90-degree corner of the box, she asks the horse's inside front foot to lift and step sideways instead of forward by lifting the inside rein as the foot is leaving the ground. As the outside front foot is leaving the ground, the rider "pushes" that foot over one step to the inside (crossing over the inside front foot) by laying the outside rein on the horse's neck where it joins the shoulder. Timing is immensely important as the rider can only influence the horse's front feet through the reins as the feet are beginning to leave the ground. Knowing where the feet are and getting in time with the feet is the key to success in this exercise. Then the horse should be immediately ridden forward in a straight line.

By working on this exercise in small, bite-sized pieces and incorporating forward movement, the horse eventually learns to step correctly through the complete turn-on-the-haunches. Having your aids in time with the horse's feet is imperative to the success of schooling the turn-on-the-haunches. The reins are connected directly to the horse's front feet and can virtually "lift and place" them where they should be through the turn.

Turn-on-the-Forehand

The turn-on-the-forehand is the opposite of the turn-on-the-haunches. The forehand stays stationary with the horse stepping in place while the hindquarters walk a circle around the front end (fig. 8.6). The outside hind foot steps over and in front of the inside hind foot in the circle. The horse stays straight through the forehand with slight counter-bend in the head and neck (fig. 8.7).

The purpose of the turn-on-the-forehand is to teach the horse to move the hindquarters over while also acting to shorten the horse's frame. This turn prepares the horse for the more advanced lateral maneuvers and helps to begin to establish a shorter frame from the hindquarters.

8.6 – The turn-on-the-forehand asks the horse to step the hindquarters around the stationary forehand. There is typically little to no bend in this maneuver. Generally, the horse's head is tipped slightly away from the direction of the turn. This horse is showing just a little more bend than is desirable, but it doesn't adversely affect the quality of the turn. Often, young horses will need to have a little more bend through the head and neck when learning this maneuver.

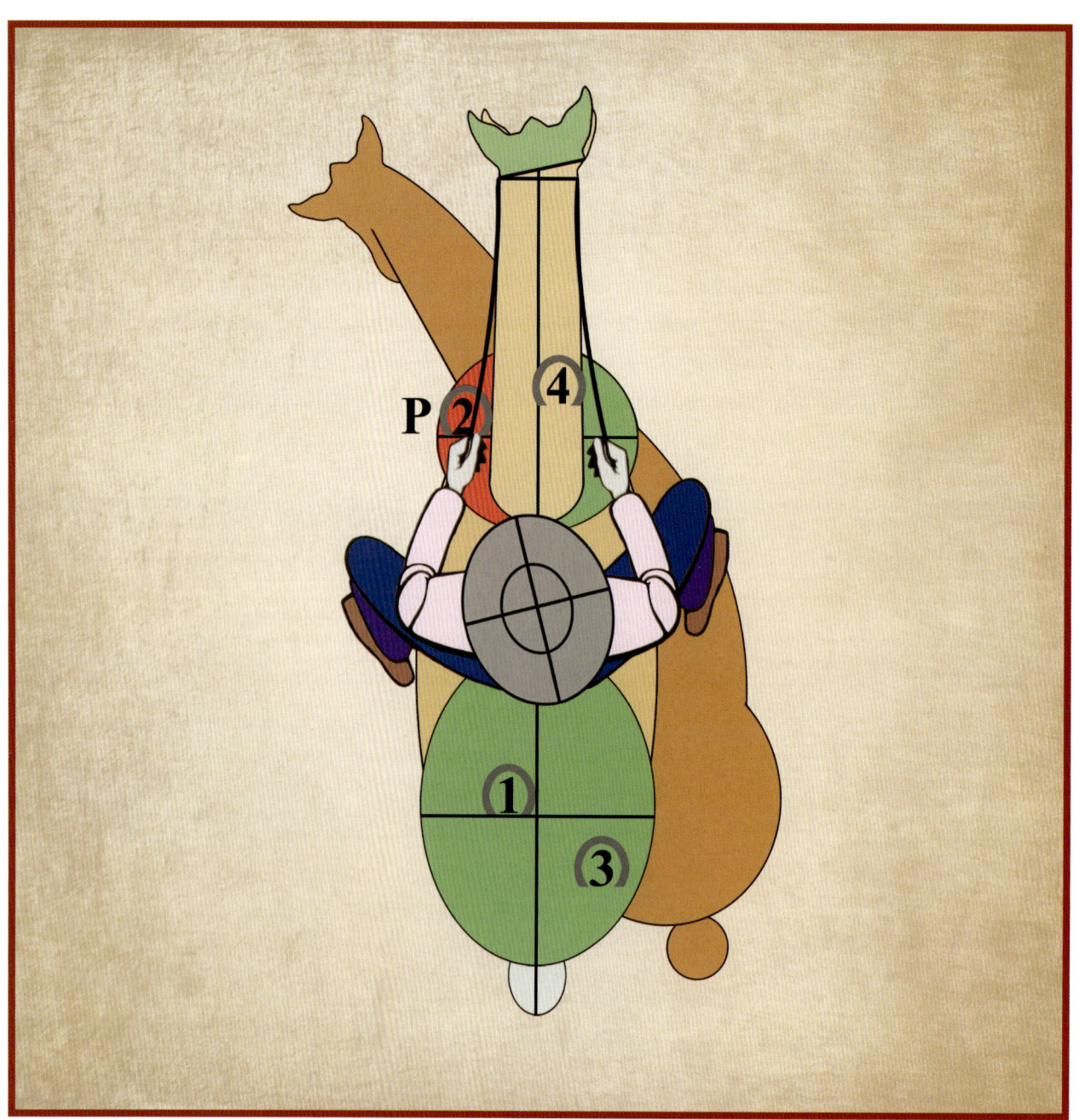

8.7 – The turn-on-the-forehand is also a walking maneuver like the turn-on-the-haunches, so again the footfalls are the same as they would be for the walk. The only difference is that the momentum of one foot is halted and the horse is asked to walk around that weight-bearing foot (in red). The footfall pattern for the turn-on-the-forehand starts with: 1) The inside hind leg as it steps up under and in front of the outside hind leg. 2) The inside front leg is the stationary leg and may step in place, but the horse should shift his weight to that leg. 3) The outside hind leg steps forward and out. 4) The outside front leg steps forward to balance the turn.

Cue for the turn-on-the-forehand by "holding" the movement of the front half of the horse with a slight contact made via the inside rein while encouraging the hindquarters to step up under the horse with your outside leg and hip. There is very little bend in the horse's head and neck. The slight contact made on the outside rein can create slight lateral flexion to the opposite direction of the travel. Because there is little to no bend in this maneuver, the *outside leg* is the one *outside* the direction of travel. Your body stays centered in this exercise, keeping the horse's balance focused on the forehand.

Teaching the Turn-on-the-Forehand

You teach the turn-on-the-forehand in small increments, just as you taught the turn-on-the-haunches. "Ride a box"—walking the shape of a square—with a turn-on-the-forehand at each corner, requesting just the quarter turn, and then asking the horse to step directly out of the maneuver. This will help keep the horse "thinking forward" in this maneuver. Even though the turn-on-the-forehand is a stationary movement, because the hind leg is stepping *over and in front of* the other hind leg rather than behind it, it is still considered a forward movement. By asking the horse to carry the momentum forward out of the turn, you continue to encourage that forward movement.

The turn-on-the-forehand is not considered a strengthening exercise because the rider's balance stays centered through the movement, but it is essential for helping to gain control over the hindquarters en route to building straightness in the horse. It is a valuable tool to help prepare the horse for some of the other advanced maneuvers.

Shoulder-In

The *shoulder-in* is the most basic and most used of the forward-traveling lateral maneuvers in Cowboy Dressage (figs. 8.8. & 8.9). This is a maneuver performed on three tracks. If you remember the discussion of the horse's anatomy in the bend, it was established that the horse, when moving

8.8 – *In the shoulder-in the horse's shoulders are moved over one track so that the inside front leg is on the inside track. The inside hind leg and outside front leg are on the middle track, and the outside hind leg is on the outside track.*

8.9 – *When the horse is straight he is traveling on two tracks. The hind legs are following in the same track as the front legs. Many of the lateral maneuvers ask the horse to travel on three or four tracks.*

horse looks into the direction of travel with bend in the head, neck, and shoulders. Visualization of this maneuver is the key to successfully riding a shoulder-in.

Physical Benefits and Teaching the Movement
If you consider the anatomy of the horse, you can see which muscle groups this maneuver is helping strengthen. By traveling in a straight line with bend through the front of the body, the horse's outside or leading shoulder has to reach forward while the inside shoulder has to take a slightly shorter step. In order to keep the horse traveling in cadence in a straight line, the inside hind leg is required to step deeper to compensate for the shorter step of the inside front leg. This strengthens the hip flexors of the pelvis, which are important muscles of balance.

The horse's balance shifts from the evenly distributed four-beat walk on two tracks to carrying more weight on the diagonal pair that is traveling on the same track. In this way, you can isolate and strengthen the muscles on the diagonal pair, one side at a time. If the horse moves from three tracks to four tracks in the shoulder-in, you lose some of this strengthening of the diagonal in the maneuver as each leg then carries even weight. In much of the lateral work that shifts the horse's weight from two tracks to three tracks, you can see this same strengthening phenomenon of the diagonal pair. Holding the horse to just three tracks can be more difficult than moving the horse onto four separate tracks because he is then evenly carrying his

evenly on all four legs, moves as if on two parallel tracks like a train track (p. 124): The left front and hind legs are on one track while the right front and hind legs are on another track. In the shoulder-in, you ask the horse to create *three tracks* in his direction of travel: Both hind legs stay in their original tracks while the shoulders of the horse are "lifted and moved over" one track. If you are doing a shoulder-in to the left, the *right front foot* moves to the left to travel in the same track as the *left hind foot*, while the *left front foot* moves to the left to travel in its own track (figs. 8.8 & 8.9). In the shoulder-in, the weight on all four legs again.

Once you understand what is needed from the horse to ride the maneuver correctly, you have to think about what is required in the rider's body in order to create the maneuver. Probably the easiest way to teach the shoulder-in to both the horse and the rider is by using 10-meter bend (fig. 8.10). When riding forward out of a 10-meter circle, hold slight bend through the horse's shoulders, head, and neck while releasing bend in the hindquarters. Weight the horse's diagonal pair of legs by driving the energy forward from the inside hind leg to the outside front leg. Maintain contact with the inside leg to prevent the horse drifting to the inside of the maneuver. Your outside leg helps maintain propulsion in the maneuver. Think about concentrating the balance in your body, and therefore, in the horse's body, on that middle track, driving the energy forward through the movement.

When creating a shoulder-in from a straight line, continue to ride straight and forward, making slight contact with your inside leg to hold the horse on a straight line. Then, ask for bend by making a slight contact with the inside rein and "pushing" the horse's outside shoulder over with the outside rein.

In the beginning, many horses will want to fall to the inside, following the bend of the head and neck. You can correct the horse by supporting with the inside rein and shifting his weight to his outside hind leg. Another technique is to drive the horse forward and release the bend, while straightening the horse back to two tracks.

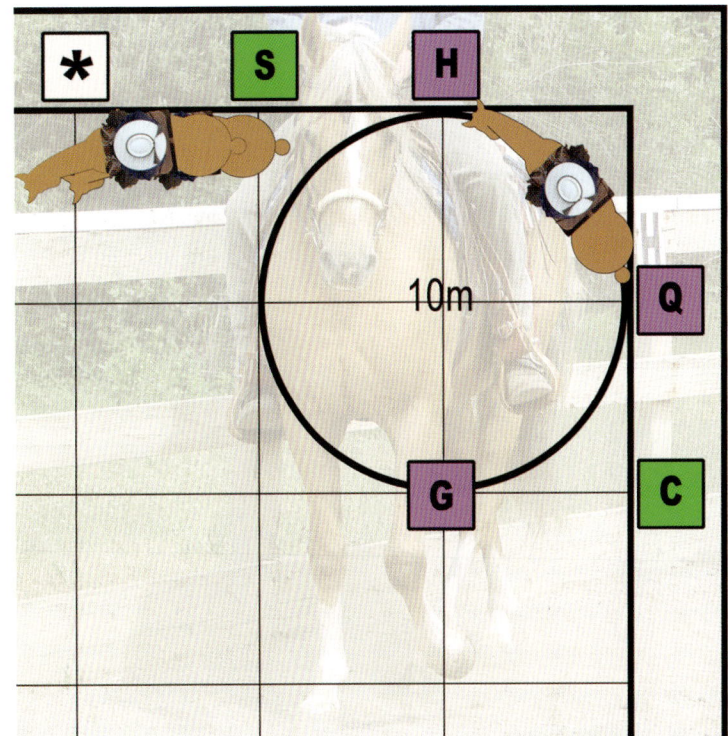

8.10 – *Teaching the shoulder-in from the 10-meter circle: Ride a full 10-meter circle with good consistent bend, then at H ride forward, holding the bend in the forehand while keeping the hindquarters traveling straight down the track. Ride the horse's inside hind leg toward his outside front leg.*

Then ask again for the shoulder to step just one track over to the inside. Once the horse has softened and is moving on three distinct tracks, release the horse to a free walk on a straight line. As the horse is learning to balance through this maneuver, it is important not to ask for too much at one time.

Shoulder-Out

The *shoulder-out* is performed in exactly the same way as the shoulder-in except the shoulders are moved *away from* the direction of travel rather

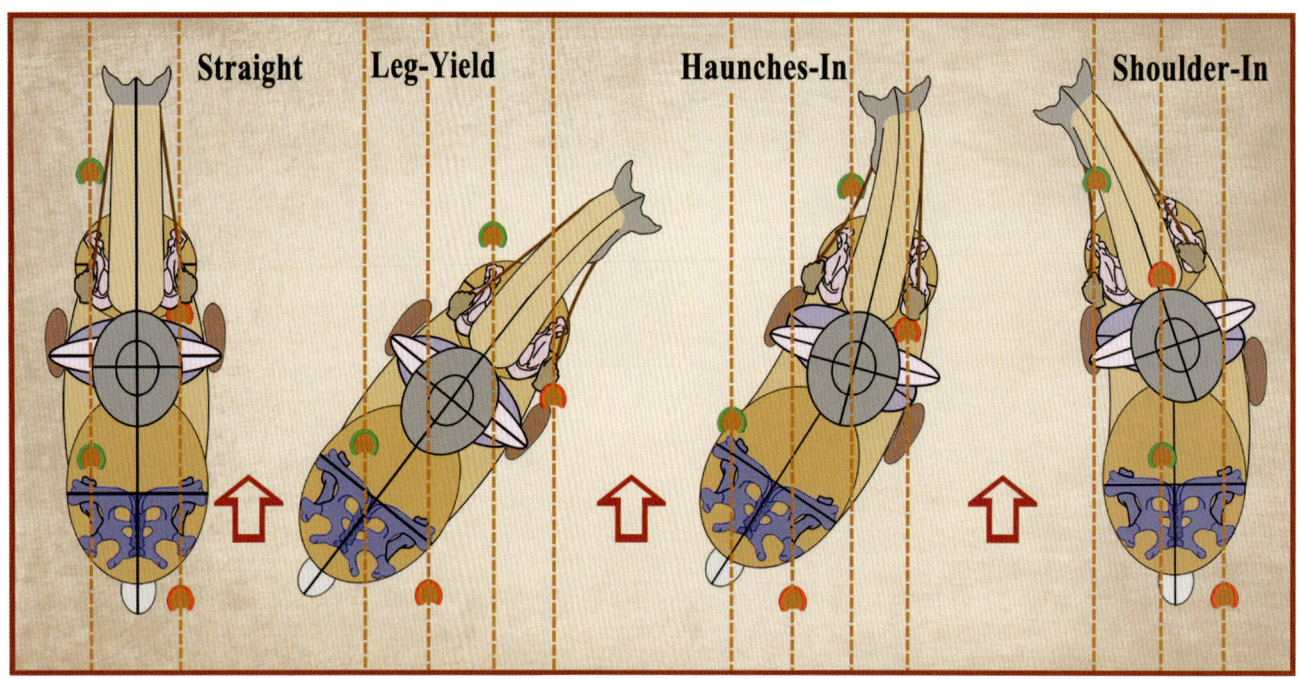

8.11 – The leg-yield differs from the shoulder-in (see p. 147) and haunches-in (see p. 151) maneuvers in two important ways. First, the leg-yield is not a maneuver performed with bend. There is flexion in the jaw but not true bend through the neck and body. The horse's body stays straight so the movement of the maneuver is sideways. You can either perform the leg-yield along the rail by moving the horse into lateral position and riding the horse forward, or you can keep the horse straight and travel diagonally across the track.

than *into* the direction of travel. A horse traveling around the track to the right performs a shoulder-out by moving the forehand over one track to the left. If you were to ride a 10-meter circle in counter-bend (see p. 135), and then continue straight down the track holding that counter-bend, you would be riding a shoulder-out on three tracks.

Shoulder-Fore

The *shoulder-fore* is useful to have in your toolbox. The shoulder fore is like a "baby shoulder-in." While the shoulder-in is performed on three distinct tracks (the inside front foot on the innermost track, the outside front foot and inside hind on the same track, and the outside hind on the track closest to the rail), the shoulder-fore asks for the horse to just *prepare* for a shoulder-in, moving the inside front foot just slightly off the two tracks. Instead of three distinct tracks, the horse's inside front foot moves just to the inside of the inside track. The horse maintains slight bend to the inside but the line of travel is straight down the rail. A shoulder-fore is not the kind of maneuver that is readily appreciated by anybody other than the horse and rider riding it! It is the perfect tool to use before a lope transition or to transition from the track onto the diagonal on the Court. The shoulder-fore is also useful for helping correct a horse that has trouble staying straight on the rail. You never want to pull the horse to the rail with the outside rein as that can cause the horse to look to the outside of the Court. You always want your horse to be looking just a little to the inside of the direction of travel around the track.

Leg-Yield

To perform a leg-yield, start at a walk along the track with the horse straight (fig. 8.11). Make a slight contact with the outside rein and move the hindquarters over one track so that the outside front leg is on one track, the outside hind leg and inside front leg are on another track, and the inside hind leg is on a third track. You can think of the leg-yield as riding a turn-on-the-forehand forward along the track. Note that if the energy in the leg-yield shifts from being directed straight ahead through the diagonal pair of legs to instead reaching out through the horse's inside shoulder, the movement shifts from three tracks to four. When ridden on four tracks, there is equal sideways and forward movement with the horse always leading through the outside shoulder. Your weight stays centered in the leg-yield.

The leg-yield is especially useful for developing "reach" through the horse's front legs and shoulders. Because the outside shoulder leads, the quality of the maneuver depends on the reach of that shoulder. This builds strength and suppleness through the front of the horse and drive through the hindquarters. Improved reach in the forehand helps with balance in bend, better and more fluid turns, and eventually, will create the kind of strength and drive through balance that lead to flying lead changes and pirouettes. While the leg-yield is a good maneuver for building reach, balance, and suppleness, the lack of bend means there is little engagement.

Haunches-In

In order to ride *haunches-in*, begin on a 10-meter circle with good bend, then ride forward along the rail (figs. 8.12 & 8.13). Maintain inside bend in the head and neck while allowing the front

8.12 – *The haunches-in is a forward maneuver performed on three or four tracks with the horse looking into both the direction of travel and the bend. Like the shoulder-in, it is sometimes helpful to teach both horse and rider the haunches-in from the 10-meter bend.*

feet to travel on their individual tracks. Ask the hindquarters to move to the inside so that the horse's *outside front* foot is on the track by the rail, while the *outside hind* foot and *inside front* foot are on the same track. The *inside hind* foot is then on the track to the inside.

You must have patience in helping the horse to step into this position, and take care to reward when the position is attained so the horse understands what is being asked. Haunches-in is an additionally challenging task for the horse because it requires deep flexion of the hip flexor on his inside hind leg, as well as elevation of the back to accommodate the bend in the head and neck. The haunches-in strengthens the diagonal pair of the outside hind leg and inside front leg.

Haunches-Out

Haunches-out is performed in exactly the same way as haunches-in except the haunches are on the line of travel and the forehand is moved to the inside of the track. The horse is traveling in the direction of the bend. Haunches-out is a suppling maneuver and a body-control maneuver. Because of the position of the haunches on the line of travel with the forehand inside the track, it serves to disengage the haunches rather than engage the haunches. For this reason, this maneuver is not used as a preparatory lateral maneuver but only as a body-control maneuver.

Half-Pass

In a *half-pass*, all the horse's feet are on separate tracks (fig. 8.14). When performed correctly, the four tracks in the dirt could be labeled from top to bottom as: outside front foot, inside front foot, outside hind foot, and inside hind foot. Unlike the commonly performed side-pass where there is only lateral movement and no forward movement, the horse should move equally forward and sideways on the diagonal, creating a perfect blend. The direction of the slight bend in the horse's body is *toward* the direction of travel, so the head and neck look just slightly toward

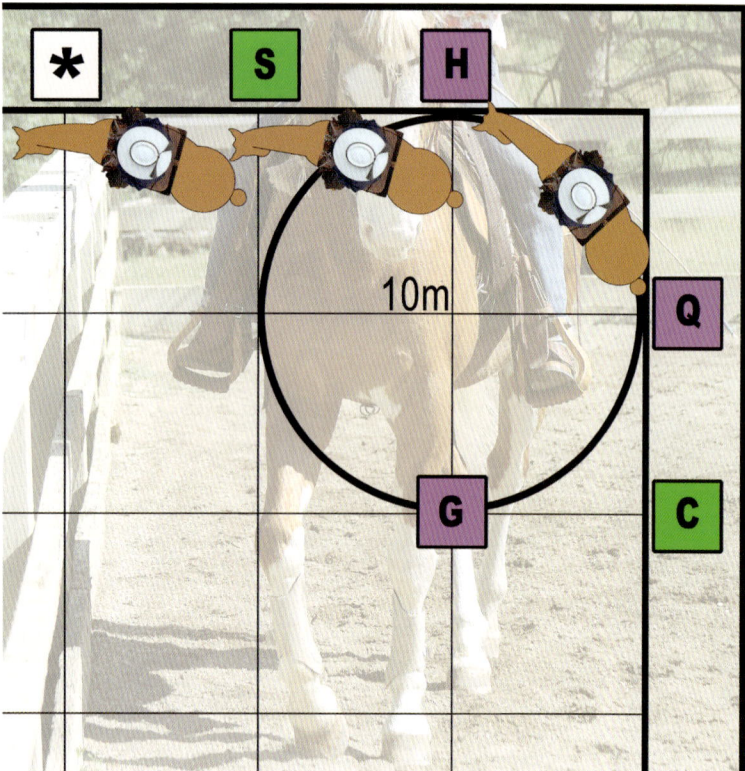

8.13 – The haunches-in can also be taught from the 10-meter circle. Ride a complete 10-meter circle, then at H, ride forward, holding the forehand on the track and allowing the hindquarters to continue with the 10-meter bend to the inside.

8.14 – *The half-pass is a lateral maneuver performed on four tracks with the horse moving into the direction of the bend. Here you see the leg-yield on the left, as compared to the half-pass on the right.*

the inside front foot.

The half-pass differs from the leg-yield performed on four tracks in a couple of important ways. First, there is bend through the body from head to tail in the direction of travel. Secondly, the half-pass calls for equal reach on the part of the forehand and hindquarters. The half-pass is a combination of shoulder-in and haunches-in, moving equally forward and laterally. It should only be attempted once all the other lateral maneuvers are comfortable for the horse.

Like the 10-meter circle, lateral maneuvers should be a part of your daily warm-up routine at the walk. Most riders do not spend nearly enough time at the walk during their warm-up, but a quick run-through with bend and counter-bend and lateral maneuvers on a straight line and in a circle will ensure that your horse's muscles are warm, limber, and ready for advancement to the more difficult gaits and exercises.

9

SHORTENING THE FRAME

"Ride the horse up to heaven, not down into the ground."

EITAN BETH-HALACHMY

Once the horse understands Soft Feel and can exist and work happily in the working frame, he is ready to begin to be schooled in the shortened frame (fig. 9.1). The short frame is to Cowboy Dressage what collection is to classical dressage. Short frame work is very important in teaching the horse compression and balance but it cannot be schooled too early or too aggressively without having adverse effects on the "try" and mental health of the horse. This chapter will discuss exercises and concepts that are important in the horse's education, but they are not to be taken lightly. Be sure that you have brought your horse along slowly through the basic elements of working frame and free frame and have established a firm grasp on Soft Feel and release *before* introducing the concept of short frame to your horse.

Short frame is the compression frame that tells the horse to shift the weight to the hindquarters and prepare for a transition (fig. 9.2). It's the frame of "Ready, set…" in preparation for the "go." The "go"

9.1 - *The three frames of the Cowboy Dressage horse are, from left to right: short frame; working (medium) frame; and the free (lengthened) frame.*

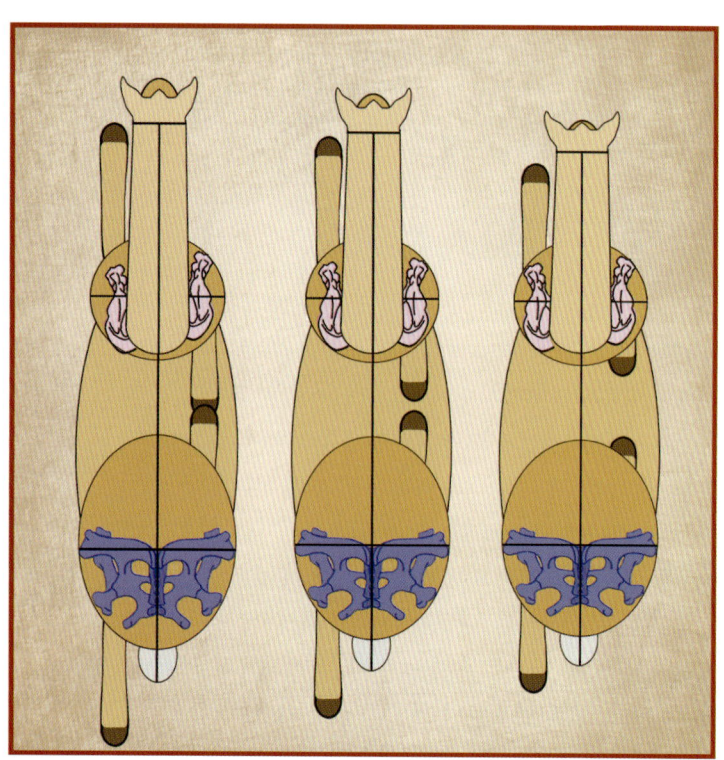

9.2 - *A good illustration of the shortening of the frame from a length of stride standpoint: (from left to right) free frame, working frame, short frame. The short frame should retain the energy of the other frames but compressed in a shorter stride so that the horse becomes a coiled spring.*

may be a lope transition or a shortening of the stride before a ground pole. The "go" may be a change in lead. The "go" may be a stop and back up. The short frame is an advanced frame of readiness. At its culmination, it becomes the lope pirouette.

There are not any requirements for the short frame in the current Cowboy Dressage tests. However, successfully transitioning between gaits on the Court is improved through use of the short frame. Take, for example, the Bow-Tie maneuver (found in the Challenge Walk/Jog/Lope Test #2): a pattern requiring the horse to lope a 20-meter half-circle, then cross the short diagonal over ground poles, change leads through the jog within the octagon, complete another 20-meter half-circle, and lope through the box in the new lead. The stride lengths required to successfully navigate the ground poles and changes of lead through a single jog stride within the octagon require the horse to be in the shortened frame across the diagonal (fig. 9.3).

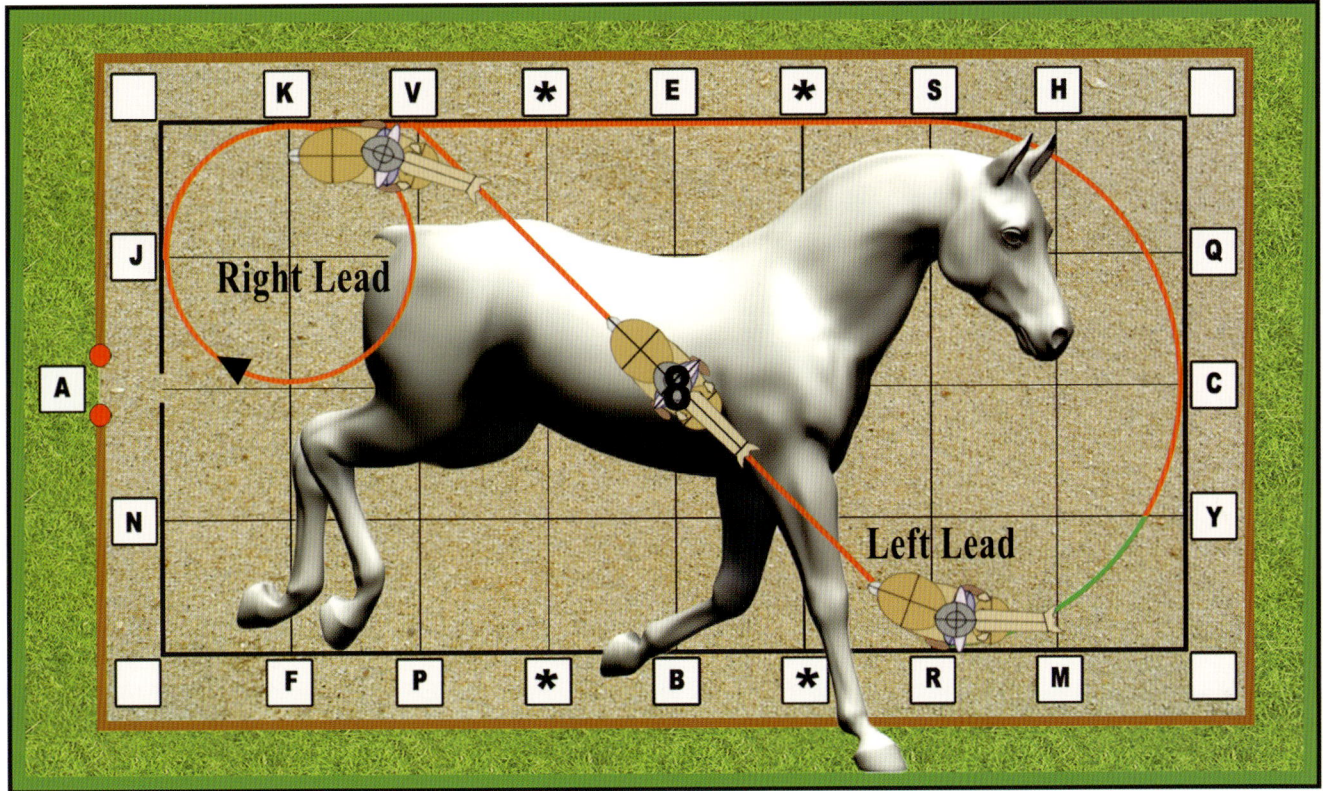

9.3 - *The Bow-Tie maneuver on the Court requires use of the short frame to be successful. The horse has to learn to hold his gait and frame through the ground poles and the lead change in the octagon.*

Teaching the Short Frame

You begin education of the shortened frame in small, bite-sized pieces for the horse. It is helpful to work on the short frame in a controlled setting, such as along a fence line or rail, or in a round pen. From the working walk, shorten the reins, asking the horse to elevate at the withers, and break and soften at the poll. Then deepen the seat by rocking your pelvis back and setting the center of gravity back in the saddle toward the hindquarters. Through tightening and elevation of your core, ask the horse to step upward underneath you. The legs and seat encourage the horse to carry the forward momentum upward into the shortened frame.

When the horse accomplishes the shortened frame at the walk, it should feel like his feet suddenly get lighter, he tucks his hindquarters under, and his forehand is lighter and elevated in your hands. This brief glimpse of short frame at the walk should be rewarded by releasing the aids and allowing the horse to transition into the working frame, and then into the free frame (figs. 9.4–9.6).

If you build on those brief moments of shortened frame with good timing of the release, it should take less and less to ask the horse to step into the shortened frame. Once he is doing so

9.4 - *The short jog is lofty with shortened stride but still features light soft contact and drive from the hindquarters with good use of the back.*

9.5 - *The medium frame shows a longer stride and less compression.*

willingly, you can begin to carry the frame for a few steps at a time. From there, build toward asking for upward transitions to the jog and the lope through the shortened frame, moving up through the gaits and then back down through transitions, just as a violinist practices musical scales. As the horse builds confidence in the shortened frame, you should always be looking for that moment of release and rewarding him before he fatigues or gets frustrated.

9.6 - *The long frame displays an extension of the stride and lengthening of the topline.*

Forward/Forward, Forward/Back

Shortening the horse's frame and shifting his weight back onto his hindquarters can also be accomplished by backing the horse, both in a straight line and on a 10-meter bend. If the horse is engaged in the hindquarters through the backup, he will shift the weight backward; if, however, the horse is dragged backward through the backup, he will shift his weight to the forehand, pulling it backward and hollowing his back. Properly backing the horse in engagement is a very important part of development in the shortened frame: The horse's center of gravity shifts backward as the back lifts, the hindquarters reach forward under the horse, and the forehand elevates with the head and neck.

One of the elemental exercises in engagement of the horse and reading intention in the body of the rider is the exercise often called "Forward/Forward, Forward/Back." This is most commonly ridden in the working frame and is used when the horse has a good understanding of self-carriage within the working frame. At the working walk, ride the horse forward into a stop with slight compression. Holding the frame without undue pressure, shift from riding the horse forward to riding the horse backward.

This exercise asks the horse to focus on the intention and energy of the rider's seat while the hands hold Soft Feel and the frame through the maneuver. The benefit of this exercise is engagement of the hindquarters. With good timing and feel, you can stop one of the horse's feet in flight and change the energy in the foot from forward to backward. Ideally, you don't dwell or settle in the stop, but instead just shift intention in your body, asking the horse to step backward a few steps, and then, without releasing the reins or the frame of the horse, ride the horse forward again at the working walk.

This exercise can be varied by changing the gait through the backup, as well. Working walk to backup to working jog or lope can be a valuable tool to help the horse compress the short frame into an upward transition (fig. 9.7). It is important

9.7 - *The short frame helps to put the horse together for a lope transition and build quality in the lope.*

not to release the frame either in the upward or the downward transition. Note, however, that if the horse is not operating on Soft Feel, this exercise can build a brace in the horse and frustration.

Backing on a 10-Meter Bend
Backing the horse on a bend is another compression exercise and is part of the development of the horse in several of the more advanced Cowboy Dressage tests (fig. 9.8). Asking the horse to back with bend ensures he is engaged in the hindquarters and not dragging the front end. Once the horse has a clear understanding of body position in the 10-meter bend, and will back up lightly on a straight line, the horse is ready to begin to back on a 10-meter bend. Working on

9.8 - *Backing the horse from M to Y on the Challenge Court while maintaining a 10-meter bend.*

bend through the backup is similar to working on the "Forward/Forward, Forward/Back" exercise in that the horse should respond to intention in the rider's body position and not just rein pressure. This is one of the reasons why I don't like the more traditional term used in classical dressage: the "rein-back." This implies that backing is solely a function of the reins, whereas a good backup has much more to do with the picture painted by all the aids used together.

On the Cowboy Dressage Court, backing on a bend is best practiced on the Challenge Court as the obstacles will often help the horse focus on his backup. However, some horses become overly nervous backing with obstacles, and for these horses, a corner of the arena may be used in lieu of the cones and ground poles of the Challenge Court.

Like everything you do in Cowboy Dressage, it is important not to rush the horse or ask for too much. When you begin teaching the horse to back on a bend, it is not wise to push him through the entire maneuver. Instead, if you can get one or two steps with softness and quality of bend, ride the horse forward again and release.

Working on a 10-meter bend, circle to the right at Y, ride the horse forward in the working walk. Stop the horse at M. Do not release the bend in your body. Instead, ride the bend backward for a step, wait for the horse to soften, then ride forward on the circle again. If the horse remains willing and isn't anticipating a stop again at M, try again. If the horse is anticipating the stop and backup, vary where you stop on the

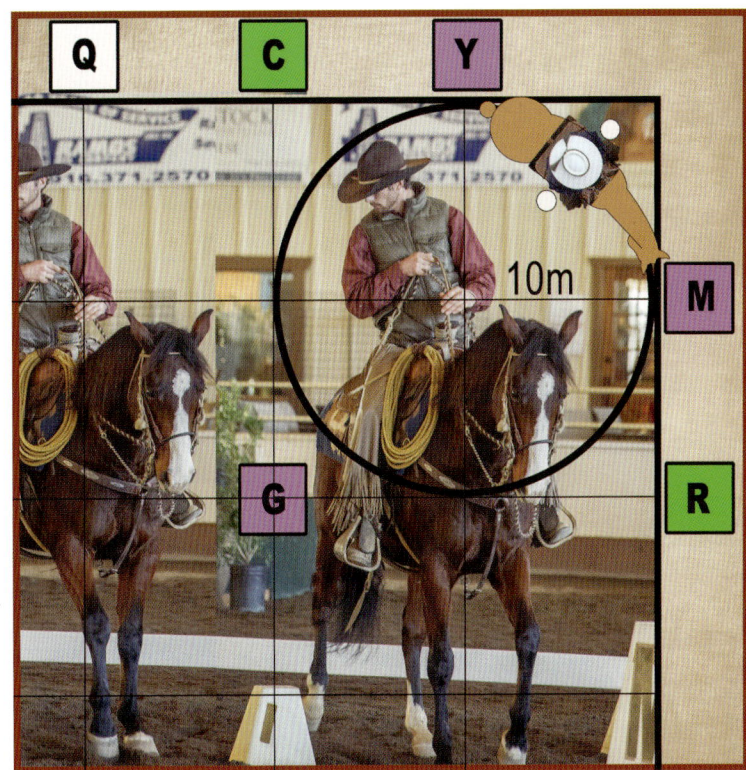

9.9 - *At M stop and back to Y. Wait for the horse to soften before riding forward on the circle again.*

circle so that sometimes you stop at Y or G, or even halfway between the markers. When you can successfully ride forward and backward on a bend with softness a few steps at a time, you can begin to add more steps until the horse can ride a quarter of a circle backward in bend.

Maintaining the bend in your body as you ride forward and back is key to riding the backup correctly. The most common mistake made on the Cowboy Dressage Court when backing a quarter of a circle with bend is that the rider releases the bend in the stop and backs up straight, then moves the hindquarters over, creating an L-shape to back through the cones. While this satisfies the requirements for the maneuver from

9.10 - *When training the short frame, it is always important to pay attention to the horse and make sure he isn't "behind" the bridle. Left to right: "in front of" the bridle; "on" the bridle; and "behind" the bridle.*

a geometry standpoint, it is incorrect in the execution and defeats the purpose, which is to help shorten the horse for the upward transition.

Working Through the Frames

Once your horse has begun to understand the compression of the shortened frame and is comfortable, you can work through the frames at the walk and the jog on the Cowboy Dressage Court. Here's a good sample exercise:

- Beginning in a working walk at C, ride forward through the corner at Q to H, finding the shortened frame through the bend.
- Ride 5 meters of short frame walk from H to S. At S, release to a working walk, continue to E.

- At E, shorten to a short walk and if the horse is soft, transition to short jog at V.
- At K, working jog, then working walk at J.
- At F, change direction through the free walk, then repeat the exercise going the other direction once you are again at C.

By working with specific goals for your transitions at the letters of the Court while working with short frame, you can both learn to prepare your horse for these transitions as well as help the horse understand the intention and difference in your core aids through the frames. If the transition doesn't happen right at the letter, it is likely a failure to prepare the horse properly.

Do not force the transition but rather be sure to more carefully prepare the horse for the next one. When working within a short frame, it is very important not to frustrate the horse nor remove the "try." Reward for self-carriage and try is very important.

Throughout, remember that when working in the short frame, the horse should be "on" the bridle (fig. 9.10). When you first begin schooling in the short frame, you may find the horse wanting to go "behind" the bridle. In Cowboy Dressage frames, the horse should always be working "in front of" the bridle or "on" the bridle, but never "behind" the bridle.

10

THE GATHERINGS

*"A Gathering isn't about riding horses.
It's about sharing the lifestyle."*

EITAN BETH-HALACHMY

Cowboy Dressage Gatherings are the events held throughout the country where like-minded Cowboy Dressage Handshake members can meet, share, ride, and embrace the lifestyle that is such a large part of the Cowboy Dressage community. While at its core a Gathering is indeed a horse show, it is unlike any show you have participated in.

Family

When we attend a Gathering it feels like a family event. It is where we get to see all the people that are scattered across our Cowboy Dressage community and catch up on their lives, their horses, and where they are in their journey to better horsemanship. The Final Gathering of the year is like a big reunion, bringing together our Cowboy Dressage families from across the world. Some of these folks we may only see once a year, but we would miss them dearly if we didn't get that annual visit.

The community feel at a Gathering is unique. While wandering the shed rows, you will find individual barns proudly displaying their colors, but you will also see members of multiple barns in an alleyway, assisting each other with tack changes, holding horses, and reading tests. Members that compete goodnaturedly at a regional show will join forces at the Final Gathering, rooting for each other's successes. Team Idaho or Team Germany, we are all Team Cowboy Dressage at the end of the day (fig. 10.1).

Education

One of the things that sets a Gathering apart from a typical horse event is the focus on education. Most include learning opportunities in conjunction with the judging of tests. Whether a question-and-answer session with the judge or a mini-clinic from a local professional, these teaching sessions are as important as the judged tests. Cowboy Dressage World continues to strive to provide the tools for success for every Handshake member to meet his or her goals. The

10.1 - *Cowboy Dressage in Germany in 2016. This group hosts annual clinics and Gatherings with a Cowboy Dressage professional clinician and judge. Building the Cowboy Dressage community starts with education.*

10.2 - *The World Finals Gathering awards ceremony is the highlight of the week. We share songs, stories, and laughs as we give out the awards earned by hard work and "try" over the course of the event's tests, and of course, for the previous year's hard work and focus on horsemanship and partnership.*

Cowboy Dressage World professionals, judges, and partners are happy to give tips and pointers to riders both new and seasoned. In the end, it isn't about who wins or has the highest score. It is about who learned and grew because of attending a Gathering.

Celebration

Unlike a typical horse show, the awards ceremony at the end of a Cowboy Dressage Gathering is a celebration of the accomplishments of each participant (fig. 10.2). While we can't all go home with the big prize, Cowboy Dressage is very good at celebrating accomplishments both large and small. While the typical highpoint awards will celebrate the horse and rider who had a very good and consistent round of tests, the Judge's Choice, Most Improved, and Soft Feel awards often given out reward the riders who have prevailed against challenges.

There is typically a wealth of awards in different categories at each Gathering, making it feel

10.3 - *This group in Germany continues to share Cowboy Dressage with new people every year, hosting clinics and spreading the message of Soft Feel and kindness.*

as if the accolades are more evenly shared by members that attended and participated. Everybody will tell you that it isn't about the ribbon, the buckle, or the prize at the end of the night. It is about the recognition of a job well done. It is about the progress and growth in partnership between a horse and rider (fig. 10.3). Most of all, it is about tearful hugs and goodbyes as the family reunion winds down and we part ways until the next time.

Divisions

There are eight divisions currently at Gatherings. They are Partnership; Walk/Walk; Walk/Jog; Walk/Jog/Lope; Challenge; Gaited; Freestyle; and Vaquero. Each of the divisions offers its own challenges and goals for the horse and rider.

Partnership

The Partnership division utilizes half the Court for the test. This allows the rider to stay more focused and perform a completely mirrored pattern. This division is designed for youth, amateurs, young horses, or any horse-and-rider pair that is new to Gatherings and would like to build confidence on the Court and with each other.

The Partnership on the Ground classes allow a horse and handler to demonstrate the foundation of groundwork and softness, working through a series of maneuvers on both sides of the horse. The Partnership under Saddle test is the same test that was performed on the ground but with the rider mounted. This helps build a seamless transition between groundwork and under-saddle work, again with the aim of building confidence in the horse-and-rider pair. This division is performed on the half Challenge Court, allowing both horse and rider to more easily visualize the patterns and markers for the 10- and 20-meter circles.

Picking Your Tests

By Jenni L. Grimmett, DVM

When I signed up for my first Gathering, I was at a loss as to which classes I should attempt. While sitting comfortably at home, I think many of us either vastly overestimate or underestimate our abilities, depending on our personality types. I am firmly in the overestimation camp. I guess you can call it positive thinking! (My husband, Dan, seems to feel it's better described as delusional.) While over-confidence and the drive that typically accompanies it is good for the rider, it can often be detrimental to the horse and to your partnership.

Let me tell you about my first Gathering.

Never having attended a Gathering or even watched a test being ridden before a judge, I had no way to really know where our skills were on the Court. It felt good to me, and I was passionate about the Vaquero tradition, so that is where I started with my horse. I also started out in traditional Vaquero gear straight up in the bridle. Our first test was respectable with a score in the high 60s. This fueled my confidence, and I was sure we were on our way to stardom. Unfortunately, this is when the pressure of the Gathering began to catch up with my horse.

While he started out relatively calm, after a few trips through the Court with me unable to provide adequate support due to my gear choices, he began to get more and more nervous, and our test scores suffered. I took my pretty silver bridle bit out of his mouth and went back to the hackamore where I could provide him a little more support. Thanks to the help of other Cowboy Dressage Handshake members and encouragement from the judges, I was able to end on a good note, and he walked quietly out of that Court after our last test.

Ultimately, it really isn't about gunning for the big prize or proving how fancy you and your horse are. It's about riding at the level of test that your horse can be most successful, with an eye on building up to the next division. There are no "levels" in Cowboy Dressage. You may ride any test that you and your horse feel comfortable with. The tests you choose to ride at home and tests you choose to ride at a Gathering may not be the same.

It's only natural for horses to have more nervous energy at a Gathering. Helping the horses learn to adjust and deal with the pressures of travel and leaving home and buddies makes your partnership stronger and makes your horse a better mount. It's one of the fringe benefits of attending a Gathering. It is your job, as the rider, to make sure the experience is as pleasant as possible for the horse by allowing him to feel success in his performance.

After my first Gathering experience, I decided what was best for my horse was to build his confidence from the very beginning, and we entered the Walk/Jog division at our next show. The easier tests and slower pace of the transitions built his confidence as he grew used to the travel and new sights and sounds. We stayed at that level, riding in a snaffle (even though he was 13, and even though I had previously had him straight up in the bridle) until we mastered those tests and were consistently scoring in the 70s. Only then was it time to move on to the next level. I didn't gauge our success by our ribbons. I gauged our success by our Soft Feel and partnership scores. As those scores went up I could also feel my horse and I riding as one. That's when we were both ready to advance—together.

We are all going to have those tests that don't go well. That's okay. We can get over it. But remember, your horse knows when a test doesn't go well, too. He can feel the tension in your body, the quickness of your commands, and the failure of good timing in your dance together. Ride the tests your horse can feel successful at. It will keep him trying to do better with you.

Walk/Walk Division

The Walk/Walk division is a new division and has grown organically from Cowboy Dressage members who have learned that sometimes the very best growth happens when you concentrate on building your horse's walk. There are several reasons why you might choose the Walk/Walk division: It is ridden on the Challenge Court and can be a great way to build a horse's confidence on this Court. The Walk/Walk division also focuses on partnership by asking for quick transitions. There is less time for preparation between the execution of maneuvers than what is seen in some of the more advanced tests. For horses or riders that have physical limitations at the faster gaits, this allows them to still participate in the Gatherings. This is also another class where gaited horses can compete on the same tests as non-gaited horses. Building a good walk in your horse helps to build a good jog, and then a good lope. Success in the Walk/Walk division will mean success in the other divisions as you and your horse advance.

Walk/Jog Division

The Walk/Jog division has four tests that each build in difficulty and length of test maneuvers. This is performed on the flat Cowboy Dressage Court. The relative simplicity of these tests allows the horse and rider to focus on the basic elements of Cowboy Dressage, mastering the gaits, bend, and circles as well as some of the lateral maneuvers as you progress to Tests 3 and 4. While the Walk/Jog Test 1 is the simplest ridden test other than the Partnership under Saddle test, you might choose to ride Test 3 or 4 instead. Knowing your horse and your partnership, and your strengths and weaknesses in your riding, helps you choose tests that both challenge your horse and reward his strengths, giving both of you a feeling of success.

Riding these tests at home will help you to determine which suit you and your horse, and which challenge you. You would do well to choose some of each when filling out your entry form for the next Gathering. If you ride only the tests that challenge you both, you and your horse can feel frustrated. But, if there is a nice confidence-building test thrown in the mix, it reminds you and your horse of how you have progressed, and gives the horse the confidence to continue to try.

Walk/Jog/Lope Division

The Walk/Jog/Lope division is ridden on the flat Cowboy Dressage Court and currently has the most tests written for the horse and rider to explore. Aside from including the working lope, these tests challenge horse and rider with more difficult maneuvers as you build your horse's balance. The standards for judging become more stringent. While it is a good idea for the horse and rider to experience success in the Walk/Jog division prior to entering the Walk/Jog/Lope division, this is a suggestion and not a requirement. If you believe you and your horse have the skills necessary to excel in these tests, then you may enter them.

Cowboy Dressage Worldwide

10.4 - *Sharing Cowboy Dressage at the Americana event in Germany.*

10.5 - *Cowboy Dressage in South Africa.*

10.6 - *A Cowboy Dressage Gathering in the United Kingdom.*

10.7 - A Cowboy Dressage Gathering in Canada.

10.8 - A Cowboy Dressage Gathering in Denmark.

10.9 - Cowboy Dressage in Europe.

10.10 - A Cowboy Dressage Gathering in Australia.

Challenge Division

The Challenge division includes both Walk/Jog tests and Walk/Jog/Lope tests ridden on the Cowboy Dressage Challenge Court. These tests include maneuvers that are performed over and around ground poles and—in the more advanced tests—require horse and rider to open a rope gate prior to entering the Court. As the tests advance in difficulty, horse and rider are asked to lope over the ground poles, change leads within the octagon, and lope out again.

Vaquero Division

The Vaquero division is designed to showcase and honor both the tack and training traditions of the California Vaqueros. This is the division where hackamore horsemen and bridle horsemen can show off the hard work that has gone into making a traditional bridle horse. Of course, there is no rule against showing in the other divisions with traditional gear, but in this division it is a requirement. This helps build comradery and friendly competition between folks that adhere to the traditional training programs. The Vaquero division is ridden on the Challenge Court and includes both Walk/Jog and Walk/Jog/Lope tests.

Gaited Division

The Gaited division allows all gaited horses to ride tests designed especially for the horse that gaits instead of jogs. The working jog and free jog requirements have been replaced with a working gait and intermediate gait. As long as it is a four-beat gait it doesn't matter if it's a Tennessee Walker, Rocky Mountain Horse, or Paso Fino. The horse is judged on the regularity and freedom of movement with that particular gait, for that horse. Gaited horses are welcome to ride in any other division in Cowboy Dressage, but this is the only division where they are not asked to jog.

Freestyle Division

The Freestyle division is a crowd favorite. The horse and rider perform a test set to music to show their skills and abilities on the Court. There are classes available for both Walk/Jog and Walk/Jog/Lope freestyle performances. There are required maneuvers for each of the classes, and additional maneuvers may be added to show the advancement of the horse. You are allowed props in your freestyle performance, and this is the place where you can see riders use the long *garrocha* pole in their rides. (For a more in-depth discussion of the Freestyle division, see p. 186.)

Judging

One of the very best things about participating in a Gathering and riding in front of a judge is the judge's score card you receive at the end of your ride. Think of the Cowboy Dressage judge as your very candid friend. The judge's job is to help you and your horse become as successful as possible. Every Cowboy Dressage judge wants your ride to be a good one. Judges are looking for what is *right* with your ride, just as much as they are looking for where you can improve.

Aside from successfully navigating the required elements of the test, the judge is also watching your Soft Feel, partnership, harmony, and effectiveness of aids. The judge will give your horse a score for the quality of his gaits (based on his potential and not on an arbitrary breed standard of perfection). The judge's feedback is as valuable as a private lesson between you, with the added benefit of being able to take that lesson home in the form of the score card.

Reading Your Score Card

At the very top of every test you can find some important information. You will see the purpose of the test, the required elements of the test, and the conditions under which the test is ridden, meaning which of the Cowboy Dressage Courts you ride in, possible points to be awarded, and average time taken to ride the test.

As you move down the score sheet, each of the elements of the test is broken down into directives that receive a single score of 0–10 from the judge. What the judge is looking for—for example, an ideal maneuver or transition at each of these directives—is listed, as well. Then there is a section for the judge's comments. The horse and rider are scored on the following scale:

> **SCORING SCALE OF MARKS FOR COWBOY DRESSAGE**
>
> | | |
> |---|---|
> | 10 | Excellent |
> | 9 | Very Good |
> | 8 | Good |
> | 7 | Fairly Good |
> | 6 | Satisfactory |
> | 5 | Marginal |
> | 4 | Needs Improvement |
> | 3 | Multiple Minor Mistakes |
> | 2 | Significant Mistakes |
> | 1 | Multiple Significant Mistakes |
> | 0 | Not executed |

With this scale, for a score of 6 or above, the judge isn't required to provide any written comments, but for any score of 5 or below, the judge will give comments to help the rider understand what needs to be improved in the maneuver to gain a higher score. Each test ridden in front of a Cowboy Dressage judge is like a mini-lesson: it helps the rider to understand where the areas needing improvement are; and the positive comments keep the "try" in the rider just like you always strive to keep the "try" in the horse. While the ribbon and the placings are fun and we all love pinning that blue ribbon to the front of the stall, it's the judge's score sheet that is the real treasure from the Gatherings.

The Cowboy Dressage Horse

By Jenni L. Grimmett, DVM

Describing the Cowboy Dressage horse is difficult. We are not looking for a type of horse or certain look as much as we are looking for a certain willingness and skill set. Because Cowboy Dressage is helping to build correctness of form and improve athleticism and balance in both horse and rider, it is more important to talk about what the horse can do than what the horse should look like. It is the environment of inclusion of Cowboy Dressage that draws so many people to the Gatherings.

The Cowboy Dressage horse is not just a prancing show pony. Before the 1950s, it was almost unheard of for a horse to specialize. Versatility, ability, and even endurance were prized beyond just a pretty face. As the horse-show world grew and became less a friendly opportunity to test your skills and more a realm of fierce competition, the jack-of-all-trades horse was replaced by the specialist that could excel in just one area. Today that is more evident than ever before. Cutters are trained to cut. Period. Reiners are trained to rein. Western

10.11 - *Jenni and Chico. Partnership between horse and rider is more important than raw talent.*

Pleasure horses are trained to move with almost painful slowness around the show ring. Nobody expects these same horses to also move cows, climb a mountain, or clear a jump course.

All horses of every breed that are prepared to give Cowboy Dressage a try are welcomed. The training principles used on the Cowboy Dressage Court should help *any* horse of *any* breed excel in *any* other discipline. Just like yoga is useful for the professional athlete, Cowboy Dressage is useful for the Western performance horse.

That said, if you are interested in Cowboy Dressage as your primary riding discipline and would like to choose a horse that will excel at the Gatherings, there are some characteristics that a potential buyer should keep in mind. First of all, a kind and willing horse will do better. While the Gatherings are generally very low key and encourage horse and rider to remain quiet and calm, some horses are just naturally suited to the environment. A nervous or worried horse that is easily distracted is going to take some time to adjust, but to be sure there is nothing like the support at a Gathering to help an anxious horse get over that!

Balance of conformation is the next thing to consider. No matter what type of horse best suits your riding style and personal goals, you want a horse that is going to be able to more easily move and bend and shorten his frame for self-carriage. A horse that is able to step up underneath himself and has comfortable gaits will be more fun to show than one that is heavy on the forehand and has a lagging gait.

Each horse on the Cowboy Dressage Court will be judged on his own potential for movement rather than judged against a generic standard. The Cowboy Dressage judges are schooled on this and are instructed not to punish the short-legged horse for being short-strided and choppy, or to overly favor the horse that has large lofty gaits. On each score sheet there is a single score (with a coefficient of 2) for evenness and regularity of gaits. Cadence and balance with good rhythm are important for any Cowboy Dressage mount, and the Cowboy Dressage schooling and tests should help the horse become more balanced and cadenced as he progresses.

10.12 - *Eitan sharing a special moment with Cheyenne.*

Because partnership and harmony are so important both on and off the Cowboy Dressage Court the prospective shopper is encouraged to spend time considering the personality and potential for partnership when selecting a Cowboy Dressage mount. Finding a horse can be similar to finding a spouse. You want a horse that complements your personality and enjoys the same things that you do. Some horses really like the challenges of the Cowboy Dressage Court while others are better suited to climbing mountains.

They say that the outside of a horse is a reflection of the inside of a person. I find that to be true, especially when you look at the very best partnerships in Cowboy Dressage. For example, my husband Dan has a string of soft, quiet, lovely mares that are a joy to be around. They are all very similar in personality and exemplify the perfect equine personality match for him. My geldings are all goofballs that are extroverts looking for and often demanding attention. They can be challenging to keep channeled and focused on a task, but they perfectly suit my equally busy, active mind. Sometimes it takes some trial and error, but I think the best advice I can give a prospective horse shopper is to do some deep soul searching to determine what equine personality suits you best.

Eitan insists that he could pick a horse out by touching him. Something special happens when you lay hands on a horse and allow your spirit to connect with his spirit—you can tell a lot about a horse by the way he makes you feel when you touch him. With a special connection and "try" in the horse, you can overcome other hurdles such as training, conformation, and lack of natural ability. It doesn't mean it will be easy, but "try" in the horse is maybe even more important to a successful partnership than anything else.

The final thing to consider if you are interested in the competitive aspect of Cowboy Dressage specifically is "handiness." Because Cowboy Dressage is designed with more handy athletic horses in mind, the small Court and maneuvers can be challenging for large horses with a huge stride. The Challenge Court, especially, can be difficult for some to shorten to the stride length of the ground poles both on the quarterlines and across the diagonals. But, that being said, there are several large horses that excel at Cowboy Dressage, so it is ultimately the individual, the partnership, and harmony that make the biggest difference.

I don't want to give the impression that there is a perfect Cowboy Dressage horse type. Maybe the things mentioned above will help you to make it a little easier to find success on the Court, but the idea of Cowboy Dressage is that the principles are good for every horse and the rider of every discipline. There are not suitability classes or breed preferences in Cowboy Dressage. You will see all breeds, sizes, and colors, and all are welcome at the Gatherings. The goal is to simply improve the horses that cross the boards at A.

11

BEYOND THE COURT

"You cannot get that 'being as one' with a horse in the arena that you can out on the trail together. The arena can build the partnership but the trail unites the souls."

EITAN BETH-HALACHMY

The cowboy in Cowboy Dressage is very important to us. The Western idea of the cowboy is synonymous with freedom, the open range, and a spirit of adventure. In Cowboy Dressage, we continue to embrace the traditions of the American cowboy and individuals around the world who are looking for something more than just the confines of the arena and the Court. The true test of a Cowboy Dressage horse and the partnership that we are building is not the higher Cowboy Dressage tests. It is the application of the knowledge and what you and your horse can do with it *outside* the Court that really matters in the long run (fig. 11.1).

All of the maneuvers, softness, lightness, and balance that we are teaching our horses in the "classroom" are just as important off the Court as they are on the Court. The options for what you and your horse can do together are limitless but here are a few things that our

11.1 - *There is so much more to be experienced when you step out of the arena and into the world.*

Cowboy Dressage members enjoy outside of just riding and practicing the Cowboy Dressage tests.

Trail Riding

Any horse can benefit from time spent on the trail. Trail riding is so often not given its due. Outside the confines of the arena rails, who knows what you and your horse may encounter or what obstacles you may be asked to overcome? Partnership on the trail isn't just about lightness and ease of communication, it is also about safety. In our area, we do a lot of mountain riding. This means that the horses are quite often on single-track trails where turning around in a pickle isn't always an option. This means that you and the horse must traverse whatever terrain is presented.

The horse must trust you that the trail is safe, and you must trust the horse to go over the terrain safely. Why wouldn't you want a horse that is highly trained and maneuverable out there on the trail? The ability to place your horse's feet right where you want them is even more important when there are multiple obstacles to consider. The arena is practice. The trail is the real world. We are firm believers in taking our show horses out into the hills (fig. 11.2). It just makes them better and more well-rounded, as well as helping to build muscles that aren't used as commonly in the arena.

Partnership established on the Cowboy Dressage Court can help you on the trail. Having a horse that "feels" back to you and knows you are listening can help soothe a nervous horse on the trail. Teaching a horse how to bend and use his body in balance with himself and the rider can help in navigating those tight switchbacks.

Building muscles of self-carriage will help the horse to better travel over uneven terrain without strain. You'll find that spending more time in the arena will make your horse more comfortable to ride if you participate in long trips in the backcountry, less fatigued (especially through his back and loin) after a 25-mile day, and an absolute joy to ride, wherever your trails lead.

In addition, all of the things that we practice in the Court can also be practiced on the trail with the aim of adding practical purpose for the horse. We practice transitions, bend, and backing up, as well as lateral maneuvers, as we travel down the trail. Like in the arena, the training opportunities are limited only by your imagination.

Mountain Trail

An offshoot of the trail-riding culture is the new equine discipline of Mountain Trail. Mountain Trail offers the intricate maneuvers, obstacles, and challenges you can see on the trail without the long hours in the saddle or the travel. There are several Mountain Trail competitive venues where riders can participate. The qualities you might want in a Mountain Trail horse pair well with all of the qualities that you are attempting to build in your Cowboy Dressage horse, including balance, partnership, and cadence between maneuvers and over obstacles (fig. 11.3).

11.2 - Eitan and Cheyenne enjoy the water outside their ranch in Grass Valley, California.

11.3 - *A horse and rider navigate a bridge together. Working with obstacles can give purpose to many of the maneuvers that you practice on the Cowboy Dressage Court. Here you can see where learning to keep your horse straight over the quarterline ground poles might come in handy.*

Self-carriage is also a large part of Mountain Trail. While this is a different type of self-carriage than what you are looking for in Cowboy Dressage, the long contact that many Mountain Trail riders use to show their horses off requires the horse to move and respond to the seat and leg aids, and not rely on the bridle.

If long trail rides aren't feasible for you, consider putting together an obstacle course to practice on as a way to put the skills you have acquired to practical use.

Cattle Work

Of course, the cowboy wouldn't exist without the cow, nor would many of the traditions and uses to which our Western horses are bred and trained. Across the world, the traditions of the horse and the gear and training used have been shaped by the desire to more efficiently raise and herd cattle over varied terrains. Most of our Western equine-training traditions are traced back to horses being used to chase cattle. Today, many horsemen use cow work to train the horse, rather than training the horse to do cow work (fig. 11.4).

Working cattle helps to give the horse purpose and a job that he seems to just understand. Athletic maneuvers, balance, and quick turns and stops are essential when working cattle. The focus of the other animals helps the horse be "in the moment" and respond with more "try" and effort than he might show in the arena.

11.4 - *Riding around a rodear of cattle adds purpose to a 20-meter circle.*

More About Musical Freestyles

While the Freestyle is indeed performed on the Court, we also wanted to include it in this chapter because it can be so much more than the judged performance that you will see at Gatherings. Riding to music is good for the horse and the rider, and can help to build both cadence and rhythm.

There is something about riding to music that speaks to many people. Music moves us and creates a rhythm within us that cannot be denied. There have been ample studies on music's effects on animals, and there is no denying that they can and do respond to the beats and rhythms created. To be able to dance with your horse seems to many to be the ultimate culmination of your time spent in the saddle. A good musical Freestyle can move you to tears, inspire you and make you laugh. A good musical Freestyle makes you feel all of the wonders of partnership and harmony and Soft Feel as if you were right in the saddle with the rider. A good musical Freestyle is a celebration between the horse and rider, and it serves as both a bookmark and a certificate of achievement along the journey of growth and discovery that is as individual as each one of us. Because in Cowboy Dressage we place more importance on partnership, harmony, and Soft Feel, the Freestyle should be a showcase of those things above all others. While the Freestyle division also offers a place to display skills and maneuvers that are not yet part of the Cowboy Dressage tests, Soft Feel must never be compromised or the purpose of the Freestyle is lost.

When the Freestyle division was conceived by the partners of Cowboy Dressage World, it was imagined to be the pinnacle of the Cowboy Dressage rider's skills. The musical Freestyle for many folks is a place

11.5 - *A winning musical Freestyle performance at the Final Gathering in Rancho Murieta, California, in 2014.*

for celebration of not how far you and your horse have come in terms of riding level, but of where you are as partners, and where you are going together into the future.

We have started using musical rides during Introduction to Cowboy Dressage clinics. On the last afternoon, everybody who has an interest in riding to music has a chance to play with the timing and transitions, and ride while feeling the music. After spending the weekend working so hard on teaching bend, straight lines, transitions, and softness, when the music comes on, that's when everyone is finally able to really focus on the partnership and harmony, and we can all get a little misty-eyed watching the partnerships blossom to the music as horse and rider do their thing in the arena.

Even if you never plan on performing a Freestyle ride at a competition, we feel that the use of music in your riding can be a very import-

11.6 - *Demonstrating the skill required to master the garrocha pole during a musical Freestyle.*

ant tool for developing rhythm and timing. For some people the music allows them to just *be* with the horse *in the moment*. The forethought involved in planning out a ride that includes the required movements, and timing those movements to music, is a useful exercise for preparation and execution of transitions.

There are now three different classes in the Freestyle division: the Walk/Jog Freestyle, the Walk/Jog/Lope Freestyle, and the Drill Team Musical Freestyle for two or more riders performing in a group. For all of these classes, the ultimate goal is the same. Your ride should showcase Soft Feel, partnership, and harmony at its best. There are required movements in the Walk/Jog and Walk/Jog/Lope Freestyles that must be choreographed into the ride, making the selection of the perfect song that much more challenging. The new Drill Team Freestyle is a class that we are very excited about. Drill-team-like maneuvers are often used in clinics to allow riders to explore the Court and teach them how to maneuver across the diagonals and straight lines. The purpose of the Drill Team in Cowboy Dressage is to showcase partnership—both with the horse and with your fellow rider. Think not so much of the fast-paced drill teams that you might have watched do intricate exciting patterns in the rodeo arena, but the synchronized and beautifully perfect quadrilles of the Spanish Riding School.

Choosing the music for a Freestyle, whether it is a group performance or individual, is so important. The music must both move the rider and the audience, and provide a sensual background for the visual beauty of the ride. If the music distracts from the ride, or if the ride doesn't match the music, it is uncomfortable to watch (and it must be hard to judge as well). You are highly encouraged to carefully and thoughtfully select your music. While mixed music (if done well) can create a beautiful Freestyle, the Freestyles performed to a single well-selected song tend to be more moving to me as an audience member. The song often tells a story or sets a mood for the ride, and it is enjoyable getting to know the riders through their musical selections.

When selecting a song, it is important to find one that has a good consistent rhythm, with changes in the music that can be used for

11.7 - *Dancing to music with your horse requires timing, feel, a sense of rhythm, and probably most importantly, a sense of showmanship. Eitan is the master of showmanship.*

transitions between the gaits. For the Walk/Jog Freestyle especially, finding that song that has the perfect change from working jog to free jog is essential for the seamless look of the ride. The Walk/Jog Freestyle can often be the most difficult to choreograph because it has the most required elements. Choosing the song that allows you to flow through these elements is key.

While the Musical Freestyle division is not a costume class, many riders feel that costumes add to the overall performance. There are folks on both sides of that debate when it comes to costumes in the Freestyles. Many feel that it can take away from the ride, turning it from a celebration into a spectacle. Others feel that it is all in good fun and the costumed rides are often the ones that are remembered by the audience over all others. If you choose to wear a costume for your Freestyle ride, we encourage you to remember that the costume should not detract from the partnership and harmony of the ride. Any costume that interferes with the horse's movement or sight is not allowed. Less is often more when it comes to costuming. Just remember to place Soft Feel, partnership, and harmony first, and your ride should be a success.

Retreats and Getaways

One of the growing activities for Cowboy Dressage enthusiasts is to put together a fun retreat that combines one of the disciplines mentioned previously with a Cowboy Dressage clinic or play day in a unique setting (fig. 11.8). This combines all the very best attributes of Cowboy Dressage together in one weekend. Community, good horsemanship, education,

11.8 - *Hanging with good friends and good horses is the very best way to enjoy a weekend. Add some quality time on the Cowboy Dressage Court and a trail ride or cattle drive, and you have the makings of cherished memories.*

11.9 - *Practicing riding down the centerline on the beach.*

11.10 - *The Northwest Saddle Sisters laying out their Court on the beach, during a retreat in Long Beach, Washington. The miles of sand were perfect for riding circles and straight lines.*

11.11 - *A Cowboy Dressage Court set up in a mountain plateau for a combined cattle work and Cowboy Dressage retreat.*

and fun! You can use these retreats to build Cowboy Dressage in your area, as well as enjoy some time with other Cowboy Dressage members. It is also an excellent way to bring people together to try Cowboy Dressage and learn in a fun and stress-free setting.

The Cowboy Dressage Court can be set up in any flat setting. Set up your Court on the beach, in a hay field, or even a mountain pasture (fig. 11.9). You can ride 10-meter circles and straight lines around natural obstacles like trees or rocks. Asking your horse to listen and function in a setting other than the arena can be a test of your partnership, but is one of the great freedoms that Cowboy Dressage offers (figs. 11.10 & 11.11). We don't need rails. All we need is a tape measure.

12

THE FUTURE OF COWBOY DRESSAGE

"Right now is our future. Kindness is our future."

EITAN BETH-HALACHMY

What started out as the dream of Eitan and Debbie Beth-Halachmy has become a budding industry. As Cowboy Dressage continues to grow and expand, the small organization struggles to keep up with its ever-widening reach. To cope with the growth, Cowboy Dressage is looking toward the future with the establishment of several associations to help to build the Cowboy Dressage network and provide support for members, educators, and judges.

The first addition to the Cowboy Dressage family that helped to take some of the burden of the organization of Cowboy Dressage off the shoulders of Eitan and Debbie was the foundation of Cowboy Dressage World. This association serves as the organizational leadership of all things Cowboy Dressage. At the head of this association are the Cowboy Dressage World partners that currently include Eitan and Debbie, Lyn Ringrose-Moe, Garn Walker, and Wyatt Paxton. These leaders are responsible for steering the fate of Cowboy Dressage,

12.1 - *Eitan and the Cowboy Dressage World Partners strive to keep education at the heart of Cowboy Dressage.*

assessing rules and changes made in the competition, and providing focus for the future through the recruitment of new folks into the Cowboy Dressage fold.

The focus of Cowboy Dressage World is the dissemination of education to make sure that everybody is receiving the same materials and methods across the country and around the world (fig. 12.1). The hard-working partners are constantly reassessing where they are and where they are going, to make sure that Cowboy Dressage continues to be a community that is steeped in kindness and the code of the West as Cowboy Dressage faces the inevitable growing pains.

The Cowboy Dressage Professionals Association is the organizational arm of the professional Cowboy Dressage educators and judges. The future of Cowboy Dressage hangs heavily on how Cowboy Dressage is presented to future riders at clinics and "play days," and how those riders are scored at the Gatherings they attend. We know from watching trends and fads pass through the other equestrian disciplines how much power the judges, especially, have to alter the course of any area of specialty. Because we believe so strongly in Soft Feel and kindness as the guiding principles of Cowboy Dressage, we need to be sure that our judges are also rewarding this *above all other things*. Our judges' training "boot camp" is an intense educational program that ensures that they are seeing the same things when they sit at C and judge the rides. They must go through

12.2 - One of the first Cowboy Dressage judging "boot camps" designed to make sure that the judges are looking at the same things the Cowboy Dressage World Partners are when rewarding and instructing members at the Gatherings. Judging is a very big and important job that is essential for the future of Cowboy Dressage.

several stages of scribing and judging schooling shows to work up to being a fully recognized judge. We are very proud of our Cowboy Dressage judges. The decision to become a certified judge requires no small amount of dedication. Our judges believe in the future of Cowboy Dressage and want to safeguard that dream for future generations (figs. 12.2 & 12.3).

The Professionals Association is also where the certification of educators occurs. There are three levels of professional educators, as well as an entry-level membership and ambassador level. The ambassador level is designed to include those important individuals that are out there coordinating and hosting clinics and Gatherings. Their inclusion in this association ensures that events

12.3 - Cowboy Dressage World Professional Association members and recommended clinicians at one of the first Professionals Workshops in Texas, 2015. It is important to Cowboy Dressage World to continue to ensure that people new to Cowboy Dressage are receiving competent instruction that includes the message of kindness first.

12.4 - *A Cowboy Dressage Professional Association lecture on bridles and bitting at the 2017 World Finals Gathering.*

are publicized as much as possible through the Cowboy Dressage community and that each event has the necessary coverage for insurance and liability.

Professionals are required to demonstrate proficiency in a skill set by attaining a qualifying score on a test ridden in front of a Cowboy Dressage certified judge. The professionals are also required to complete annual educational hours, internship hours, and volunteer hours in support of Cowboy Dressage (fig. 12.4). This is so much more than just a paid membership organization. The dedication of Cowboy Dressage professionals is clear proof that they both believe in and practice the principles of Cowboy Dressage. When you seek instruction from a Cowboy Dressage professional, you know you are getting the very best instruction available, and that the material covered is all based on the same principles of Soft Feel and kindness.

We continue to drive the focus of Cowboy Dressage and our Gatherings toward more education, spreading the word on how to build the very best partnership with our horses (fig. 12.5).

Cowboy Dressage has quickly grown from very small beginnings in Grass Valley, California, now reaching coast to coast in North America, as well as across oceans to Europe, Australia, and Africa. One of the reasons that it has spread so quickly is that all of the materials that you need to set up a Court and try your hand at some of the tests are available online (www.cowboydressageworld.com). Anybody with a flat piece of ground can sketch out a Court, print out some tests, and get to work! You can set up a Court in a hay field, on a natural plateau, on the beach or a river bank. All that matters is that you have markers to help you with your geometry and accountability.

If you are frustrated with the lack of Cowboy Dressage activities in your area, we encourage you to grab some markers and a tape measure and set up your own Court. If you build it, they will come. You can take turns calling tests for your friends and before you know it, you'll have a group of folks ready to embrace Cowboy Dressage. Perhaps you can host a clinic and bring in a Cowboy Dressage professional to help you and your friends get more of the basics and a firm start on your journey to Soft Feel. All across the country, every time we have introduced Cowboy Dressage to open-minded riders, it has taken hold like wildfire. Once you try it, you are hooked! With enough support in the smaller communities, you'll soon have schooling shows, then larger Gatherings will follow. All because you had a flat piece of ground and a tape measure.

12.5 - *Cooperation and sharing between our Cowboy Dressage professionals promotes cooperation and learning among all our Handshake members. Kindness first, learning second...competition fifth!*

APPENDIX I:
GLOSSARY

A: The marker on the centerline at the opening of the Court where the horse and rider enter and exit for all tests.

Action: Used to describe the character of the movement of the horse in the gait. Some breeds have more action in their movement then others, such as Morgans and Saddlebreds.

Aids: The rider's hands, seat, legs, voice, weight, and energy that work together to create direction for the horse both on the ground and in the saddle.

Amateur: A term used to describe a rider who does not get paid for riding, training, or teaching another rider.

Armitas: Leather-fringed outerware similar to chinks but typically longer, with a square bottom and full belt upper.

B: A marker on the midline of the Court across from E.

Balance: The ability of the rider to use her center of gravity to ride in harmony with the horse.

Bend: The creation of a lateral arc through the horse's spine from head to tail. Typically referred to as 10-meter or 20-meter bend, indicating the size of the curved line being traveled.

Blanks: Five meter markers on either side of E and B that do not have letters but are used to help the rider visualize the 5-meter gridlines.

Bosal: A rawhide or leather stiff, braided noseband. Traditional gear used by the California Vaqueros.

Bow-Tie: A maneuver on the Court that includes a half of a 20-meter circle at each end of the Court connected by straight lines on the short diagonals.

Box: Often used to refer to the octagon on call sheets.

Broken Arrow: A maneuver on the Court that features a broken line and places you back on the line of travel without a change of direction. On the Open Court: F–8–M or K–8–H or F–8–K. On the Challenge Court: V–8–S, P–8–R, or P–8–V.

C: Marker on the centerline opposite of A.

Call Sheet: The list of directives that the caller uses to help the rider execute a test.

Caller: During a Gathering, the person who reads the test for the rider during the ride.

Cavesson: A leather or rawhide noseband worn around the horse's muzzle. In Cowboy Dressage, it is worn loosely and used as decoration.

Cadence: The musical beat of the horse's gait. See also Rhythm.

Center of Gravity: The balance point in the body at which rotational forces equal zero. In the horse at rest, the center of gravity is just behind the elbow. Through collection and elevation of the forehand, you attempt to move the center of gravity farther back toward the middle of the rib cage.

Centerline: The line cutting the Court in half lengthwise from A to C. This is the line of entrance for all tests.

Challenge Court: The standard Cowboy Dressage Court that also includes ground poles on the quarterlines and short diagonals, as well as cones marking the corners and G. A 12-foot octagon marks the center of the Court at "8."

Chaps: (Pronounced *SHAPS*) Long, leather outerwear that may be fitted or flared at the bottom. May be fringed.

Chinks: Short, leather outerwear, often fringed, that falls just below the knees. Traditional gear worn by working cowboys.

Clinician: A Cowboy Dressage Professional Association member who has met the requirements of both education and skills, and is approved to teach Cowboy Dressage to other Handshake members. There are three levels of achievement that a professional can strive to obtain.

Collection: The process of shortening and elevating the horse from tail to nose for the purpose of advanced maneuvers. A collected horse has a topline that is arched from back to front.

Counter-bend: Traveling in the opposite direction of the bend. For example, riding a 10-meter circle to the right while the horse is bent to the left.

Court: The 20- x 40-meter gridded arena that is ridden in Cowboy Dressage.

Cue: The use of a single aid to create a specific response in the horse.

D: Invisible marker on the centerline on the gridline between F and K.

Disengagement: The portion of the stride of the hind leg that occurs behind the hip. Also used in Natural Horsemanship to describe the horse stepping around in a circle with the back inside hind leg crossing in front of the outside hind leg.

Dressage: In the simplest form, this refers to training from basic to elevated.

E: Marker on the midline across from B. Forms midline E–8–B.

Energy: The quality of the gait that makes the gait appear "snappy" and forward. "Needs more energy" is a common comment on Cowboy Dressage score sheets when the horse is not exhibiting enough drive and engagement or forward movement.

Engagement: The portion of the stride that is weight-bearing and propelling the horse forward. In the hind legs, it is the portion of the stride that occurs up under the horse's body until the hoof moves behind the hip.

Error: Typically occurs when a rider goes off course during a test at a Gathering. The judge signals the error and asks the rider to continue. Each error is a deduction of 2 points from the total. Three errors results in dismissal.

F: Marker in the lower left corner of the Court on the long diagonal F–8–H.

Figure 8: A maneuver that requires two 10-meter circles that meet at a single point with a change of bend on the centerline.

Flexion: Bending through the spine. May be either lateral (side to side) or vertical (up and down).

Flying Lead Change: A transition from one lope lead to the other without dropping to the jog. The horse should change leads between lope strides.

Forequarters: The portion of the horse to include the head, neck, shoulders, and front legs of the horse. Also known as the forehand.

Forward: The willingness of the horse to propel himself.

Free Frame: A lengthened frame that asks the horse to stretch over the topline while maintaining engagement of the hindquarters. The cadence should be similar to the working frame though the stride is longer. A longer, not faster, gait.

Fresh Rein: The rider releases all contact on the rein and allows the horse to relax and settle, then picks up the reins again to establish contact with the horse.

Freestyle: A test performed and choreographed by the rider and ridden to musical accompaniment. The Freestyle is meant to be a showcase and celebration of the horse and rider's accomplishments to date.

G: Invisible marker on the centerline on the H–M gridline. Marked by two cones on the Challenge Court. Serves as the initiation point for the establishment of bend when turning from the centerline to the track.

Gait: The movement of the horse that is characterized by rhythmic footfalls. Typically Walk, Jog, Lope. In naturally ambling horses, the gait is characterized by a unique four-beat movement where each foot strikes the ground separately but at a faster pace than the traditional walk.

Garrocha: A long wooden pole that was traditionally used by the Spaniards for working cattle and is now used as an accompaniment by many Cowboy Dressage members in the Musical Freestyle.

Gate: On the Challenge Court a 4-foot opening that is defined by two upright posts and a rope. The rider must open the gate by lifting the rope and placing it on the other post.

Gathering: An event in the Cowboy Dressage community that brings the members together to celebrate Soft Feel and the Handshake, while enjoying the opportunity to ride tests for a score in front of a certified Cowboy Dressage judge.

Ground Pole: A 4-foot-long pole typically 4–6 inches in diameter that is used on the Cowboy Dressage Challenge Court.

Groundwork: Any of multiple exercises for the horse where the rider is not mounted.

H: A marker on the corner of the Court that is used on the long diagonal H–8–F.

Hackamore: Used to refer collectively to the headgear that consists of a braided bosal, rope mecate, and leather headstall or hanger.

Handshake: The agreement made between members of Cowboy Dressage World and the Cowboy Dressage Partners that is our word and bond to uphold the values of Cowboy Dressage and the code of the West for the betterment of the Western equine community and welfare of the horse.

Harmony: A state of being between horse and rider where each is content and happy in their relationship.

Haunches-In/Out: A lateral maneuver with bend that moves the haunches one track either to the inside or outside of the direction of travel but always into the bend.

Hindquarters: The portion of the horse to include the hip and hind legs of the horse. Also known as haunches.

I: Invisible marker on the Court on the centerline on the S–R gridline.

Impulsion: The quality of the gait that propels the horse upward.

Inside Rein/Hand/Leg: Refers to the body part of either horse or rider that is on the inside (shortened) side of the horse (inside the bend). This may or may not also be inside the direction of travel.

Intermediate Gait: For the gaited breeds this is a four-beat gait that should exhibit regularity, cadence, a supple back, and engaged hindquarters.

J: Quarterline marker connecting J and Q.

Jaquima: The Spanish word for hackamore.

Jog: A two-beat diagonal gait.

Judge: The Cowboy Dressage Approved individual that sits behind C and scores the test maneuver by maneuver.

Judges' Boot Camp: The intensive training program that all our Cowboy Dressage judges must attend prior to being approved to officiate at a Gathering.

K: Corner marker on the long diagonal K–8–M.

Kindness: The guiding principle of Cowboy Dressage. Treating others, both human and equine, with respect and courteousness. In all things Cowboy Dressage, kindness comes first.

L: Invisible marker on the centerline on the P–V gridline.

Lateral Maneuvers/Lateral Work: Refers to any movement that asks the horse to step outside of the straight travel and places the feet on three or four tracks instead of two tracks. The lateral maneuvers are used as strengthening and suppling exercises for the horse.

Lead: In the lope, it refers to the leading leg in the three-beat gait. When traveling on the left lead it is the left front leg that strikes the ground last.

Lead Change: To switch from one leading leg to the other. May be either "simple" or "flying."

Leg-Yield: A lateral maneuver performed on four tracks without bend. The horse can either move forward along the rail with the hindquarters pushed to the inside of the rail, or move diagonally across the Court with the forehand and hindquarters both reaching equally.

Lope: A three-beat gait.

Loping Hackamore: A piece of tack similar to a traditional hackamore that is constructed of rope and rawhide. It is an approved piece of tack for Cowboy Dressage.

M: A corner marker on the long diagonal M–8–K.

Maneuver: A figure performed on the Court.

Mecate: A single, long piece of rope attached to either a snaffle or a bosal that also has a section that may be used as a lead.

Midline: The line from E–8–B that breaks the Court into halves horizontally.

N: A quarterline marker marking the Y–N quarterline.

Octagon: The eight-sided box in the middle of the Court on the Challenge Court.

Open: A rider division at the Gatherings that includes professional horsemen or anybody that earns money teaching, instructing, or coaching Cowboy Dressage.

Outside Rein/Hand/Leg: Refers to the body part of either horse or rider that is on the outside (lengthened) side of the horse (outside the bend). This may or may not also be outside of the direction of travel.

P: Marker 10 meters from the corner that marks the short diagonal P–8–S.

Partnership: The quality in the relationship between horse and rider that embodies understanding, trust, and willingness.

Propulsion: The quality of the gait that pushes the animal forward.

Q: Marking the quarterline and connecting the line between Q and J.

Quarterline: Horizontal lines 5 meters on either side of the centerline that divide the Court into four equal quarters.

R: A marker 10 meters from the corner marking the short diagonal R–8–V.

Rhythm: The musical beat of the horse's gait. See also Cadence.

S: A marker 10 meters from the corner marking the short diagonal S–8–P.

Salute: The acknowledgment of the rider to the judge at the beginning and conclusion of a Cowboy Dressage test. Can be done with a tip of the hat or a drop of the hand, with either the right or the left hand.

Scribe: The person sitting to the right of the judge that takes notes during the test and records the judge's comments on the score sheet.

Serpentine: A maneuver that includes connected half-circles with a change of bend. May be ridden as a 10- or 20-meter serpentine.

Short Frame: A gait used primarily as a transition and strengthening gait. It asks the horse to shorten and elevate the stride beyond what is asked in the working frame. This is like the collected frame in classical dressage but refers more to the shortening of the frame than the elevation associated with collection.

Shoulder-In: A maneuver performed on three tracks where the horse's inside hind leg and outside front leg are on the same track while the outside hind leg and inside front leg are on their own separate tracks. This is a strengthening and suppling exercise.

Simple Lead Change: Transition from one lope lead to the other through a soft relaxed jog. Clear jog steps must be demonstrated.

Snaffle: A bit that consists of two jointed pieces and single rings for the attachment of the headstall and reins.

Soft Feel: The wordless communication between horse and rider that allows the two to become one, thinking and acting as one unit.

Square: A maneuver that calls for a 20-meter box that is ridden with 5-meter bend in the corners.

Test: The series of maneuvers that are designed to challenge both horse and rider in the development of their skills on the Cowboy Dressage Court.

Top Hand: The elite competition in Cowboy Dressage that uses Cowboy Dressage Challenge Walk/Jog/Lope Test 2 as the qualifying test. The top five riders then compete by riding a mystery test, first on their own horse and then on their competitors' horses, through a random draw. Only takes place once a year.

Track: The path horse and rider follow around the Cowboy Dressage Court that includes the straight lines down the sides of the Court and the 10-meter arcs or bend in the corners.

Transition: Moving the horse from one gait to another either up or down or from one frame to another, as in working frame to free frame within the jog.

Turn-on-the-Forehand: A lateral maneuver that asks the horse to move the hindquarters around the forehand while keeping the inside front leg in place. The horse should turn around the inside front leg, keeping a walking-forward rhythm to the footfalls.

Turn-on-the-Haunches: A lateral maneuver that asks the horse to move the forequarters around the hindquarters while keeping the inside hind leg in place. The horse should turn around the inside hind leg, keeping a walking-forward rhythm to the footfalls.

Two-Handed Bit: A Western bit that is broken in the middle in either two- or three-jointed pieces and also consisting of shanked side pieces. It functions both as a direct and leverage bit.

V: A marker 10 meters from the corner marking the short diagonal V–8–R.

Vaquero: Classically, it refers to the cattlemen of Spanish descent that worked the mission cattle herds in the California foothills. In Cowboy Dressage, it is a division that honors the traditions of the Vaquero and includes requirements for traditional gear.

Vertical: Typically used to describe the degree of flexion in the horse's poll. A straight perpendicular line from the horse's ears to the nose to the ground means the horse is on the vertical. The horse's head should never go behind the vertical line. In the free gaits, the horse should be in front of the vertical line.

Walk: A four-beat gait.

Whip: A soft flexible tool carried by the rider either in the saddle or on the ground. Used as an extension of the aids. (As a side note, Eitan Beth-Halachmy hates the term "whip," and for Cowboy Dressage suggests alternate terms like, "flicker," "motivator," "schtick," and "flip.")

Wild Rag: A colorful silk square of material worn tied around the neck. It is worn as an accoutrement at a Gathering and is a part of the historical working cowboy's outfit.

Working Frame: A medium frame that asks the horse to accept contact with the bit and soften at the poll while taking slightly shorter steps than in the free frame. It is a springy and energetic, though shortened gait.

Y: A quarterline marker on the same line as N.

Youth: Refers to any rider under 18 competing at a Cowboy Dressage Gathering.

APPENDIX II:
COWBOY DRESSAGE EXERCISES AND MANEUVERS

Practice makes perfect and it takes multiple times performing these maneuvers before horse and rider will excel and be in sync. All these maneuvers may be found in one of the Cowboy Dressage tests. While we strongly believe that the Cowboy Dressage tests can and will help train your horse, it also helps to ride the maneuvers individually to help your horse master a concept or help to strengthen a weakness. Your horse is your very best coach and the Cowboy Dressage Court is your very best classroom. Here are some of the ways in which you can put that classroom to work to get the most out of your time in the saddle.

10-METER FIGURE EIGHT

This maneuver can be performed and practiced several places on the Cowboy Dressage Court. The 10-Meter Figure Eight includes two 10-meter circles with a change of bend on the centerline where the circles meet. For example, the 10-Meter Figure Eight performed at H would include a change of bend at G. You can also perform a 10-Meter Figure Eight at E or B with a change of bend at "8."

Start by practicing this maneuver at the working walk. Pay attention to your bend and your markers, making sure that your outside stirrup grazes the markers on your circles. As you make your change of bend at G there is a slight leg-yield beforehand to move your outside stirrup to the other circle before. This happens within one stride at the point where the circles meet. There is no straight line between the circles nor do they form a teardrop diagonal change of bend where they meet.

When yours are the first hoofprints on the Court, it helps to see how your change of bend

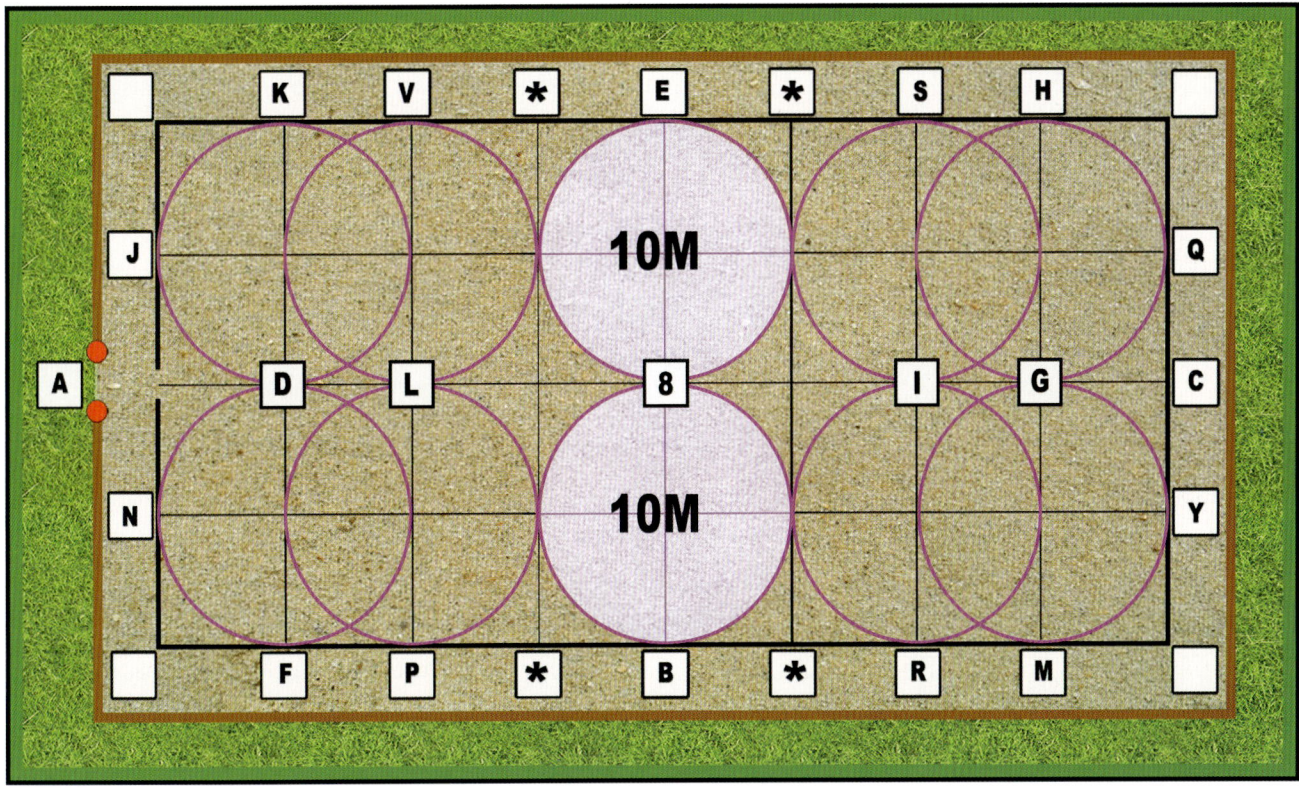

Exercise 1: *The 10-Meter Figure Eight*

is happening. Are you early? Are you late? If the figure eight circles flatten out at the point of the change of bend, then you are taking too long to make the change happen. How closely can you make your two circles meet?

Once you feel that you are able to change bend smoothly at the walk, try this maneuver at the working jog. This figure eight is another way to change directions on the Court during your warm-up ride other than using the diagonals.

You can also use this maneuver with counter-bend during your suppling exercises for your warm-up. Instead of changing bend where the circles meet, you can go to counter-bend through the 10-meter circle and then back to regular bend at the centerline.

The 10-Meter Figure Eight is a common feature in most of the upper-level Cowboy Dressage tests because it is difficult to do correctly. However, the combination of 10-meter circles also makes this an easy exercise for young horses and with the endless variations for riding the figure eight, make sure this maneuver is part of your daily workout with your horse.

QUARTERLINE LOOP

The turn down the quarterline at Q and Y is a useful maneuver and one that is used in several of the Cowboy Dressage tests. It incorporates bend, straight lines, ground poles (when used on the Challenge Court), and lateral maneuvers, as well as change in frame or gait if the rider desires.

You can use this pattern without the lateral maneuvers, as well as with the lateral maneuvers you will find more commonly within the Cowboy Dressage tests. Keep mixing this up so your horse doesn't get bored and doesn't anticipate the exercise.

One way to use this exercise is for practicing the working frame through the aid of the 10-meter bend, followed by a release into the free frame on the straight line. For a horse that may want to speed up or get ahead of the rider, I find this exercise useful because the free frame is a relatively short period of release, followed by the return to a working frame. You can start this exercise in the walk with a change in frame between working walk and free walk, and then in the jog between working jog and free.

Traveling down the track from M to C you turn left down the quarterline at Q. That is a quarter of a 10-meter circle from C to the intersection of Q–H to make that turn. Then straight down the quarterline to the midline. Stop and do either a half turn-on-the-forehand or half turn-on-the-haunches, or a combination of half turn-on-the-forehand to full turn-on-the-haunches. Then continue back to C and turn right down the quarterline at Y again, making a quarter of a 10-meter circle on that turn.

The key to successfully navigating this maneuver is a good 10-meter bend.

You can vary this exercise by using it to do short working jog to free walk transitions. You can do a working jog from C to the quarterline then transition to working walk or free walk. You can also do this entire maneuver at a working jog. You want to remember that the important part of this maneuver is to have a clear 10-meter bend and nice straight lines with a square stop before the lateral maneuver.

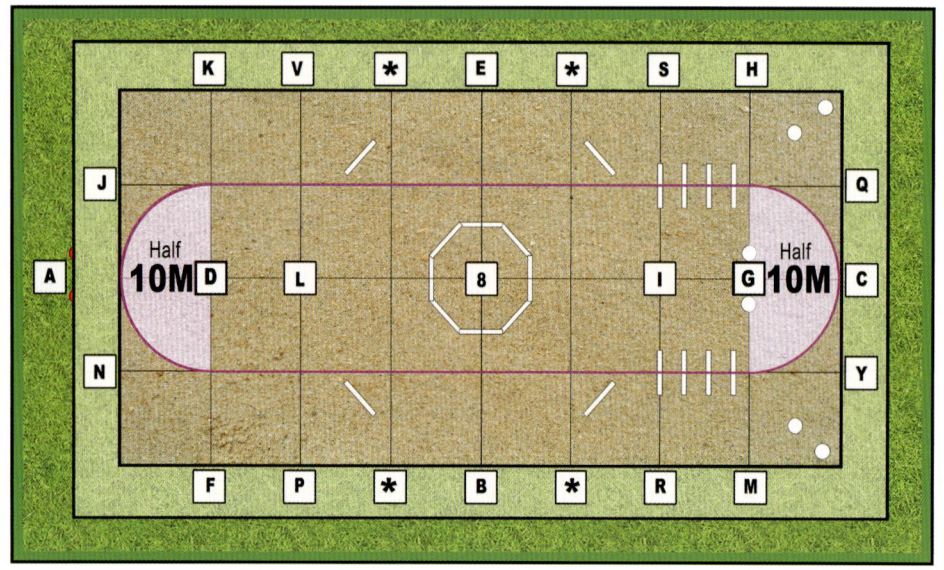

Exercise 2: *The Quarterline Loop*

20-METER CIRCLES

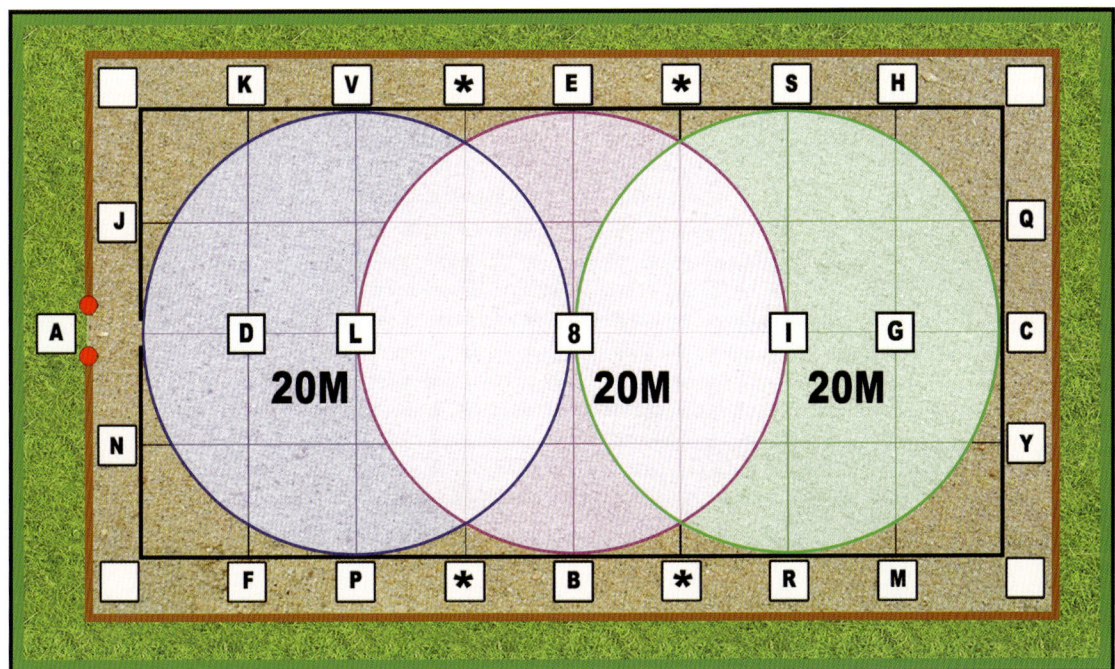

Exercise 3: *20-Meter Circles*

The 20-Meter Circles are an excellent exercise for cadence and developing the free frame. You can use the two circles at A and C as a large 20-meter-circle figure eight. Adding the 10-meter circles at several points along your 20-meter circle will help to mix up the large circles and is an excellent tool for practicing rein management, as well as change in frame for the horse and rider.

For the horse that lacks "forward," the large 20-Meter Circles exercise allows for the time and space to drive the horse forward and really lengthen the gait to teach the horse to wait on your seat to rate back down to the working frame. For the horse that likes to rush in the free frame, adding the small circles can help to break up that rushing and teach the horse to seek the 20-meter circle as a place where the work is a bit easier than multiple small circles.

If you are on the 20-meter circle at A, you can add a 10-meter circle in at A, P, "8," or V. The 10-meter circle at "8" is a great way to change bend as well as frame: You can do a small 10-meter circle figure eight at "8" and transition onto the large 20-meter circle at C, or the middle circle at B and E. There are not currently any tests that ask for the 10-meter circle at "8," but when you are creative and can read the 5-meter grid of the Court, there are no limits!

SQUARE WITH 5-METER BEND

You will find the Square with 5-Meter Bend maneuver on the upper level Walk/Jog/Lope tests on the Cowboy Dressage Court. It is an excellent exercise for building straightness and it introduces the 5-meter bend to your horse. Typically, all the bend on the Court requires the horse to be in a 10-meter bend, but the square maneuver has a much tighter bend.

To build success when riding the 20-meter square, ride the entire thing at the working walk. Ride deep into the corners while encouraging the horse to bend around your inside leg. Your outside leg will help to hold the bend in the corner and prevent the hindquarters from drifting out. A shoulder-fore prior to entering into the bend can help prepare the horse for the 5-meter bend. If you are having trouble figuring out where the 5-meter bend is in the corner, it will be halfway between your 10-meter bend line and the corner of the Court.

You can add transitions into this exercise, working with both working jog and working walk. The maneuver performed in the test asks for the rider to make the transitions between working jog and working walk at S and R. You can vary that routine by asking for those transitions at "8" and C.

The Square with 5-Meter Bend is an excellent exercise for balancing your working gaits in a straight line. There are few other maneuvers in the Cowboy Dressage tests that ask for more than 20 meters of working walk. Keeping a good, consistent working walk with good soft contact and snappy forward momentum is not as easy as it sounds.

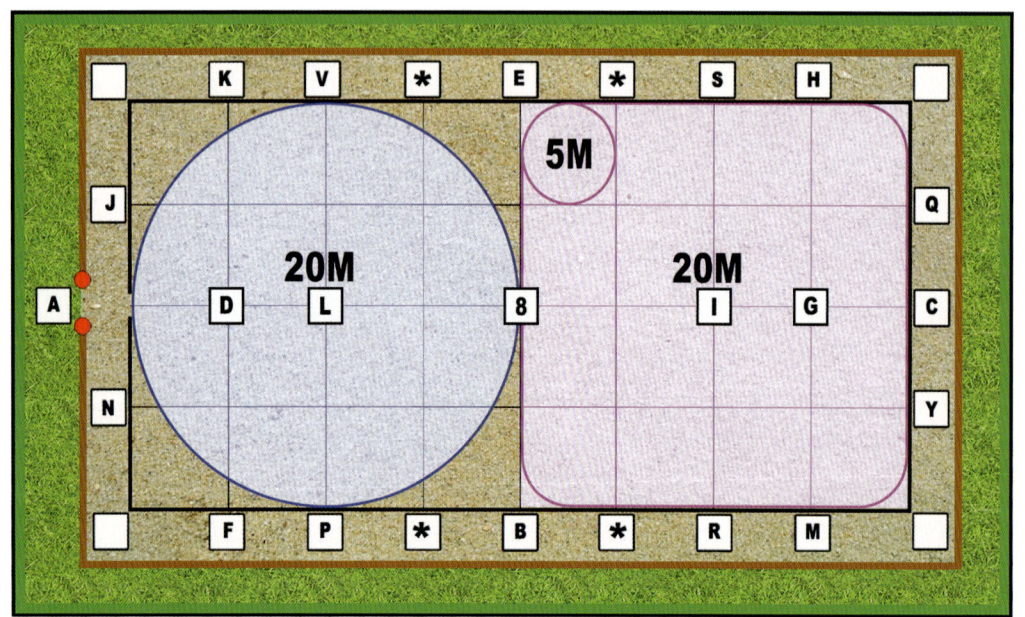

Exercise 4: *The Square with 5-Meter Bend*

20-METER DIAMOND

The 20-Meter Diamond exercise is another great one for straightness. In this exercise, you ride the 20-meter circle touch points with a straight line and 90-degree turn in the corners. This exercise can help teach the turn-on-the-haunches in small increments. By riding toward the marker you can use it to help encourage your horse to turn over the hindquarters as you push the shoulders over; then when the new direction is attained, you ride right out of it.

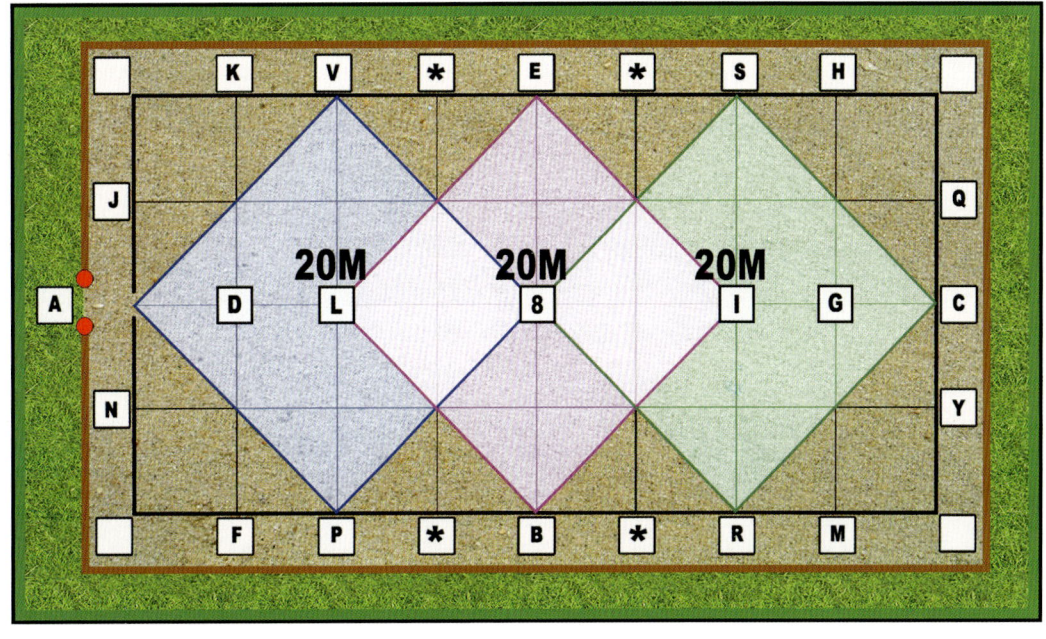

Exercise 5: *The 20-Meter Diamond*

The key to success in this exercise is to ride right into the turn, use the forward momentum to help make the turn, and ride right out of it again. You do not want to stop the horse and then push the shoulders over. It should be a fluid movement through the entire diamond.

You can do this maneuver in either free frame or working frame, but we encourage you to start in the free walk. Get in time with your horse's feet in the free frame, and as you come to the marker, push the shoulders over in time with the horse's footfall. You cannot influence the horse's foot when it is on the ground. So if you are going to influence the outside shoulder to move over, you will get ready to cue as the outside hind foot hits the ground—you know that the outside front foot will be following.

You can see how you can follow the grid pattern to change direction on the diamonds so you can be sure to work the horse evenly in both directions.

10-METER SERPENTINE

The 10-Meter Serpentine is probably one of our very favorite exercises. We use the serpentine in warm-ups every ride. There are three different 10-meter serpentines you can do on the Cowboy Dressage Court. This diagram shows the two serpentines along the long sides of the Court, but you can see how you can also do a serpentine down the centerline bordered by the quarter-lines.

The most challenging thing for new riders to see on the Court is the change of bend that occurs on the serpentine. No matter which serpentine you are doing, whether it is along the E side of the Court, the B side of the Court, or down the centerline, the change of bend will always happen in the same place on the Court.

There are three changes of bend in the 10-meter serpentine. The change of bend will always happen on the P–V line, the E–B line, and the R–S line. For the serpentine on the centerline, the changes of bend are at I, "8," and L.

The 10-Meter Serpentine is an excellent exercise for practicing change of bend and for working on cadence in the working gaits. You can use the serpentine to work on counter-bend. For instance, starting at Y, tracking right in the working jog in the right bend, you can hold the right bend through the entire serpentine, so two of your half-circles are in counter-bend. Then you can switch bend and work your way back the other direction all in left bend.

You can also use the 10-Meter Serpentine to work on lope departures. Using the short frame and the 10-meter bend in the transitions, you can work on transitions between working jog and working lope on the 10-meter bend. This is a great way to work a few lope strides at a time and build a slow balanced gait.

There aren't currently any serpentines in the Cowboy Dressage tests other than a short serpentine in the Partnership on the Ground Test 2, but it is a very common exercise for warming up, and you will often see the serpentine in the Musical Freestyle division.

Exercise 6: *The 10-Meter Serpentine*

BROKEN ARROWS

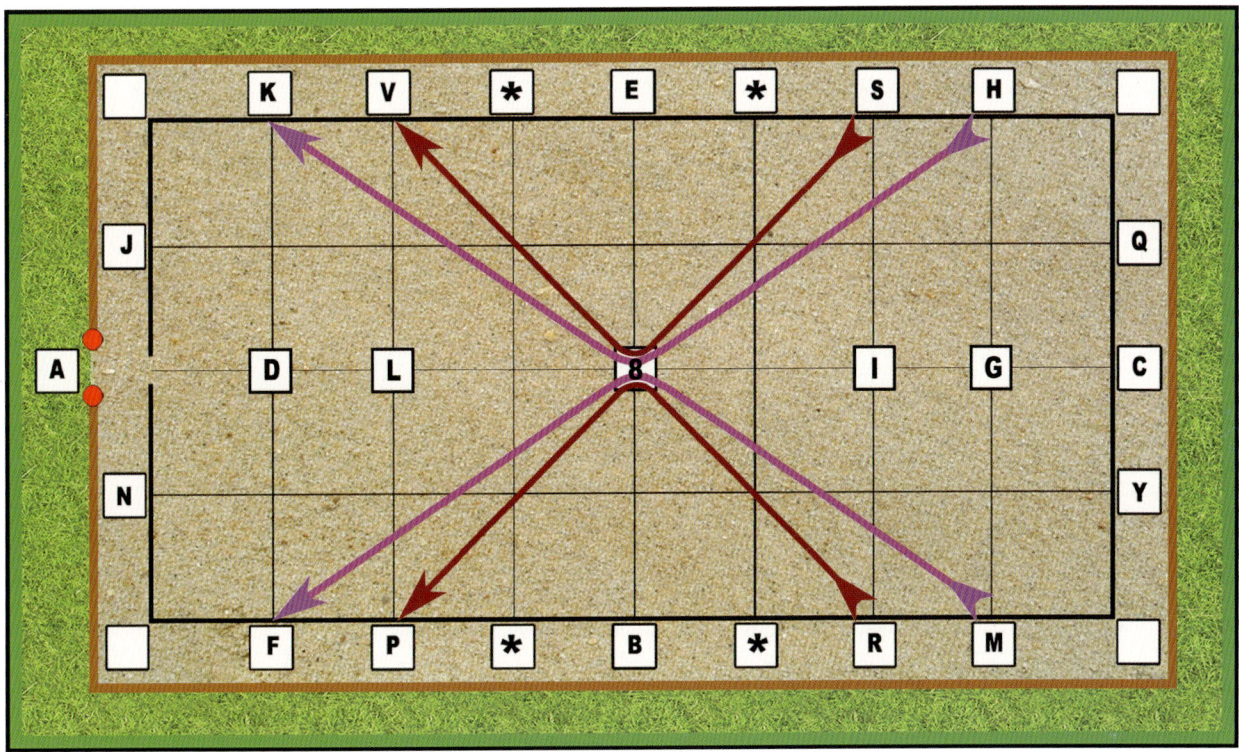

Exercise 7: *Broken Arrows*

There are several Broken Arrow maneuvers that are included in the Cowboy Dressage tests. These maneuvers are generally performed in the free walk. The Broken Arrows exercise is performed on the diagonals on the Court. Broken Arrows is very similar to the 20-Meter Diamond pattern in that you want the horse to maintain forward momentum through the turn, keeping the hindquarters engaged and the shoulders pushed over onto the new line of travel, like a mini turn-on-the-haunches.

On the Challenge Court, Broken Arrows is ridden on the short diagonals P–"8"–R and V–"8"–S. You can also turn Broken Arrows on its side and ride from P–8–V. On the long diagonal, Broken Arrows is ridden F–"8"–M and K–"8"–H.

The Broken Arrows adds variety for both horse and rider. It's an excellent addition to your maneuvers and your warm-up.

213

CIRCLE INSIDE THE BOX

The Circle Inside the Box is a maneuver that you will find in the Walk/Walk Challenge Test. We talked about the value of using the octagon for building bend in chapter 7 (see p. 132). This exercise asks for a full circle inside the box in a free frame.

You approach the octagon on a loose rein, enter at the center of the pole, and leg-yield

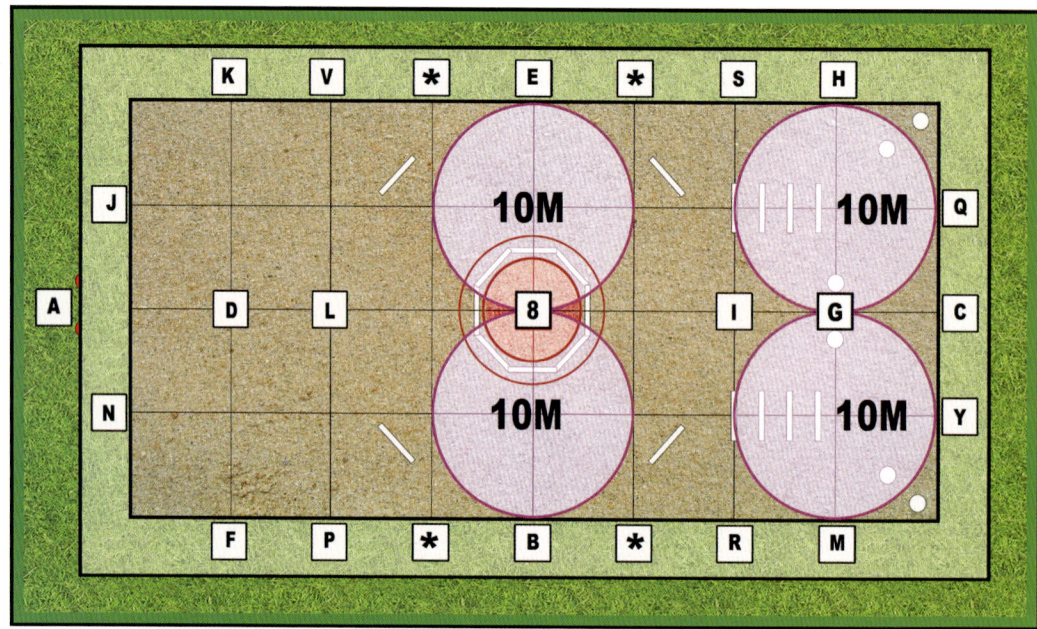

Exercise 8: *Circle Inside the Box*

over to the poles to walk a full circle inside the octagon. You want to have good forward and consistent bend through the entire circle. When you close your circle by reaching the point at which you entered the octagon, you "lift" the shoulder back onto the centerline to exit the octagon directly on the centerline.

Using the octagon in your 10-Meter Figure Eight, you can also change bend through the octagon. The added difficulty of using the poles through the change makes this maneuver that much more challenging to keep from going too straight through the octagon. You can see on this diagram where you exit the octagon just beyond where the two 10-meter circles of the figure eight meet. Be sure you don't go straight out of the middle of the octagon when you are on a 10-meter bend.

On this diagram, you can also see the circle you can use on the outside of the octagon. All of these circles are useful for building bend and making use of your Court.

BOW-TIE

The Bow-Tie is a very common maneuver found on the Walk/Jog/Lope tests both on the regular Court and on the Challenge Court. This maneuver makes use of the short diagonals and half of the 20-meter circles at each end of the Court.

We use the Bow-Tie maneuver for many different things on the Court. When practiced at the free jog, it can help develop "forward" and consistency of gait, as well as making the difference between a 20-meter bend and straightness more obvious to the horse.

At the lope, the Bow-Tie is a useful maneuver for schooling simple lead changes through "8." You can also use the centerline for a downward transition without a lead change if the horse begins to anticipate. In Walk/Jog/Lope Test 5 the Bow-Tie maneuver calls for the counter-lope, holding the lead through the entire maneuver, so that one-half of the Bow-Tie is on the correct lead, and the other half is in the counter-lope. The key to successfully navigating the Bow-Tie in the lope or counter-lope is to make sure you have a straight line across the diagonals right to your markers. If you do not make that diagonal all the way across, your turn onto the half circle will be too tight, and it can throw the horse off balance.

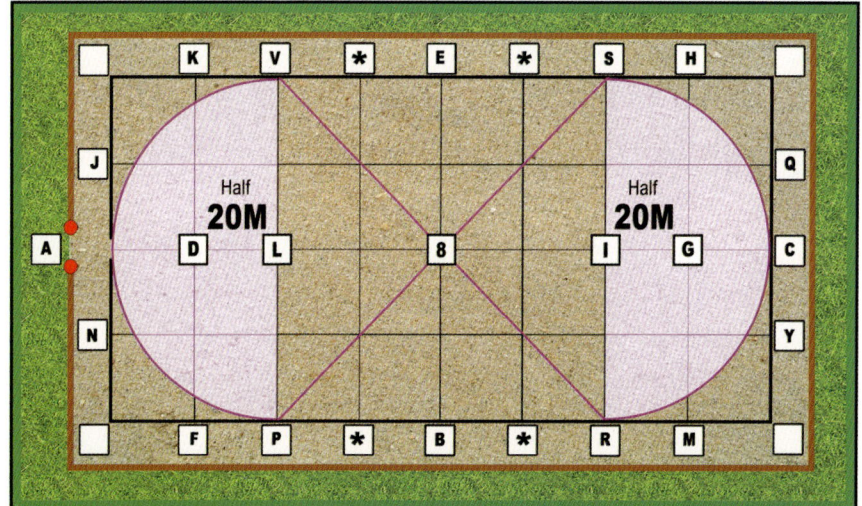

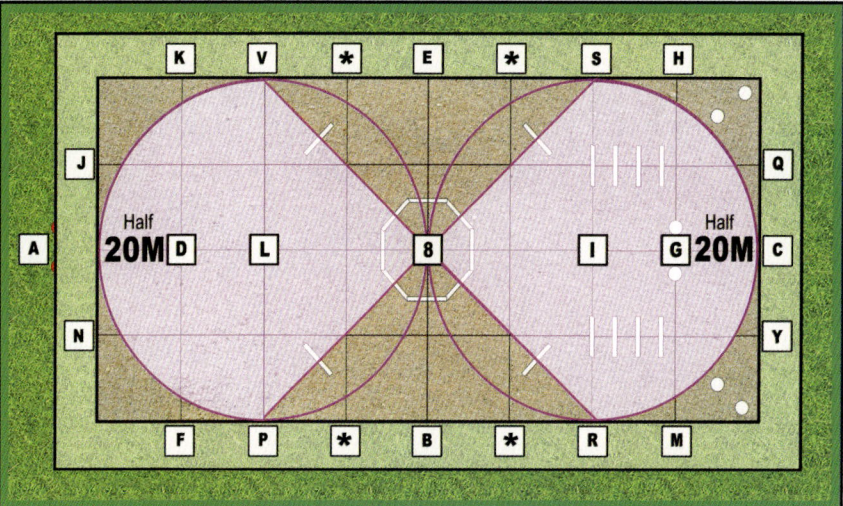

Exercise 9: *The Bow-Tie on the Cowboy Dressage Court (top); The Bow-Tie on the Challenge Court (bottom).*

The Bow-Tie maneuver on the Challenge Court requires very precise timing when the lead change is made through the octagon. Schooling this maneuver on the regular "open" Cowboy Dressage Court, *before* adding the ground poles, can improve success. You are also wise to add one or two of the diagonal ground poles without the octagon in the early stages of schooling the Bow-Tie and lead change across the diagonal.

CIRCLES

There is no end to the number and variation of circles that can be ridden on the Cowboy Dressage court. In this exercise we put together several different size circles using the octagon and cones on the Cowboy Dressage Challenge Court. This is a great exercise for a horse that is having difficulty maintaining bend or understanding the changes in bend. The many different size circles in this exercise will help to further shorten the horse, as well as give him something to focus on as he performs the smaller circles. We then reward the horse for all that bending with a final free jog circle on a 20-meter bend. Remember, bend is important for building suppleness and shortening the horse, one side at a time, but it can also make a horse reluctant to move forward. The conscientious rider is always looking to balance the development of bend and forward in her horse.

In this exercise you enter at A in either a free or working walk. All of the circles in this exercise will be ridden to the same direction, so you can decide if you are circling left or right as you enter. In this diagram all of the circles are to the left. At the octagon make one circle around the outside of the octagon, then one circle to the inside of the octagon. Exit on the centerline and continue to G. At G make a small circle around the cone then continue to Q. Ride a 10-meter circle at Q, then follow with a small circle around the corner cone. Shoulder-in from H to E. At E make a 20-meter circle to the left and continue to A. When you get to A turn down the centerline and repeat the exercise to the right.

Exercise 10: *Circles*

TURKEY TAIL

This is an exercise of concentration and small movements for the horse. It is excellent for helping the horse develop balance and strength through the use of shoulder-in on a circle, as well as asking the horse to wait and not rush through the maneuver, as there are multiple opportunities to rebalance and refocus the horse at the junction of the octagon.

Begin by riding a circle around the outside of the octagon. Then ask the horse for a shoulder-in on the circle. At each junction of the octagon you will do a small turn-on-the-forehand to keep the horse's forequarters on the octagon. Once you have gone halfway around, ride through the octagon, and maintain the same bend, but ride in the opposite direction in a counter-shoulder-in. Now you will be doing a mini counter-turn-on-the-haunches at each junction.

This is an exacting and challenging maneuver for the horse, and you may only get a few steps of either shoulder-in or counter-shoulder-in in the beginning. Remember not to ask for too much too soon and build up to the full maneuver slowly. You can ride just the length of one of the sections of the octagon in shoulder-in before releasing and riding forward. Soft Feel and balance within the horse are the ultimate goals. Reward for softness in the horse, and build on this maneuver one step at a time.

Exercise 11: *Turkey Tail*

ACKNOWLEDGMENTS

The body of work presented in this book would not be possible without the help and guidance that both Eitan and I have received in our lives and along our journey to better understanding of these amazing animals we have chosen to share our lives with.

Eitan would first like to acknowledge and thank his lovely wife, Debbie, without whom the dream of Cowboy Dressage would have remained a dream. Eitan also acknowledges the horses that have helped to instruct and shape him as a horseman, from the very first equine he was privileged to ride as a boy in Israel to the hundreds that have been in his life since. There are two horses that stand out for Eitan and he would like to thank them first and foremost: Holiday Compadre, the talented powerhouse of a Morgan stallion, was the first to really give Eitan a platform to showcase his unique style. Compadre and Eitan showed the world what a little Morgan stallion could do. The second horse that Eitan would like to recognize is Santa Fe Renegade. Another Morgan stallion of immense presence and talent, Santa Fe is all heart. He performs as he does out of a mutual love and respect for the rider who has so patiently and artfully helped to sculpt the horse that he is today. Both amazing stallions have helped Eitan to better understand the nature of horses and the relationship that we share with them, as well as the potential that lies at the heart of each equine—if we just learn to listen.

I never got to meet or ride Holiday Compadre. He was retired by the time Eitan was part of my life. Santa Fe, however, has as much to do with the strides I have taken in understanding the concepts of Soft Feel and partnership as does Eitan. These two masters have helped shape me in ways that I didn't know were possible and hadn't even dared to dream. I am humbled and grateful for their patient teaching.

I would also like to acknowledge my husband, Dan, who has been so supportive in my pursuit of Cowboy Dressage. It's not like we didn't already have enough going on! I couldn't do any of this without his unending love and support. Thank you to my mom and dad who recognized the passion in a young girl and bought me my first Morgan all those years ago. And finally, thank you to Dr. Ahmed Tibary, a fine horseman in his own right, who helped to make me the veterinarian I am today.

And of course, none of this would be in your hands at all without the folks at Trafalgar Square Books. Thank you for believing in Cowboy Dressage and this project, and for making our vision a reality.

Jenni Grimmett, DVM

PERSONAL NOTE FROM DAN GRIMMETT

My journey with Cowboy Dressage began as the role of the supportive husband. I participated in our Thursday "ride nights" where we opened our home and our Court to friends looking to give Cowboy Dressage a try. I continued to ride the tests and could see how they helped me improve the things I had already been working on.

Then in November of 2014, Jenni and I loaded up our horses and headed to the Finals in California where Jenni was one of the evening educational presenters. After my first ride, 8 came up to me and said, "You surprised me. I thought you were just a supportive husband who didn't know how to ride." Then he gave me his mischievous grin and said, "Why are you giving points away to the judges?" He proceeded to give me the pep talk of my life. I won't go into the details as there may have been a few expletives involved, but the gist was, why would I come all the way down to the Finals and not try any harder than that? As I rode in for my second test, I could see 8 eyeballing me, and you can bet I did not give points away to the judges. My first test was a score somewhere in the mid 50s; my second test was an 80. When I rode out after the second test, I got the nod of approval from 8, and I was hooked. He had said the right thing, at the right time, in the right way.

I am lucky enough to have the opportunity to ride with 8. It's a yearly trek for us to Wolf Creek Ranch for five days of Cowboy Dressage Horsemanship School. Two years ago I went without a horse and was very much looking forward to riding 8's horses. On the first day we started in the "pressure cooker." This is a round pen where you ride alone in front of the rest of the students while 8 tells you all the things you should be able to do even though you may not be able to. While we were all sitting there, Santa Fe Renegade is brought in and warmed up. Of course, we were all thinking we would be watching 8 put on an amazing demo, but he looks right at me and says, "Climb on, Cowboy."

Hold on here a minute! My wife loved this horse and had spent a week riding him a month before (and hadn't quit talking about it). I was now in a situation where if I rode him better than she did I was an idiot...and if I didn't...still an idiot. But no sense protesting—8 said get on, so I got on.

Eitan began giving me commands: "Shorten your rein...shorter...shorter...shorter!" Okay, so now the reins were good. "Move your legs back...farther...farther!" Now my legs were good. Then he said, "Pick up a jog to the right, move your outside leg back, and cluck." So I was loping... oops, not loping anymore. Again, he said, "Pick up the jog, move your outside leg back, and cluck." Loping again...and...not loping. He asked, "Why do you quit riding? You gotta keep riding." I repeated the steps and picked up the lope once more. Beautiful, soft, incredible loping. So now

8 said, "Down to the walk. Lengthen your rein...longer...longer...longer! Not bad, Cowboy; that was really pretty." He again took what for me was a bit of a stressful, difficult situation and made it a very valuable lesson by saying the right thing, at the right time, in the right way.

I can't remember a day in my life where my thoughts didn't start and end with horses. Today, I live upstairs in a barn with horses below. We live and breathe each day with horses and their care as our living, our recreation, and our passion. Finding Eitan is the fulfillment of a dream—to learn and ride with a true horseman, the mentor I've waited for since childhood. He has given me the tools and the drive to push myself to become much more than I could have on my own by saying the right thing, at the right time, in the right way...a horseman.

I've had a front row seat as 8 and Jenni have worked so hard to bring you this book. I will tell you they've gone over every word, picture, and diagram with a fine-tooth comb to ensure that it is as close to perfect as humanly possible. It has been an incredible experience and one we will always remember as invaluable time spent with Debbie and 8. I consider them family.

And I always knew Jenni was destined to do great things. I'm extremely proud of her.

Dan Grimmett

INDEX

Page numbers in *italics* indicate illustrations.

5-meter bend, square with, 210, *210*
10-meter bend/circles
    backing up on, 160–62, *160–61*
    court layout for, 79, *79*
    exercises using, *133*, 214
    figure eight using, 206–7, *207*
    straightness in, *128*
    for stride adjustments, 107–8
    for teaching lateral movements, 149, *149*, *152*
    in warm-up, 130–33, *131*
10-Meter Figure Eight maneuver, 206–7, *207*
10-Meter Serpentine maneuver, 212, *212*
20-meter bend/circles
    court layout for, 79, 80
    exercises using, 133–35, *133–34*, 209, *209*, 215
20-Meter Circle maneuver, 209, *209*
20-Meter Diamond maneuver, 211, *211*
20-meter square, 210, *210*

Abdominal muscles, 103–5, 123
Aids. *See also* Rein aids
    overview, 49–50, 55–56
    acceptance of, *32*, 34, *34*
    in Ask Ride Ask, 64
    leg aids, 63–65, *63–65*, 129–130, *129*
    PERR series in, 94–95, *95*
    seat/weight as, 65–70, *66–69*
    as sentences, 49
    timing of, *56*, 90–93, 114
    used in combination, 56
    voice, 70
Anthropomorphism, 53
Apparel, for Gatherings, 22, 174, 191
Ask Ride Ask, 64
Asymmetry, 11. *See also* Crookedness
Attention span, of horse, 32–33

Back, of horse
    anatomy, 10, 98–100, *99*, *103*
    engagement of, 117–18, *117*
    hollowing of, 11–12, 73, 118
    lateral mobility, 98
    muscles of balance in, 96, 97–105, *99*, *101*, *103*
    skeletal maturation, 27–32
Backing up
    on 10-meter bend, 160–62, *160–61*
    as correction, 40, 52–53
    for loading hindquarters, 100
    for shortening frame, 159
Balance
    in gaits, 177
    muscles of, 96, 97–105, *99*, *101*, *103*
    of rider, 12, 58–59, 67
    in Wisdom Tree, *32*, 35
Barrel, of horse, 93, 123–27, *125*, *127*, *129*
Behavior issues, 11–12, 38–39, 53–54
Behavior modification, 51–55
Bend
    biomechanics of, 123–27, *124–27*
    bit/rein action and, 14
    changes of, 131–32, *131*, 212
    counter-bend, 135–37, *136*
    development of, 35, 130–35, 216
    in groundwork, *33*, 42–45, *43–44*
    importance of, 102, 114, 123, *123*
    leg aids and, 63–65, 129–130
    rider alignment in, 124–27, *125–26*
    straightness and, 121–23
Beth-Halachmy, Debbie, 1–3, 195
Beth-Halachmy, Eitan, 1–3, 195
Biting, 54
Bits
    leverage action of, 17–19, *18–19*
    one-handed, 21, *21*
    selection considerations, 16, 17, 21
    snaffles, 13–16, *13*, *15*
    two-handed, 16, *16*
Body language
    aids and, 50
    in groundwork, 39–42
    horse's sensitivity to, 107

intention in, 50, 55
rider position as, 124–27
signs of tension in horses, 73
Bone, Martina, 4
Boots, 22
Bosal hackamores, 17–19, *18–19*, 20–21, *20*
Bow-Tie maneuver, 155, *156*, 215, *215*
"Box." *See* Octagon; Ride a Box exercises
Bracing, 14, 105
Breathing, 107
Bridles
with bits, 13–19
hackamores, 20–21, *20*
rein types, *15*, 21–22
Broken Arrows maneuver, 213, *213*
Bucking, 11–12

Cadence, 88, 177, 212
Cattle work, 184
Center of gravity
of horse, 97–105, 107
of rider, 67, *67*, 69, *69*
Challenge Court
layout of, 81–85, *81*
maneuvers using, 208, 214–17
Challenge Division, 174
Changes of direction. *See* Direction changes
Chewing, 71, *71*
Children, 40
Circle Inside the Box maneuver, 214, *214*
Circles. *See also specific dimensions*
court layout for, 79–81, *79–80*
exercises using, 130–35, 216, *216*
in groundwork, *33*
shoulder-in on, 46, *46*
Circles maneuver, 216, *216*
Classical dressage, 26
Collection, 31, 155. *See also* Short frame
Communication. *See also* Aids
from horse, 50, 70–73
role of tack in, 7–8
in Wisdom Tree, *32*, 33–34
Conditioning, 97, 182–84
Cones, *82*, 83
Conformation, 10, 177
Contact, 59, *59*
Contiguity, 53
Contingency, 53

Costumes, in musical freestyles, 191
Counter-bend, 135–37, *136*, 207
Counter-bend rein, 61–62, *61*
Counter-lope, 215
Courts
overview, 75–76
alternate locations for, *192–93*, 199
half-court configuration, *84*, 85
setups for, 76–79, *76–77*, 198
Cowboy Dressage
associations, 195
Gatherings, 165–175
glossary of terms, 200–205
horse selection for, 176–79
international scope of, *166*, *168*, 172–73
judging of, 174–75
mission of, 4
Cowboy Dressage Professionals Association, 196–98, *197*
Cowboy Dressage World, 166–67, 195–96
Cowboy tradition, 181–82
Crookedness, 123–24, 139. *See also* Straightness
Crowding, 40
Cue, as application of aid, 49. *See also* Aids

Diagonal ground poles, *82*, 83, *83*, *84*
Diagonal lines, in courts, 78, 213, *213*
Diamond figures, 134–35
Direct rein, 60, *60*
Direct rein of opposition, 62–63, *62*
Direction changes, 131–32, *131*, 206–7, *207*, 212
Disengagement, 91–93, 118–19
Disrespect, 52
Downward transitions, 111, 115–16
Dressage. *See* Classical dressage; Cowboy Dressage
Dressage whips, 40
Drill Team Freestyle, 189
Drilling, 44
Driving position, 38–39, *39*
Driving reins, 44

Education
certification for, 197–98
at Gatherings, 166–67, *199*
Emotionality, pitfalls of, 54, 55
Energy core, 69–70, 107
Engagement, 91–93, *91*, 159
Execution, in PERR series, 94–95, *95*

Extension, muscles of, 96. *See also* Long frame
Eyes, of horse, 72–73, *72*

Fearful horses, 55, 73, 177
Feet
    moving of, *32*, 33–34
    placement of, 44, 45, *45*, 182–83
Fight or flight response, 73
Figure eights, 131–32, *131*, 206–7
Fitness, 97, 182–84
Flexor muscles, 100, *101*
Foaming, at mouth, 71
Footfall patterns
    overview, 88, *88*
    head movement and, *92*
    rider awareness of, 90–91, 92–93
    in turn-on-the-forehand, *146*
    turn-on-the-haunches, *142*
Forehand
    bit/rein action on, 14, *56*, 58–59
    developing reach in, 151
    falling onto, 115–16, 126
    turns on, 145–47, *145–46*, 217, *217*
"Forward"
    aids for, 65, *65–66*, 68
    in bending, 129–130, 133, 136
    exercises for, 209, 216
    in groundwork, 33
    importance of, 32
    loss of, 95, 134
    in turn-on-the-forehand, 147
    in turn-on-the-haunches, 144
    in Wisdom Tree, *32*, 34, *34*
Forward/Forward, Forward/Back, 159–160
Frame
    overview, 89–90, *89*
    adjustability of, 107–8, *155*, 162–63
    influence of hands on, 57–58, *57*, *58*
    long, 89, *89*, *112*, *158*
    medium, 89, *89*, *111*, *158*
    short, 155–163, *159*, *162*
Free gaits
    exercises using, 208, 209
    frame in, *106*, *116*, 117–19, *117*, *119*, 134
    jog, 111–13, *117–18*
    lope, 116–17, *116–17*
    as release, 107
    walk, 96, *96*, 105–8, *106*

Freestyle Division, 174, 186–191
Futurities, 26, 27, 31

Gaited Division, 171, 174
Gaits
    overview, 87–88
    cadence of, 88
    footfall patterns, 88, *88*
    "forward" in, 89–90
    jog, 109–13
    lope, 113–17
    quality of, 177
    walk, 90–96, *90*, 105–9
Gallagher, Megan, 5
Garrocha pole, *133*, 174, *188*
Gate obstacle, 83
Gatherings
    celebration and, 167–68, *167*
    divisions of, 168, 171, 174
    educational components, 166–67
    as family events, 165–66
Getaways, 191–93
Glossary of terms, 200–205
Going together position, 39, *39*
Grimmett, Jenni L.
    on Cowboy Dressage, 1–3, 5
    on horse selection, 176–79
    on picking tests, 169–170
    on skeletal maturation, 27–32
Ground poles
    in Challenge Court, 81, *81*, *82*, 174
    exercises using, 47, *47*
    in stride adjustments, 108–9, *108*
    for young horses, 44
Groundwork
    for bending, 42–45, *43–44*, 127–28
    benefits of, 8
    body language in, 39–42
    from both sides of horse, 41
    exercises using, 45–47, *45–46*
    as foundation for under-saddle work, *38*
    leading, 37–42
    for walk development, 95
    as warm-up, 33
    in Wisdom Tree, *32*, 33, *33*
    for young horses, 26
Growth plates, 28–29, *30*

Half-pass, 152–53, *153*
Halters, 8–9, *9*
Halts and halting, 41–42, 62, 65–66
Handedness, in horses, 11, 123
Handiness, of horse, 179
Handling. *See also* Groundwork
    from both sides, 41
    leading, 8–9, *9*, 37–42
Hands. *See also* Rein aids
    effective use of, 56–59, *57–59*
    influence on horse's feet, *56*
    position of, 14, *57*
Handshake principles, 3
Harrison, Marcia Moore, 4
Hats, 22
Haunches-in/haunches-out, *140*, 150–52, *151–52*. *See also* Hindquarters, loading of; Turn-on-the-haunches
Head
    balance role, 104
    movement of, 92, *92*
    rotation of, 126
Head position
    in center of gravity, 105
    fixed/set, 93, 104
    in frames, *89*, 107, *119*, *162*, *163*
    rein influence and, 14, 57, *57*
Head-shy horses, 54
Helmets, 22
Hindquarters, loading of, *57*, 100–105, *109*, *117*, 155–56
Hips, 100
Horses. *See also* Young horses
    domestic vs. wild, 97
    selection considerations, 176–79
    Soft Feel as commitment to, 5
    specialization of, 176–77

Indirect rein, 60–61, *61*
Indirect rein of opposition, *62*, 63
Inside/outside aids, 14, 140
Intention, 55, 133, 159

Jog
    overview, 109, *109*
    footfall patterns, *88*, *109*
    frame in, *158*
    free gait, 111–13, *112*, 117–18
    in hand, 41
    posting of, 112, 134
    through the Octagon, 45
    working gait, 110–11, *110*
Joint injections, 31
Judges and judging, 174–75, 196–98, *197*

Kicking, 11–12
Kindness, as guiding principle, 3, *3*, 196, *199*
Knees, "closing" of, 28–29, *30*

Largent, Nonny, 5
Lateral flexion
    in bending, 127–29, *128*
    bit/rein action and, 14
    overuse of, 57, 58, *58*
Lateral movements
    benefits of, 100, 102, 139–140
    described, 140–153
    on quarterlines, 208
    in warm-up, *153*
Lead changes, 215
Leadership, 54
Leading
    equipment for, 8–9, *9*
    handler position, 38–39, *39*
    manners and, 39–42
Lead-line classes, 40
Leads and lead changes, 113, 215
Learning to learn, 26, 31
Legs, of rider
    aiding with, 63–65, *63–65*, 129–130, *129*
    influence on horse's feet, *56*
    in lateral movements, 140
    position of, *63*, 65, *65–66*
    rein aids and, 60–63
Leg-yielding, 131–32, *150*, *151*, *153*
Lengthening, of stride, 44, 105, 116. *See also* Long frame
Licking, 71, *71*
Lightness
    of rider's seat, 66
    in Wisdom Tree, 32, 34, *34*
Long frame, 89, *89*, *112*, *158*. *See also* Free gaits
Long lines, 44
Lope
    overview, 113, *113*, *115*
    counter-lope, 215
    departures, 212
    footfall patterns, *88*, *113*
    four-beat, 113

free gait, 116–17, *116–17*
lead changes, 215
transitions, *159*
working gait, 114–16, *114–15*
Loping hackamores, 20, 21
Lungeing, equipment for, 8

"Manana" tradition, 25–26
Maneuvers
    in court configurations, *80*
    described, 206–17
Manners, 11–12, 38–39, 53–54
Mecate reins, *15*, 20–22
Medium frame, 89, *89, 111, 158*. *See also* Working gaits
Mental maturity, 31
Meyers, Dee, 5
Miller, Robert, 55
Monaghan, Phil, 5
Motivation, 54
Mountain Trail, 183–84
Mouth, mobility of, 71, *71*
Movement, directed by rider, *32*, 33–34. *See also* "Forward"
Musical freestyles, 186–191

Natural horsemanship, 30, 51–52, 55–56
Neck
    balance role, 104
    bending and, 124
    flexion of, 30–31, 57, 58, *58*, 128
    position of, 105, 107
    "telescoping" of, 104–5
Negative reinforcement, 52
Nervous horses, 55, 73, 177
Non-weight-bearing phase, of stride, 91–92

Obstacles, 83, 184, *184*
Octagon
    in court layout, *82*, 84
    exercises using, 132–33, *133*, 214, *214*, 216
    in groundwork, 45–47, *45–46*
    turn-on-the-haunches in, *141*
"Old Man Walk," 40–41
One-handed Western bits, 21
One-rein stops, 30
Outside/inside aids, 14, 140
Over-bridling, 14

Partnership
    as foundation of training, 32
    rider/horse suitability and, 178
    on the trail, 182–83
    in Wisdom Tree, *32*, 33, *33*
Partnership Division
    overview, 174
    on the ground classes, 37, *40*, *42*, *84*, 174
    under saddle classes, 174
Patience, importance of, 25–26
Paxton, Wyatt, 5, 195
PERR series, in communication, 94–95, *95*
Pivoting, vs. turning, *142*
Poll
    bit action and, 17–19, *18–19*
    position of, *101*
    suppleness of, 104, 105
Positive reinforcement, 51–52
Posting, 112, 134
Predatory behavior, 55
Preparation
    in PERR series, 94–95, *95*
    for transitions, *159*, 163, 189
Pressure. *See also* Release
    bit action as, 17–19
    horse's response to, 32
Pressure points, 11
Punishment, 52–55

Quarter Horses, 10, 31
Quarterline ground poles, 47, *47*
Quarterline Loop maneuver, 208, *208*
Quarterlines, 77, 78, *82*

Race horses, 27–28
"Recliner" position, 13
Rein aids. *See also* Reins
    in bending, 128–130
    influence of, 13–19, *18–19*, 22, 56–59, *57–59*
    inside/outside, 14
    overuse of, 161
    release of, 59
    types, 60–63, *60–62*
"Rein-back," 161. *See also* Backing up
Reining, 28, 140
Reins. *See also* Rein aids
    position on snaffle, 14, *14*
    styles of, 21–22

Relaxation, 94–95, *95*, 107
Release
    free gaits as, 107
    in lateral movements, 140
    as negative reinforcement, 52
    in PERR series, 94–95, *95*
    from shortened frame, 158
Respectful ground manners, 38
Retreats, 191–93
Rhythm, in musical freestyles, 189
Ride a Box exercises, 143–44, 147
Riders
    commitment to Soft Feel, 5
    horse's mirroring of, *50*
    position of, 12–13, *66*
    relationship with horse, 178
    straightness role, 122, *122*
Riding
    of each stride, *64*, 116–17
    vs. guiding, 129–130
Ringrose-Moe, Lyn, 195
Rope halters, 8–9, *9*
Rumens-Partee, Dale, 4

Saddles, 9, 12–13
Score cards, 175
Seat
    aids from, 65–70, *66–69*
    driving role, *68*
    position of, *66*
Self-carriage
    conditioning for, 183, 184
    defined, 4–5
    rider commitment to, 5
    in Wisdom Tree, *32*, 35
Shanked bits, 17–19, *18–19*
Short frame
    overview, 89, *89*, 155–56
    benefits of, *159*
    development of, 157–162
    head position in, *162*
Shoulder-fore, 150–51
Shoulder-in
    overview, *140*, 147–48, *147*
    benefits of, 148–49
    exercises using, 217, *217*
    in groundwork, 46, *46*
    leg aids in, 64
    tracking in, *150*
Shoulder-out, *140*, 149–150
Shoulders, of horse, 126–27, *127*, 151
Simple lead changes, 215
Skeletal structures
    alignment of rider with horse, *50*, 124–27, *125–26*
    maturation of, 27–32
Snaffle bit futurities, 28
Snaffle bits, 13–19, *13*, *15*, *18–19*
Soft Feel
    as guiding principle, 196
    hands in, 59
    in lateral movements, 139–140
    in musical freestyles, 186–87
    in Wisdom Tree, 35
Spade bits, 21, *21*
Spanish tradition, for training horses, 28
Spine. *See* Back, of horse
Spins, in reining, 140
Square with 5-Meter Bend maneuver, 210, *210*
Steps, calling out of, 90–91
Stirrups
    rider's weight in, 67, 107
    saddle fit and, 12–13
Straightness
    bend and, 121–23
    development of, 139, 211
    tracking in, *148*, *150*
    in Wisdom Tree, *32*, 35, *35*
Strengthening exercises, 147–49, 150–51
Stretching, 112, 134
Stride
    length of, 44, 45, 89, *89*, 108–9, *108*
    phases of, 91–93
    rider awareness of, 67, 211
    riding of, *64*, 116–17
"Subtractive" reinforcement, 52
Suspension, 109, 113
Symmetry, 11. *See also* Straightness

Tack
    bridles, 13–16
    for Cowboy Dressage, 7–8
    halters/leads, 8–9
    saddles, 9, 12–13
Tail, 73
Tempo, 88

Tension
    in horse, 71, 73
    in rider, 59, 170
Tests, 169–170, 198, 206
Ties (apparel), 22
Time, required for training, 25–26
Timing
    of aids, *56*, 90–93, 114
    in behavior modification, 54
    exercises for, 67, 211
    in musical freestyles, 189
Topline
    muscles of balance in, 96, 97–105, *99*, *101*, *103*
    rounding of, 117–18, *117*
Trail riding, 182–83
Training
    as behavior modification, 51–55
    dressage as, 75
    natural horsemanship methods, 30, 51–52, 55–56
    Spanish tradition of, 28
    time required for, 25–26
    Wisdom Tree principles of, 25–35
Training scale, 26. *See also* Wisdom Tree
Transitions
    accuracy of, 42
    downward, 111, 115–16
    exercises for, 210
    jog/lope, 114–16, 212
    preparation for, 189
    upward, 111, 114, 116
    walk/jog, 111, 112
Treats, 51–52
Tree, of saddle, 12
Trot, 109. *See also* Jog
"Trot-a-lope," 113
Trust, 3, *3*, 182
"Try"
    behavior modification and, 53, 54–55
    importance of, 3, *3*, 32, 179
    scoring of, on tests, 175
Turkey Tail maneuver, 217, *217*
Turn-on-the-forehand, 145–47, *145–46*, 217, *217*
Turn-on-the-haunches
    overview, 140–44, *141–44*
    exercises for, 211
    exercises using, 217, *217*
    in hand, 42–44, *43–44*
Two-handed Western bits, 16, *16*

Unwanted behavior. *See* Behavior issues
Unwanted horses, 32
Upward transitions, 111, 114, 116

Vaquero Division, 174
Vertical flexion, 30–31, 57
Voice aids, 70

Waiting, 54–55
Walk
    overview, 90–91, *90*
    engagement/disengagement in, 91–93
    footfall patterns, *88*
    free gait, 96, *96*, 105–8, *106*
    through the Octagon, 45
    working, 93–95, *94–95*
Walk pirouettes, 141
Walker, Garn, 195
Walk/Jog Division, 171
Walk/Jog/Lope Division, 171
Walk/Walk Division, 171
Warm-up
    exercises for, 130–35, *153*, 212
    groundwork as, 33
Weight
    of horse, *57*, 100–105, *109*, 117, 155–56, 159
    of rider, 65–70, *66–69*
Weight-bearing phase, of stride, 91–92
Western Reined Cow Horses, 28
Whips, 40
Wisdom Tree
    overview, 25–26, 32, *32*
    levels of, 33–35
Withers, position of, *101*
Working gaits
    exercises using, 208
    frame in, 93–94, *106*, 111
    jog, 110–11
    lope, 114–16
    walk, 93–95, *94–95*
Worry, in horses, 73

Young horses
    attention span of, 32–33
    bending and, 127–28
    collected frame and, 31
    groundwork for, 44
    skeletal maturation, 26, 27–32
    starting of, 28–29